CHRONICLES OF OLD BOSTON

EXPLORING NEW ENGLAND'S HISTORIC CAPITAL

Published in the United States by:
Museyon, Inc.
20 E. 46th St., Ste. 1400
New York, NY 10017

Museyon is a registered trademark.
Visit us online at www.museyon.com

ISBN 978-0-9846334-0-1

1120959

Printed in China

To Ginny,
the light of my life

For nearly four centuries Boston has been a center of learning, literature, and innovation. John Winthrop's City Upon a Hill gave birth to American independence; it has given us the first telephone and the first e-mail message. The city of the Puritans still inspires the world in the 21st century, although not always in ways that John Winthrop would have agreed with.

—Charles Bahne

View of the city of Boston from Dorchester Heights.
painted and engraved by Robt. Havell, circa 1841

CHRONICLES OF OLD BOSTON

TABLE OF CONTENTS

WALKING TOURS

CHAPTER 1.

CITY UPON A HILL

John Winthrop established the tone for Boston before his ship even left British waters. "For we must consider that we shall be as a City upon a Hill," Winthrop told his fellow émigrés aboard the *Arbella*, as they waited for fair winds to take them to America in the spring of 1630. "The eyes of all people are upon Us." Whether it succeeded or failed, the new settlement would prove an example for all the world to observe. "A Model of Christian Charity," he called it.

The men and women who came to the Massachusetts Bay Colony were different from other European colonists of the early 17th century. Wealthier and better educated than settlers elsewhere, they were not adventurers, traders or planters. Despite positions of influence in a rising middle class, they faced religious and political persecution. Their opponents called them "Puritans" because they wanted to "purify" the Church of England. It was not a name they called themselves.

In the Puritans' eyes, the Church of England—also called the Anglican Church—was rife with corruption. The King appointed the Archbishop; the Archbishop named the bishops; and the bishops chose the parish clergy.

< John Winthrop and passengers of the *Arbella* landing in the New World

John Winthrop

"Scandalous and dumb ministers" misinterpreted the Bible, or so the Puritans thought, while "learned" ministers were suspended by their superiors. Efforts at reform were rebuffed by the upper levels of the church hierarchy, who lived royally. In 1625 a new king, Charles, acceded to the throne; he soon began to suppress the dissenters even more harshly.

It took years for the self-proclaimed "saints" to plan their escape from "this sinfull lande." They received a land grant in March of 1628, and a charter a year later. Charles may have issued the charter to the Massachusetts Bay Company simply because he wanted the Puritans to leave the mother country.

Like other American settlements of the era, the Bay Company's charter was suited to a commercial enterprise, not to a government. It was assumed that the investors and top officials would remain in England. But that wasn't spelled out in the document. Six months after receiving the charter, the Company's members agreed to transfer "the whole Government," the charter included, to America.

John Winthrop didn't plan to join that first group to come to New England. At 41 years old, a successful lawyer and a justice of the peace with a manor at Groton, he was sympathetic to their beliefs but not yet convinced to depart his home. But the colony's "Chief undertakers" persuaded Winthrop that "the welfare of the Plantation depends upon his going," and they would not go without him. In October of 1629, Winthrop was unanimously elected Governor of the Massachusetts Bay Company.

The next March, some 700 souls boarded 11 ships at Southampton, England. The first four vessels departed on March 22, carrying Governor Winthrop and the colony's other leaders. They arrived on the other side of the Atlantic on June 12. According to Winthrop, "Salem, where we landed, pleased us not," and within a week the company had moved to Charlestown. That too was unsuccessful, due to "the want of fresh water," and by the fall most of the early settlers were moving across the river.

On September 7, 1630, the Court of Assistants ordered: "Trimountaine shall be called Boston." The name refers to a town in Lincolnshire, England, from which several prominent members of the colony had come. ("Massachusetts" was a Native American term meaning "at the blue hills," a reference to the peaks south of Boston that are visible from Massachusetts Bay.) On November 29 Winthrop wrote back to England, "My dear wife, we are here in a paradise." Margaret Winthrop would follow him a year later.

The colony grew spectacularly, and it thrived under Winthrop. A thousand more arrived later that year; and within a decade over 20,000 Englishmen and women would settle in the Bay Colony. This was far more people than the colony's leaders had anticipated, and there were growing pains as new towns were established throughout the countryside.

At the beginning, John Winthrop and the other founders of the Bay Colony thought democracy to be incompatible with their goals. Sitting at the edge of the wilderness, they were keenly aware of potential enemies. Among those enemies, of course, were the church officials back in England. And there were internal enemies, too: In order to accomplish the works of God on earth, there could be no tolerance for heresy. Seeking freedom to worship in the way they saw fit, the Puritans didn't believe they could offer the same freedom to those who disagreed with them. The other New England colonies—Connecticut, Rhode Island and New Hampshire were all founded by people driven out of Massachusetts for religious reasons.

Still, democracy arose naturally. Distance diminished the king's authority, and new structures formed to replace it. Without bishops, the churches of Massachusetts became congregational: each parish was a direct covenant between God and his parishioners. When a decision had to be made, the assembled parishioners relied on their collective wisdom to reach a just one. Yet church and state were distinct. God was concerned with men's souls, not with petty matters of local government.

Secular government soon followed the congregational model, evolving into the New England town meeting, a form of direct democracy. The town

A JEZEBEL IN THEIR MIDST

Anne Hutchinson Preaching in her House in Boston

From the 21st-century perspective, Puritan Boston's darkest hour was the exile of Anne Hutchinson, expelled from Massachusetts for her outspoken religious beliefs. The Puritans, of course, saw things differently.

The Hutchinson family—Anne, her husband William and their 11 children—came to America in 1634 and built a house at the present-day corner of School and Washington Streets, across from Governor John Winthrop's home. The year after their arrival, Anne began hosting informal meetings in her house, at which she discussed Biblical passages. Originally only a few women attended, but by 1636 the crowds had grown to about 80 men and women every week. When she started disparaging Boston's male religious leaders, they could take it no longer.

The Killing of Anne Hutchinson

Tried and convicted of heresy, excommunicated from the church and banished from the colony, Anne Hutchinson walked to Portsmouth, Rhode Island in April 1638. There the Hutchinsons helped establish a new colony, populated by other exiles from Massachusetts. After her husband died, Anne and her younger children moved to Dutch New York to be free from English control. She and six of her children were killed in 1643 by raiding Native Americans, near what is now the Hutchinson River in the Bronx.

John Winthrop was chief judge of the court that convicted Anne Hutchinson in November 1637. To Winthrop and the other Puritan leaders, she was an enemy in their midst, an unlearned lay preacher who had to be cast out if the fragile colony were to survive. We might disagree.

meetings, in turn, elected delegates to the General Court, or legislature. For half a century, the people of Massachusetts Bay governed themselves, without interference from the mother country—setting a precedent for their descendants' protests against the policies of George III and his Parliament.

A key belief for the Puritans was the concept of "commonwealth," the idea that a community is interdependent: all its members share responsibility for their overall well-being, and for each other. As Winthrop said aboard the *Arbella*, "We must bear one another's burthens. We must not look only on our own things, but also on the things of our brethren ... For this end, we must be knit together, in this work, as one man." This idea was still important to the leaders of Massachusetts a century and a half later, when John Adams drafted the Constitution that still governs the Commonwealth—not the State—of Massachusetts.

John Winthrop was the guiding light of the Massachusetts Bay Colony. He helped establish principles of government that Americans now take for granted, such as the two-house legislature and the absence of hereditary titles. Twelve times he was re-elected as Governor; three times he was chosen Deputy Governor. But the people of Massachusetts did not follow his light blindly; in some elections he was defeated. When he died in 1649, he had been Governor for 12 of the Colony's 19 years.

Winthrop's words onboard the *Arbella* continue to inspire generations of Americans. Three centuries after that ship sailed across the ocean, as John F. Kennedy prepared to assume the Presidency, he recalled John Winthrop's famous words: "We must always consider that we shall be as a city upon a hill—the eyes of all people are upon us."

CHAPTER 2.

A COLLEGE IN THE WILDERNESS

The Puritans who settled Massachusetts in 1630 carried their love of learning across the Atlantic with them. Wealthier and better educated than most other 17th-century emigrants, they'd grown tired of English pastors who weren't knowledgeable about the Holy Scripture. So, less than a decade after they'd carved out settlements in the wilderness, they created an institution of learning that has become one of the greatest universities in the world.

As one of their members wrote in 1643, "After God had carried us safe to New England ... One of the next things we longed for, and looked after was to advance Learning and perpetuate it to Posterity; dreading to leave an illiterate Ministery to the Churches, when our present Ministers shall lie in the Dust."

Yet, for such an illustrious institution, the establishment of Harvard College was marked by mishaps and scandals. Perhaps no one in history has achieved so much fame from such a small monetary donation as John Harvard got from his bequest.

‹ John Harvard statue, Harvard University, circa 1904

Harvard College, Cambridge, 1762

We do know this: John Harvard was not the founder of the college. In fact, he was still in England when it was created.

Truth be told, there was no single "founder" of Harvard College. It was created by an act of the Massachusetts Bay Colony's legislature, the Great and General Court. Colonial records say that, on October 28, 1636, the Court agreed to give £400 towards a school or college. It's not recorded who proposed the measure, and the ayes and nays are similarly lost to history.

The promised £400, almost a quarter of the colony's annual budget (and about $70,000 in today's money), was to be given in installments. In the end, the "country's gift" wasn't fully paid until 14 years later, and some of that in agricultural produce instead of cash.

In agreeing to fund the college, the General Court decided "to appoint where and what building" at its following session, but the Court was preoccupied with the heresy trial of Anne Hutchinson, a matter that kept officials busy for a full year. It wasn't until November 15, 1637, that the Court ordered the college to be at "Newetowne," the community now known as Cambridge.

Five miles upstream from Boston, Newetowne had initially been planned as the colony's capital. But things hadn't worked out that way, and many of the town's first residents relocated to Connecticut, perhaps because of religious differences with other colonists. A new group of settlers came to Newetowne in 1636; the "enlightening and powerful ministry" of their leader, the Reverend Thomas Shepard, was one reason why the town was chosen for the college over Marblehead, another suggested site for "that happy seminary."

Once picked as the college's home, it was only natural that Newetowne be renamed in honor of an English university town. Many of the colony's leaders had studied at Cambridge; so in May of 1638, the General Court "ordered, that Newetowne shall henceforward be called Cambrige."

After choosing the site for the college, the Court picked a committee of overseers to operate it. The overseers bought an acre of land from a Mr. Peyntree and began construction of a college building upon his cow yard. Until that first building was completed, Peyntree's former house served as the school's temporary headquarters.

For the college's first professor, the overseers selected Nathaniel Eaton. Sometime in the summer of 1638—the exact date is lost to history—Professor Eaton began instructing nine students, the first freshman class.

As far as can be discovered, John Harvard had no connection with the college while he was living. He likely knew Nathaniel Eaton, perhaps even called him a friend; they might have met during their college years. No one is sure of the reason for his gift; we only know that, when he died on September 14, 1638, Harvard bequeathed half his estate and his entire library to the still-unnamed college in Cambridge.

Born in London in 1607, the son of a butcher, John Harvard had trained for the ministry at the University of Cambridge; but with his Puritan beliefs, he could not hope to be a clergyman in his home country. His parents and his siblings had all died young, many of them perishing of the plague; his combined inheritances made John a well-to-do member of the middle class. At his death he was described as "a Scholler and pious in his life."

John Harvard and his wife Ann arrived in Massachusetts in summer of 1637, possibly on the same ship with Nathaniel Eaton. Both families settled in Charlestown, where Harvard was named assistant minister of the church. Scarcely a year after his arrival, Harvard succumbed to "a consumption" (tuberculosis). Childless and just 30 years old, he left no written will, just a deathbed request that his estate be divided between his widow and the new college.

Sources vary greatly in their assessment of John Harvard's estate; an early college treasurer put the college's share at exactly £779 17s. 2d., the equivalent of about $140,000 in today's currency. Of this total, it's unclear

Harvard along the Charles River from Weeks Memorial Bridge, 1932-33

how much the school actually received. Some of the bequest was in the form of uncollected debts; as late as 1650 the college was still suing John Harvard's debtors in efforts to recover the money. And chief among his assets was a tavern in a busy section of London, later sold for an undisclosed price.

Based on this legacy, and on his extensive library of 329 titles (more than 400 volumes), the General Court voted the next March that the school "shalbee called Harvard Colledge," thus granting immortality to a young minister who probably would otherwise be forgotten.

Alas, Nathaniel Eaton proved to be an unfortunate choice as the college's first professor. In August 1639, he was accused of giving an assistant teacher some 200 blows with a cudgel "big enough to have killed a horse." Investigation showed that Eaton regularly whipped his students, and his wife furnished an "ill and scant diet" to them, "ordinarily nothing but porridge and pudding, and that very homely." One of his students later called Eaton "fitter to have been … master of a house of correction, than an instructor of Christian youth."

Summarily dismissed from Harvard, Eaton fled to Virginia, tossing a constable who tried to detain him overboard as he made his escape. It was then discovered that he'd amassed immense debts and had passed worthless bills of exchange. Of John Harvard's bequest, Eaton had absconded with everything he could lay hands on—at least £200, likely more. Years later he fled Virginia, abandoning his second wife there, and ultimately died in a London debtor's prison.

After just a year, the nascent college was forced to close while a new instructor was found. Its savior was Henry Dunster, chosen President of the College in 1640. Serving in that post for 14 years, Dunster was responsible for resuming classes, completing the college's first building, and putting the school in good financial standing. In 1642 he presided over Harvard College's first commencement ceremony, a graduating class of just nine students.

At the approach of its quarter-millennial celebration in 1886, the school—then known as Harvard University—wanted to honor its namesake with a statue. There are no portraits or even any written descriptions of John Harvard's appearance, so sculptor Daniel Chester French hired a student, Sherman Hoar (Harvard class of 1882) as a model. Its granite pedestal is carved "John Harvard, Founder, 1638," giving the sculpture the nickname "statue of three lies," since each line of the inscription is wrong. Tourists, told that rubbing the statue's left toe will bring good luck, have left that shoe bright and shiny; but students sometimes boast of doing unspeakable things to that shoe as well. As a university symbol, "John Harvard's" statue is a prime target for pranks by students of rival schools.

John Harvard's bequest of £779—assuming that the college even got all of it—would be worth about $140,000 today. In a day when colleges routinely name things after large benefactors, a gift of that size would probably not even merit a coatroom. But for that puny amount, John Harvard got the greatest name in all of academia.

The Overdue Book

Although the monetary portion of his bequest was either squandered or plundered by Nathaniel Eaton, John Harvard's library survived largely intact for 126 years. With other donations, it became the nucleus of a book collection that rivaled many European college libraries. But on the night of January 24, 1764, Harvard Hall and its contents, including the entire library, were consumed by fire. Only one volume from John Harvard's collection survived, because it had been checked out: *The Christian Warfare Against the Devill World and Flesh*, by John Downame.

In recent years a legend has circulated that the student who had borrowed the book was expelled, since the volume was several weeks overdue. But a check of college records shows that the book had been borrowed by Ephraim Briggs, who did indeed graduate with the rest of his class, later in 1764.

John Harvard's copy of *The Christian Warfare* is now displayed in a place of honor in Houghton Library, the university's rare books repository. It is the only piece of John Harvard's bequest known to survive today.

JOSEPH BRECK & SONS

CHAPTER 3.

THE JOLLY BACHELOR

If it weren't for Faneuil Hall, few people would remember the name of Peter Faneuil today. For five brief years he was "the topmost merchant in all the town," with a fleet of ships that traded across the Atlantic. Among those ships was one he called the *Jolly Bachelor*, a not-so-subtle allusion to his own reputation for entertaining. But today we recall Peter Faneuil as the donor of one of Boston's most cherished landmarks.

The Faneuil family were Huguenots, French Protestants who fled religious persecution in their homeland in the 1690s. Of the two Faneuil brothers who immigrated to the New World, Benjamin settled in New Rochelle, New York, while Andrew came to Boston.

Then as now, New Englanders were uncertain how to pronounce the family name. In French, it would be *fuh-noy*, with a silent *l*. But few Bostonians of his day spoke French. On Peter's tomb in the Granary Burying Ground, his name was initially carved the way the locals pronounced it: "P. Funel." Later, the pronunciation evolved into *fannel*; today, most people say *fan-yel* (like Daniel), *fan-yool* or even (horrors!) *fan-you-ell*.

‹ Faneuil Hall, circa 1920s

Andrew had escaped France with a good-sized fortune, and soon became the most prosperous merchant in New England. After his brother died in 1719, the childless Andrew and his wife, Mary Catherine, took in their two nephews and four nieces. Five years later, Mary Catherine Faneuil died, an emotional loss that weighed heavily on the widowed Andrew.

Legend has it that Andrew Faneuil—still suffering from the passing of his beloved—insisted that his two nephews, Peter and Benjamin, forego any romantic attachments with the female gender. Supposedly Andrew first planned to bequeath his business and estate to Benjamin, the younger nephew. But Benjamin fell in love, and so was disinherited by his uncle.

When Andrew passed away in 1738, his will gave Benjamin just "five shillings and no more"—the equivalent of 83 cents in American money. The bulk of the estate, many tens of thousands of pounds, went to Benjamin's brother Peter, who'd remained unwed. The inheritance included Andrew's mansion with its seven-acre terraced garden, ornamented by flowers and shrubs, and hothouses filled with tropical fruits.

Peter Faneuil became the wealthiest man in Boston, and he lived up to his newfound means. Within three weeks of his uncle's passing, Peter sent to London to order five barrels of "your very best Madeira wine … for the use of my house." Soon he was buying glass and china, silverware bearing the family crest, and "a handsome chariot."

At the time, a controversy was brewing about Boston's lack of a central food market; without such a market, farmers and hawkers strolled the streets, peddling wares from carts. Feelings on both sides were quite strong; one wooden market had been demolished in the middle of the night by a mob "disguised as clergymen."

Peter Faneuil was of the pro-market faction. He disliked the inconvenience of searching all over town for pushcart vendors selling the fine foods he wanted for his table. So in 1740 he offered "at his own cost and charge to erect and build a noble and complete structure or edifice to be improved for a market." When it was put to a vote, Faneuil's generous offer was accepted by a bare seven-vote margin: 367 *yea* and 360 *nay*.

Peter Faneuil

To appease the opposition, Peter Faneuil added a meeting hall on the second floor, above the market stalls. It has been so ever since: politics upstairs, and commerce below. As poet Frank Hatch wrote in 1958,

Here orators
In ages past
Have mounted their attack
Undaunted by proximity
Of sausage on the rack.

Artist John Smibert drew up the plans and construction took two years. On September 10, 1742, the contractor delivered the keys, at Peter Faneuil's request, to the town selectmen. Three days later, a special town meeting voted unanimously, "in testimony of the town's gratitude," to name the hall in honor of its benefactor.

Sadly, one of the first meetings held in the new hall was Peter Faneuil's own funeral oration. The Jolly Bachelor died on March 3, 1743, not quite 43 years old, leaving behind a cellar-full of wine, beer and cheese. His brother Benjamin—the one who had been disinherited just five years earlier—now received the bulk of Peter's estate.

The market under Faneuil Hall was slow to gain acceptance; it was the meeting hall that proved popular. The first market stall wasn't rented until three months after the building opened; the second stall, not until a year later. During its first two decades, the market was often closed entirely. Then in 1761, fire gutted the hall, leaving only the brick walls. A lottery was established to fund the building's restoration. When it reopened in 1763, James Otis prophetically dedicated the upstairs room to the "Cause of Liberty."

Gathered in Faneuil Hall the next year, Boston's town meeting voted to protest Parliament's passage of the Sugar Act. As they put it then, "If Taxes are laid upon us in any shape without our having a Legal Representation where they are laid, are we not reduced from the Character of Free Subjects

Faneuil Hall, 1789

to the miserable state of tributary Slaves?" It was America's first public protest against policies of the mother country in the years leading up to the Revolution.

In this sacred hall Bostonians rallied against the Stamp Act, the Townshend Acts and the landing of British troops in 1768. Funeral services for the five victims of the Boston Massacre were held here, as was the first of the Tea Meetings to discuss the fate of that "pernicious herb."

During the British occupation of Boston, the hall served as a barracks by British soldiers, then used as a theater for their officers' amusement—at a time when dramatic performances were still banned by the town government.

After the Revolution, Faneuil Hall remained the venue for Boston town meetings until 1822, when the town became a city. Since then, it's endured as a forum for political meetings of every stripe, notably some of the most important meetings of the anti-slavery movement in the years before the Civil War. It's still used regularly by political candidates and advocacy groups, as well as for student spelling bees and citizenship ceremonies, and occasional orchestra concerts. On the night before he was elected President, John F. Kennedy addressed the nation from its rostrum on live television.

In 1805, the structure was enlarged by architect Charles Bulfinch. It now takes up twice its original footprint, and is four stories high instead of two and a half. Brick walls on three of its four sides are original from 1742, as is the gilded grasshopper atop the cupola.

In 1826 Josiah Quincy, the second Mayor of Boston, built the adjacent Faneuil Hall Market complex (sometimes called "Quincy Market" in

Josiah's honor) as an extension of the food markets under Faneuil Hall itself. On their 150th anniversary those three market buildings were restored and renovated into the "festival marketplace" that now occupies them. Meat markets in the ground floor of Faneuil Hall itself also endured into the 1970s; the space is now occupied by a National Park visitor center.

Ironically, Faneuil and his family were on the losing side of the two biggest issues associated with Faneuil Hall over the centuries. Not only did Peter own slaves for his household, he traded slaves commercially, profiting from the sale of human beings. And his nephew Benjamin—the son of Peter's brother Benjamin, and the third generation of his family to bear that name—was one of the East India Company's consignees, whose cargo of tea leaves was destroyed in 1773.

Peter would be surprised. His gift, the "Cradle of Liberty," has long been one of America's foremost centers for political debate. From taxation without representation to abolition of slavery, from tea to health care, it's all been discussed in Faneuil Hall. Yet politics was an afterthought when Peter Faneuil donated the building to Bostonians in 1742. He only wanted a convenient place to buy food.

Peter Faneuil's Grasshopper

Surmounting the cupola of Faneuil Hall is a gilded grasshopper. Many theories have been proffered over the years for the choice of this insectiform weathervane, but it appears to have been Peter Faneuil's idea, copied from the Royal Exchange building in London. Faneuil was a member of that exchange and he had a similar, but smaller, vane atop the summerhouse in the gardens behind his Tremont Street house.

Shem Drowne, deacon and master craftsman, fashioned the weathervane out of copper and gold leaf, with glass doorknobs for eyes. It's 52 inches long and weighs 38 pounds. In 1755 it crashed to the ground in an earthquake; in 1761 it survived a fire. Drowne's son, Thomas, repaired the weathervane in 1768.

A mysterious note was once found, folded up inside the "vest" attached to the grasshopper's thorax; in that handwritten note, the grasshopper explains that he escaped the 1761 fire by "hopping Timely from my Publick Scituation," coming off "With Broken bones, & much Bruised." Later in the note, which is now in the Boston Public Library, the insect promises to "Discharge my Office, yet I shall vary as ye Wind."

CHAPTER 4.

THE HOUSE OF HANCOCK

He was the richest and most popular man in Massachusetts. Yet today no house or statue, no poem nor even a beer recalls his life. Only an insurance company and its office tower are named after him. John Hancock today is known best for his autograph, a flourish of ink so bold that his very name is a synonym for the word signature.

John Hancock was born the first son of a minister, himself the eldest son of another clergyman, and the traditions of the day would have had John Hancock follow his elders to the pulpit. Then his father died when John was 7 years old. Soon afterwards, the boy was adopted by his father's brother. Thomas, the uncle, had achieved spectacular success in business at a young age, but he had no children. John Hancock, his nephew, was chosen to be his business partner and heir.

Young John studied at Boston Latin and Harvard and then learned business at his uncle's side. An education of another sort came in London, where he was sent by his uncle to establish trading contacts. Even his prosperous uncle balked at the reports of John's lavish living—a habit the lad would maintain for the rest of his years.

‹ *The Declaration of Independence, July 4, 1776* (detail) by John Trumbull. John Hancock is seated at the table on the right-hand side

Hancock mansion before its demolition in 1863

John's rise to prominence came suddenly. On August 1, 1764, his uncle Thomas collapsed inside the Town House, today's Old State House. John Hancock, age 27, became the wealthiest man in the province, with an inheritance nearing £70,000, perhaps $12 million in modern U.S. money. (Thousands more would come 12 years later, at the death of his Aunt Lydia.) He got the business, the fleet of six ships, the house on Beacon Hill, thousands of acres of land throughout New England—he got it all.

It was a time of change for Boston and for the merchant trade. Thomas Hancock had earned much of his wealth pursuing government contracts in time of war. Now in peacetime, there were no more military procurements. John changed the focus of the family business to consumer goods. Although the town was in an economic recession, the House of Hancock profited immensely. John bought his own wharf and renamed it after himself. He expanded his fleet and named one of his new ships *Liberty*, displaying his political views to all.

Hancock had learned to use wealth as a tool to win popularity. As one of the town's biggest employers, he paid good wages. As a merchant, he offered competitive prices and fair credit terms. He helped establish a number of other young men in business. He improved the town through real estate development. And like his uncle, he donated to charity, not only to churches and institutions, but also to individuals who needed help.

As his later enemy, royal Governor Thomas Hutchinson, would write, "The nephew's ruling passion was a fondness for popular applause. He changed the course of his uncle's business, and built and employed in trade, a great number of ships; and in this way, and by building at the same time several houses, he found work for a great number of tradesmen, made himself popular, was chosen select man, representative, moderator of town meetings, etc."

On news of the repeal of the Stamp Act, John Hancock gave a "grand and elegant Entertainment." A huge display of fireworks was set off from his house, visible to all who gathered on the Common, and he "treated the populace with a pipe of Madeira wine." When that first cask ran dry, Hancock's servants rolled out a second.

Was John Hancock the biggest smuggler in Boston, as his enemies claimed? Was he even a smuggler at all? Perhaps; perhaps not. For obvious reasons, the records say nothing. But smuggling was a way of life in Boston, and Hancock was probably no exception. Sea captains would often negotiate bribes with junior-level customs officials or unload cargo secretly before government agents could perform their inspections. Such was the setting for the government's seizure of John Hancock's sloop *Liberty* in June of 1768.

The Townshend Acts

After the Stamp Act was repealed in 1766, officials in Britain still felt a need to raise revenue from their American colonies. Charles Townshend, Chancellor of the Exchequer, proposed taxes on certain goods that were shipped from the mother country to the colonies. The 1767 legislation adopting these taxes was called the Townshend Act; the duties applied to lead, paint, paper, glass and tea.
Colonists in Boston and elsewhere reacted with what would now be called a boycott. They refused to buy, not only the taxed goods, but any goods imported from England. While these protests were ultimately successful, they caused economic problems at home. Fewer imports from Britain meant less activity on the waterfront, in turn creating joblessness and poverty.
The colonists' actions meant lost business for British manufacturers, and Parliament responded by repealing the Townshend Act duties in 1770—except for the tax on tea, which was retained.

Smuggler or not, royal officials had their eye on John Hancock. His politics made him their obvious target; his legal maneuverings had outwitted them before. Worse, he led a successful effort to shun the officials at social occasions. The embarrassed Customs Commissioners wanted to make an example of King Hancock.

They saw their chance with *Liberty*. A month after its arrival, a customs agent made a belated claim that he had witnessed foul play on its landing. By this time, *Liberty* was ready to depart again, laden full with outbound

cargo. A naval vessel seized *Liberty* and towed her away, to be auctioned off, along with her rich cargo. Mobs at the wharf pelted the customs officials with rocks and filth, then stoned their houses. Francis Bernard, the royal Governor, appealed to the King to send troops to keep order in the town.

While all this was going on, Hancock stayed at his mansion. There could be no claim that he had a role in the violence. Yet within five months, the troops that Bernard had requested were marching up Long Wharf. Within two years, those soldiers would be involved in the Boston Massacre.

Hancock's businesses were forced to close at the beginning of the Revolution. They never reopened. Effectively, John Hancock retired at the age of 38. He would live the rest of his life—just 18 more years—on interest from his investments, sales of his vast real estate, and small salaries from government offices.

His popularity established, Hancock was regularly elected to public office for the rest of his life, first as a town official, then as a representative in the Massachusetts Assembly, and later in higher positions. After the Revolution, he became Massachusetts's first popularly-elected governor and served 11 years in that post.

It was fate, perhaps, that Hancock was President of the Second Continental Congress on July 4, 1776—as the presiding officer, he was, in fact, the only man to sign the Declaration on that day. Most of the Declaration's signatures were affixed a month later to a formal copy that had been prepared by a calligrapher in the intervening weeks.

The landing of British troops in Boston, 1768

Legend has it that as Hancock put his embellished mark on the Declaration, he made a comment about George III not needing his spectacles to read it. Like many legends, the story is unlikely. As a Boston schoolboy

Hancock had studied with Abiah Holbrook, one of history's great writing masters. Hancock's fine penmanship can be seen on countless pages of his uncle's ledger books; his florid signature adorned (and authenticated) thousands of lottery tickets issued to rebuild Faneuil Hall while he was a Boston selectman.

There is one document, though, that John Hancock never signed: a will. He died with no legal instructions for the dispersal of his estate, and with no surviving children. He was still a wealthy man, but his estate was a small fraction of what he had inherited from his uncle. It took decades for his relatives to sort out their shares.

For years after his death, Hancock's one great monument was his house, the fine granite mansion erected by his uncle Thomas. Across the street from the Common, just below the peak of Beacon Hill, it had an unsurpassed view of the city and the harbor. Everyone in town literally looked up to it. The only thing higher was the beacon itself, from which the hill had taken its name.

It is said that Hancock wanted to give the house to the state, as a governor's mansion to complement the new State House that would soon be erected next door, on his former pasture. But the lack of a will prevented Hancock's wish from coming true. Seventy years after Hancock's death, his grandnephews offered to sell the house to the state. Legislators thought the price too high, so the deal was never consummated. The mansion was sold to a developer instead, and demolished.

1 Hancock House: Beacon Street

happy BOSTON! ſee thy Sons deplore,
y hallow'd Walks beſmear'd with guiltleſs Gore:
ile faithleſs P—n and his ſavage Bands,
th murd'rous Rancour ſtretch their bloody Hands;
ke fierce Barbarians grinning o'er their Prey,
pprove the Carnage, and enjoy the Day.

If ſcalding drops from Rage from Anguiſh Wrung
If ſpeechleſs Sorrows lab'ring for a Tongue,
Or if a weeping World can ought appeaſe
The plaintive Ghoſts of Victims ſuch as theſe;
The Patriot's copious Tears for each are ſhed,
A glorious Tribute which embalms the Dead

But know, FATE ſummon
Where JUSTICE ſtrips the
Should venal C—ts the
Snatch the relentleſs Vi
Keen Execrations on t
Shall reach a JUDGE wh

The unhappy Sufferers were Meſs^s SAM^L GRAY, SAM^L MAVERICK, JAM^S CALDWELL, CRISPUS A
Killed. Six wounded; two of them (CHRIST^R MONK & JOHN CLARK) *Mortall*
Publiſhed in 1770 by Paul

CHAPTER 5.

BLOOD IN THE STREETS

Five bodies lie together in the Granary Burying Ground. Joined by happenstance in death, they probably never knew each other. We know little about their lives as well. Fate brought them to King Street on the night of March 5, 1770, and there they became martyrs, the five victims of Boston's Horrid Massacre.

It began as a dispute over a barber's bill, a business transaction that involved none of them. But after 17 months of occupation by an army from overseas, that barber's bill was just the spark needed to ignite a fatal fury. From shouted curses to jostling, to snowballs and rocks, to bullets and death—it took less than an hour.

Historian Mercy Otis Warren, a close friend of many of the Revolution's leaders, later wrote that "the American war may be dated from the hostile parade" of October 1, 1768, when two regiments of soldiers landed at Long Wharf and marched down King Street. Officials in London had ordered the troops to Boston after hearing that "the People in Town were in great Agitation" about the seizure of John Hancock's ship *Liberty* when customs officers alleged Hancock was smuggling cargo without paying import duties.

‹ *The Bloody Massacre Perpetrated in King Street Boston on March 5, 1770 by a party of the 29th Regt.*, engraving by Paul Revere

An 1856 depiction of the killing of Crispus Attucks during the Boston Massacre

The occupying force comprised about 1,200 men, compared with Boston's adult population of about 7,000; in other words, British soldiers made up about a sixth of the town's adults.

Inevitably, disputes arose. "Continual bickerings took place in the streets between the soldiers and the citizens," wrote Mercy Warren; the inhabitants "suffered almost every species of insult from the British soldiery." Rude remarks were directed at the town's women; passersby were halted for no seeming reason and had to explain, at gunpoint, why they were on the streets of their own town.

The times were difficult economically, too. To protest the Townshend Act—taxation imposed without representation—many Bostonians had pledged not to buy imports from Britain. But fewer purchases of imported goods meant fewer ships sailing across the Atlantic, and fewer workers needed on Boston's wharves. Having His Majesty's troops here just made matters worse. A soldier's small salary made no allowance for social life, so the enlisted men of the Royal Army were always looking for odd jobs, competing with residents for scarce employment.

As the second winter of the occupation drew to an end, tensions flared at Gray's Ropewalk, near Pearl Street in the present-day Financial District. Ropemaking was a labor-intensive industry requiring unskilled day laborers. With an Army barracks nearby, soldiers often helped out at Gray's.

On Friday, March 2, 1770, a soldier of the 29th Regiment happened by Gray's Ropewalk. Outside, some workers decided to poke fun at the Redcoat. One ropemaker asked the soldier if he wanted work. Yes, he replied, unaware it was a setup. "Well, then, go and clean my shithouse," laughed the worker. Angered, the soldier threw a punch. But a second ropemaker tripped him, and a third stole his cutlass. The soldier went to his barracks for some friends, and a full-fledged mêlée ensued, involving 30 or 40 people on each side.

After a weekend of minor brawls, rumors began to spread that something bigger would happen on Monday evening. The dispute over the barber bill would kindle the spark, as if one were needed.

Not long after dark on Monday, March 5, Edward Garrick, a wigmaker's apprentice, spied Capt. John Goldfinch of the 14th Regiment walking along King Street (today's State Street). Weeks earlier, Goldfinch had patronized the shop where Garrick worked. Lacking cash, the Captain wrote a promise to pay the bill later. He had, in fact, returned to pay up and had a receipt in his pocket.

Perhaps the teenaged Garrick didn't realize that the bill was settled; perhaps he just wanted to cause trouble. Whatever the reason, Garrick yelled out to Goldfinch: "There goes the fellow who hath not paid my master for dressing his hair!" Goldfinch ignored the lad and his friends.

Nearby was the Custom House, with a soldier standing outside it to guard the royal treasury within. The sentry, Private Hugh White, replied to Garrick, defending his officer. When Garrick passed by again an hour later, he resumed his argument with White, who responded by hitting the boy with the butt end of his musket.

Boston Massacre, by F.O.C. Darley

Soon word of White's assault on Garrick was spreading all over town; a crowd gathered, harassing White. A nearby church bell rang out—the usual fire alarm. Neighbors emerged looking for the fire—in those days, everyone in town was expected to help extinguish a blaze—and they joined in the fracas as well.

At first it was merely curses hurled at White. "Damned lobster son of a bitch!" "Bloody back!" Then a few snowballs flew, pieces of ice as big as a fist. White waved his loaded gun. "Fire, damn you, you dare not fire," the crowd yelled.

Across the square, Capt. Thomas Preston looked out of his office as the mob confronting White grew larger. With the sentry in increasing danger, Preston went to a barracks a few blocks away to assemble a rescue party. He returned with seven other soldiers and tried to bring White back to the guardhouse. But the angry assemblage would not allow them through.

Suddenly a thrown object—a club, a stick—arced through the air. A soldier fell, either hit by the missile or losing his balance trying to avoid it. When he regained his posture, he fired point-blank into the crowd. Then the other soldiers fired as well. There was no time to reload; each soldier fired just once, although some had loaded two balls into their muskets.

When smoke from the guns had cleared, three people were lying dead; two were mortally wounded and would die days later; and six more suffered non-fatal injuries. First to fall was Crispus Attucks, also known by the alias Michael Johnson, a tall man about 47 years of age. Of mixed African and Native American heritage, he'd escaped from slavery 20 years earlier.

Standing next to Attucks, and also slain, was Samuel Gray, a ropemaker, and one of the participants in the fight at Gray's ropewalk just three days earlier. Witnesses said Gray was shot by Matthew Kilroy, a private in the

29th Regiment, another combatant in that ropewalk brawl. Perhaps Kilroy recognized Gray and deliberately fired at him.

Also shot fatally were James Caldwell, a young mariner; Patrick Carr, a 30-year-old Irish immigrant and leather worker; and Samuel Maverick, 17, an apprentice to an ivory craftsman. The three men were in scattered locations near the edge of the crowd and may have just been spectators. Caldwell was returning home from a visit with his girlfriend.

brave Brethren in the Country, deeply affected with our Diſtreſſes, and to whom we are greatly obliged on this Occaſion—No one knows where this would have ended, and what important Conſequences even to the whole Britiſh Empire might have followed, which our Moderation & Loyalty upon ſo trying anOccaſion, and ourFaith in the Commander'sAſſurances have happily prevented.

Laſt Thurſday, agreeable to a general Requeſt of the Inhabitants, and by the Conſent of Parents and Friends, were carried to their *Grave* in Succeſſion, the Bodies of *Samuel Gray*, *Samuel Maverick*, *James Caldwell*, and *Criſpus Attucks*, the unhappy Victims who fell in the bloody Maſſacre of theMonday Evening preceeding!

On this Occaſion moſt of the Shops in Town were ſhut, all the Bells were ordered to toll a ſolemn Peal, as were alſo thoſe in the neighboring Towns of Charleſtown Roxbury, &c. The Proceſſion began to move between the Hours of 4 and 5 in the Afternoon; two of the unfortunate Sufferers, viz., Meſſ. *JamesCaldwell* and *Criſpus*

Four coffins of men killed in the Boston Massacre, as shown in the *Boston Gazelle*, 1770

Agitators or innocent bystanders, they all became heroes. Over 10,000 mourners came to their funeral at Faneuil Hall, the largest gathering "ever together on this Continent on any occasion," and the victims were buried together at the Granary Burying Ground. (A second funeral was held after Patrick Carr died on March 14.)

The town's printers issued dueling pamphlets, *A Short Narrative of the Horrid Massacre* and *A Fair Account of the Late Unhappy Disturbance* and even *Additional Observations to a Short Narrative*. Paul Revere's famous engraving of the Massacre was part of the propaganda effort, purposely distorting the scene, showing (among other things) Captain Preston standing behind his men, ordering his men to fire, when in reality Preston had been in front of them, telling them to cease fire.

Bostonians demanded a trial by a civilian jury, not a military one. Yet John Adams volunteered as the soldiers' defense lawyer, to ensure fairness. Calling the victims "a motley rabble," Adams won a surprising acquittal for Captain Preston and all but two of his men. They'd fired in self-defense,

The Sixth Martyr

Along with the five victims of the Boston Massacre, a sixth martyr lies in the same grave at the Granary Burying Ground: 12-year-old Christopher Seider (sometimes spelled Snider), "the innocent, first victim of the struggles between the Colonists and the Crown." Seider was killed, not by British soldiers but by a Boston civilian. It happened just 11 days before the Massacre.

On February 22, 1770, Seider was part of a crowd gathered in Hanover Street to protest a store that was selling foreign goods, in violation of the town's non-importation agreement. Not far from the store lived Ebenezer Richardson, a supporter of the King, who came out to pick a fight with the protesters and tried to run them down with a horse and cart. They responded by throwing rocks. Richardson then went in his house and fired a gun through a broken window, killing Seider and injuring another boy. Richardson was convicted of murder and sentenced to hanging, but King George III pardoned him and gave him a government job in Philadelphia.

Local residents had long despised Richardson, whom John Adams described as an "abandoned wretch." Not only was he an "informer" for the government, he had also fathered a child with his wife's sister.

said Adams, and no one could prove precisely which soldiers had fired the fatal shots. Privates Matthew Kilroy and Hugh Montgomery were found guilty of manslaughter, not murder. Avoiding prison sentences, they were branded on their thumbs, marks to display their guilt for the rest of their lives.

The remaining soldiers of the 14th and 29th Regiments were removed from town within days after the Massacre. Government officials, it seemed, had finally realized the folly of using military means to maintain peace in an urban setting.

For a decade and a half afterwards, the Town of Boston sponsored an annual Massacre Day oration on March 5. In 1776, George Washington and Henry Knox deliberately chose that infamous day to fortify Dorchester Heights, symbolically avenging the "horrid Massacre" by driving the British Army out of Boston once and for all.

But a century later, the final resting place of the Massacre victims at the Granary Burying Ground was still unmarked. It was Lewis Hayden, the black activist of another century, who was finally able to get a suitable monument erected in their honor in 1886.

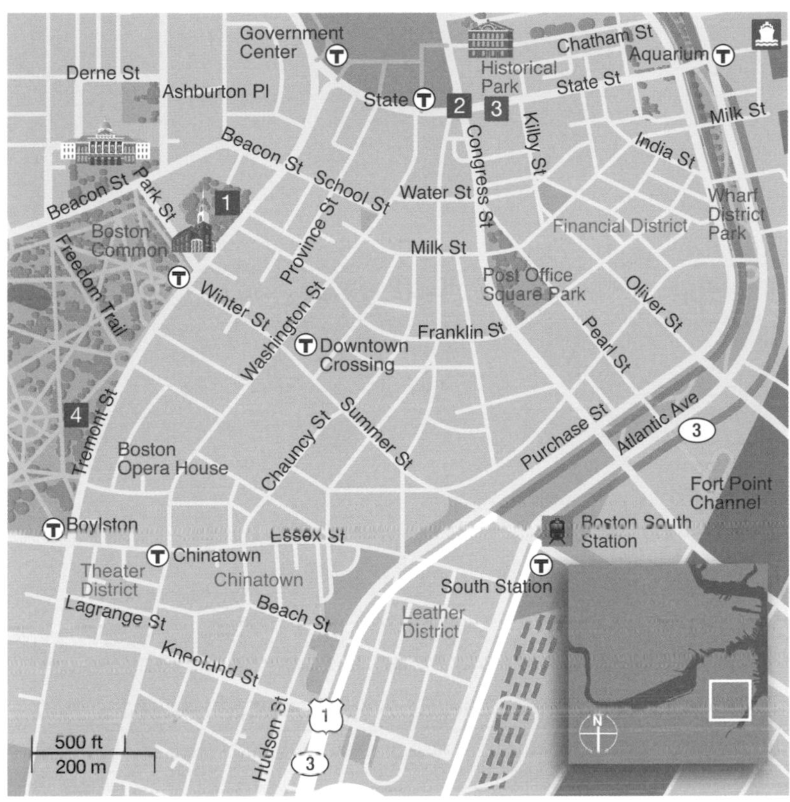

1 Granary Burying Ground
2 Massacre Site: State Street and Congress Street
3 Custom House
4 Boston Massacre Monument

CHAPTER 6.

SO LARGE A CUP OF TEA FOR THE FISHES

The destruction of the tea in Boston Harbor on the night of December 16, 1773, was the event that made a break with England inevitable. Once tea leaves had mingled with salt water, things "had gone too far to recede." Even Governor Thomas Hutchinson conceded that it was "the boldest stroke which had yet been struck in America."

As the only readily available source of caffeine in that era, tea was enjoyed by virtually everyone in England and her American colonies. By the 1760s, the average adult in the 13 colonies consumed about a cup a day, or a pound and a half of dry tea every year.

The London-based East India Company had a monopoly on importing tea into Britain, and much of their tea was re-exported to America. But that *legal* monopoly didn't prevent illegal trade. Enterprising merchants smuggled tea from Holland and sold it in the New World for less than the legal, taxed tea. By 1773, some 75 to 90 percent of all tea drunk in British America was smuggled. The East India Company neared bankruptcy, with warehouses of unsold tea rotting on the wharves of London. Still, it remained one of the largest corporations in the British Empire, with vast political influence.

Patriots dressed as Native Americans throw British tea into Boston Harbor

So the East India Company requested government aid, a bailout. The Tea Act, enacted in May 1773, actually reduced the total tax on tea sold in America, but it kept the tax established by the Townshend Acts six years earlier—the one tax that colonists had been most vocal in opposing. Instead, the Tea Act sought to lower the price of the Company's tea, so it could better compete with smuggled tea. The new law also changed the way that tea would be sold, extending the Company's monopoly into the American colonies.

Traditionally, tea had been sold in London to an exporter, who then sold it to an importer in America, who in turn sold it to retailers. Under the Tea Act, the Company would ship tea to its own handpicked agents in the colonies. The middlemen, and associated costs, were eliminated. In a political move, the East India Company chose the family and friends of Governor Thomas Hutchinson as its agents (or "consignees") in Boston.

By this time, Hutchinson had been in politics for virtually all his adult life. For 15 years he'd served as lieutenant governor, chief justice and governor, often holding multiple posts at the same time. But he'd become "the principal object of popular resentment," in repeated conflict with James Otis, John Hancock, Samuel Adams and their political allies. In 1770, King

George III appointed Hutchinson to his highest post yet, Royal Governor of the Province of the Massachusetts Bay.

Hutchinson was proud to represent "the greatest monarch on earth." He named his in-laws and friends to high-ranking positions, and curried favor with London officials in order to improve his own situation. He was a native of Massachusetts, yet he always sided with royal government policy; when he did disagree, he kept publicly silent and confided only to a few close acquaintances.

To many Bostonians, the East India Company's appointment of Hutchinson's two oldest sons as tea consignees was simply the latest example of the nepotism and corruption that had been government practice for decades. Besides the Hutchinson sons, Thomas Jr. and Elisha, the other consignees included Hutchinson's in-laws and cousins, and some family friends such as Benjamin Faneuil. The Hutchinsons and their friends would now have a monopoly on the sale of all legal tea in New England.

The popular response, advanced by patriot leaders and citizen meetings, was simple: Send the tea back to London, in the same ships it came in. In New York, Philadelphia and Charleston—the other ports receiving tea shipments following the Tea Act—the consignees all resigned; no one would accept the cargoes of "that bainfull weed." But in Boston, the family and friends of Governor Hutchinson refused to relinquish their posts. They knew they would profit from the tea when it was landed, and they knew they had the backing of the governor.

Even Hutchinson would profit if the tea were sold in Boston. The Governor's salary was paid from the tea tax; everyone in town knew that. What they didn't realize was that Hutchinson had also invested most of his savings in stock of the East India Company. His personal fortune, both financial and political, was thoroughly entangled in the tea trade.

Hutchinson used legal technicalities to thwart any efforts to avoid taxation. Once the tea ships had entered Boston Harbor, he said, the law required payment of the hated duties, even if the tea later went back to England. And no vessel could leave Boston Harbor without a "clearance," a permit signed by a government official. Hutchinson, of course, would never allow a

Fueled by Several Bowls of Punch

The preparations made by Boston's patriots before they dumped tea in Boston Harbor had to be kept profoundly secret. The plotters donned their "Indian" disguises away from the crowd, at houses and hiding places scattered about the town. One such place was revealed many years later, by a lad who'd been too young to take part: Peter Edes, an eyewitness to history in his own house.

Peter's father Benjamin was a printer and publisher of the radical *Boston Gazette* newspaper. The "Long Room" above Edes and Gill's print shop on Queen Street (now Court Street) was an important meeting place as the patriots plotted against the Crown. On one afternoon, a number of gentlemen met instead in the parlor of the Edes house on Brattle Street (now the site of City Hall Plaza). Peter, who would celebrate his 17th birthday the next morning, was not admitted into his elders' presence. His role was to make punch, in a bowl which he filled several times during the hours that they were gathered. Periodically, the door to the parlor would open, and the empty bowl would be handed out to Peter; when he passed the full bowl back, the door would shut again. After dark, Peter's father and his friends, fueled by the punch, left the house and proceeded to the wharves. Peter followed, among the 2,000 spectators who lined the shore.

Peter told the story, decades later, to his descendants. The Edes punch bowl is now in the collection of the Massachusetts Historical Society.

clearance to be issued until the tax was paid, and the Royal Navy was ready to sink or seize any ship that tried to leave without the required paperwork.

The law also required cargoes to be unloaded within 20 days after a ship's arrival. If the freight were still on board after that, the government would forcibly unload it and seize the ship too. *Dartmouth* had been the first ship to arrive, and thus the first to reach the end of the 20-day period, at midnight on December 16. Such was the deadline that all sides—patriots, consignees and government officials—faced on that fateful evening.

Hutchinson thought he had outwitted his enemies. All he had to do was wait. If the tea were still aboard *Dartmouth* on the morning of the 17th, the law would be upheld; the tea would be delivered to the consignees—his family members—who could then start selling it.

A final request for a clearance for *Dartmouth* came on the afternoon of the 16th. Sent by "the Body of the People," who had gathered that day in Old South Meeting House, the ship's owner traveled seven muddy miles to visit Hutchinson at his estate in Milton. Once again, the Governor refused. He'd had several chances to defuse the situation by allowing the tea to go back to England, but he would never relent.

Shortly after word of the Governor's refusal got back to Boston, "the War Whoop" was heard on the street outside the Old South. Few of the 7,000 people gathered in and around the meetinghouse knew what was about to happen; it was all planned elsewhere, in utmost secrecy. About 120 men and boys—many disguised as "Aboriginal Natives"—descended on the three vessels, while thousands of citizens observed from the shore. The accursed tea, that worst of plagues, that pernicious and obnoxious herb, was destroyed.

The protestors threw 342 chests and quarter-chests of tea into the sea—92,616 pounds in all, the equivalent of about 18,523,200 teabags. The East India Company's losses amounted to £9,659. In 18th-century American dollars, the tea was worth $32,000; today, it would retail for around $750,000½.

"Who knows," someone had pondered that evening, "how tea will mingle with salt water?" Afterwards, there were complaints of "the taste of their fish being altered," and newspaper reports of local fish contracting "a disorder not unlike the nervous complaints of the human body."

For Hutchinson, it was a bitter defeat. Two days before the tea was destroyed, he wrote, "Surely, My Lord, it is time this anarchy was restrained and corrected by some authority or other." Instead, the anarchy had triumphed. Hutchinson was removed from his job and exiled from his homeland. Recalled to England to meet with his King, whom he had so loyally served, Hutchinson was never able to return to Massachusetts.

1 Old South Meeting House: 310 Washington Street
2 Griffin's Wharf

CHAPTER 7.

PAUL REVERE'S RIDE

Late in the evening of April 18, 1775, a middle-aged silversmith set out from Boston on a mission that would become legend. The moon was just rising as Paul Revere and two friends climbed in a rowboat on the North End shore. With muffled oars they crossed to Charlestown, where Revere borrowed a horse and rode into history.

Thanks to a poem by Henry Wadsworth Longfellow, the midnight ride of Paul Revere has become one of the most famous events of our nation's past.

That spring, Revere was 40 years old, a successful craftsman. Because he worked with his hands, he could relate to and was trusted by Boston's other "mechanics" or artisans. And as a silversmith, his clientele came from the town's wealthiest elite. Thus Paul Revere was one of the few people in the town who communicated easily with working men and well-to-do alike.

As differences with the mother country arose in the 1760s, Revere joined the Sons of Liberty and helped lead efforts to oppose the Crown's policies. So when soldiers were posted in Boston in the summer of 1774—part of King George III's response to the destruction of the tea in Boston harbor—it was

< An illustration of Paul Revere on his ride

Paul Revere, by John Singleton Copley, 1770

only natural that Paul Revere became, as he put it later, "one of upwards of 30, cheifly [*sic*] mechanics, who formed our selves in to a Committee for the purpose of watching the Movements of the British Soldiers, and gaining every intelegence [*sic*] of the movements of the Tories."

In September 1774, the Regulars—so called because they belonged to the Regular (full-time) Army—made their first offensive excursion out of Boston. About 260 men sailed up the Mystic River, then marched to what is now Powder House Square in Somerville, where they seized 200 half barrels of gunpowder. Their mission caught the local folk by surprise; Revere's intelligence network was not yet established.

But that September raid was the Army's only successful attempt to capture the military supplies that New England residents were stockpiling. Subsequent efforts were all thwarted by the newly established spy network. Once, Paul Revere rode 60 miles to New Hampshire to alert the townsfolk of Portsmouth that soldiers were on their way.

In spring of 1775, it was apparent that His Majesty's Army was planning another mission, this time to either Lexington or Concord—Revere and his friends weren't sure of the precise destination. The midnight ride that Longfellow celebrated in his verse was in fact Paul Revere's third trip to warn those towns that April. On his first two rides, his message was more vague: The Regulars are coming soon. We don't know exactly when. Be prepared.

Using lantern signals as a backup, Revere and his compatriots created a system of redundant communications, in case messengers were physically unable to get out of Boston when the Regulars finally did march. On his second journey to Lexington, on April 16, Revere "returned at Night thro Charlestown" and agreed with some of the residents there, "that if the British went out by Water, we would Shew two Lanthorns in the North Church Steeple; & if by Land, one, as a Signal."

So—despite what Longfellow wrote—the lanterns were not a signal *to* Revere "on the opposite shore"; they were signals *from* him to the people in Charlestown, just in case Revere was unable to cross the river safely.

The lanterns were hung by Robert Newman, the sexton of Christ Church, and by Capt. John Pulling, a member of the parish vestry. For generations, descendants of Newman and Pulling have squabbled over who did what. In all probability, both men climbed the steeple. When they descended, they found a patrol of soldiers passing by the church door on Salem Street. They escaped through a window in the rear, near the altar.

While Newman and Pulling were working the lanterns, Revere was with two other friends, getting the rowboat ready. A family legend says that Revere forgot his spurs—but his dog had followed him. So, the story goes, Paul Revere wrote a note, tied it to the dog's collar, and sent the pup home. In due time the dog returned, with the spurs. The tale sounds exaggerated, but we know that Revere related it to his grandchildren, decades afterward.

One of Revere's friends also realized that they lacked cloth to muffle the sound of the oars in the water. Afraid to return to his own home, he went to his girlfriend's instead. After a whispered conversation, the young woman went inside. When she returned to her window, she threw down a flannel petticoat, still warm from the wearing.

Revere and his friends barely made it to Charlestown, rowing past the guns of the British Navy ship *Somerset*. The rising moon was not yet high enough to illuminate the scene; but astronomers estimate that if they had been 15 or 20 minutes later, they would have been seen and probably killed.

On the Charlestown shore, Revere asked if his lantern signals had been received (they had), and borrowed a horse of Deacon Larkin. Scarcely a mile after he'd mounted that steed, luck was again with Revere; he eluded a patrol of Army officers who were on the highway to stop express riders such as he. They chased Revere, but their horses got stuck in the mud when they took an off-road shortcut.

At midnight, Revere arrived at Lexington, where he'd been sent to warn John Hancock and Samuel Adams. A guard outside their lodgings did not recognize the rider and asked him not to make any noise since the occupants were sleeping. "Noise!" exclaimed Revere. "You'll have noise enough here before long. The Regulars are coming out!"

He never said: "The British are coming." Paul Revere, like everyone else in Massachusetts in 1775, thought of himself as British.

As yet another backup, Joseph Warren had sent a second rider, William Dawes, via a different route. Dawes, who left Boston before Revere, arrived in Lexington about half an hour after him. Having fulfilled their orders to warn Hancock and Adams, the two men decided to ride onward to Concord, seven miles up the road, to alert the militia there. En route they chanced on another rider on the highway: Samuel Prescott, a young doctor returning home from courting his fiancée. Prescott offered to help them carry their message of alarm.

About halfway to Concord, their luck ran out. Another Army patrol was blocking the road. Prescott escaped and carried the news to Concord. Dawes escaped too, but his horse got spooked and threw him. Revere was captured. The soldiers asked their captive's name; "Revere," he said. "What," came their reply, "Paul Revere?" Knowing him to be a leader in the rebel movement, the officers held him. But an hour later Revere was released by his captors, who were frightened by the sound of distant gunfire, and worried that their own small contingent might be outnumbered by the gathering militia.

Revere and Dawes were the only official alarm riders that night, the only ones given orders to depart Boston to warn the outside world. But they were not the only ones on the highway. Despite General Gage's best efforts, the Regulars' mission to Concord was no secret. Besides the Committee of Safety's two official expresses, upwards of 60 messengers helped spread the news in one form or another. Some of these were people whom Revere had alerted, who then rode in a different direction; others were citizens who'd seen the soldiers march by.

During his lifetime, and for four decades after his death, Paul Revere's excursion to Lexington was not well publicized. Revere himself remained active in civic affairs, and he became one of the young nation's first manufacturers, making gunpowder, cannons, church bells, and thin sheets of copper. He was known for these aspects of his life, and for his other roles in the Revolution, especially his political engravings and cartoons. The tale of Paul Revere's ride was basically one he reserved for telling his many grandchildren.

In 1797, however, Revere received a request from Jeremy Belknap of the Massachusetts Historical Society; in reply, Revere sent Belknap a letter documenting his trip to Lexington that April eve. Yet even after the Society published that letter, the midnight ride of Paul Revere remained relatively obscure, until Henry Wadsworth Longfellow made it famous in 1860.

THE MIDNIGHT RIDE OF... WILLIAM DAWES?

Listen, my children, while I pause
And you shall hear of William Dawes...

No, Henry Wadsworth Longfellow never wrote those lines. But in the century and a half since "Paul Revere's Ride" was published, many people have wondered why the poet chose Revere and not Dawes, for the hero of his poem.

There's a simple answer: Even before the story of his ride was widely known, Revere was famous for other things, while Dawes was relatively unknown. Revere was a silversmith, an engraver and a manufacturer of bells; his works can be seen in art museums and church towers around the world. Dawes was a tanner, who treated raw hides with chemicals to turn them into leather; none of his craftsmanship survives.

Revere helped secure his own legacy as well. He wrote a description of his ride that was published in his lifetime; he and his family kept volumes of letters, papers and journals. The Dawes family retained little; only a couple of his letters have been found.

In fact, Dawes was selected for his role in the midnight mission precisely because he was unknown. His route over Boston Neck required him to pass through an Army checkpoint; a rider was needed who would not arouse suspicions. Dawes was perfect for the part. He often traveled into the countryside for his work, to buy hides from farmers, so he was familiar with the roads. Yet the British officials were unaware of his activism for the Patriot cause; he easily bluffed his way past the officers who manned the gate on Boston Neck.

CHAPTER 8.

THE CASE OF DOCTOR CHURCH

Sex, intrigue, a mysterious letter written in cipher, a ship that disappeared at sea—the case of Dr. Benjamin Church reads like something out of a clichéd spy novel. Except that in Dr. Church's case, it was all true, to the dismay of George Washington and the Continental Congress. What's more, the full depth of Dr. Church's treachery wasn't even discovered until 150 years after his disappearance.

Dr. Benjamin Church, Jr., was a leading figure among Boston patriots in the decade before the Revolution. A surgeon and one of the few physicians in town who had trained in Europe, he was also a skilled poet and public speaker. As early as 1765, he wrote and published political satire to oppose British government policies. He had performed the autopsy on Crispus Attucks after the Boston Massacre and was the orator chosen to commemorate the third anniversary of that sad event.

By the eve of the Revolution, Dr. Church had risen to the top ranks of the patriot leaders, just below John Hancock and Samuel Adams. At one point he was Chairman of the Committee of Safety, the second-highest civilian position of the Massachusetts rebels; and in July of 1775, he was appointed

< *Ships Leaving Boston Harbor*, by Robert Salmon

Dr. Benjamin Church

Director and Chief Physician for the hospital in Cambridge—in effect, America's first Surgeon-General.

His downfall was one Godfrey Wenwood, a baker who lived in Newport, Rhode Island.

Not long after Dr. Church's appointment to the hospital post, Wenwood received a visit from an old lover. She had a letter for someone in Boston, she said, and she sought Wenwood's help in getting it there. Newport was still under British control and in regular communication with the military forces in Boston. But many of its residents, like Wenwood, supported the patriot cause.

Wenwood probably wondered why his old flame had showed up on his doorstep; their relationship had been a stormy one. So he put her letter aside. Several weeks later, she sent him another message, full of misspellings: "I much wonder you never Sent wot you promest to send.... I am alittle unesey that you never rote. thar is aserten person hear wants to Sea you verey much."

At some point Wenwood opened the original letter that she had given him, and found that it was written in coded characters—a mixture of malformed letters from our own alphabet, Greek letters, numbers and other strange symbols that ultimately proved to be a simple substitution cipher.

Wenwood and a friend took the suspicious correspondence to a patriot official in Providence, and soon they were conducted to Cambridge, to show the letters to General Washington. Wenwood's ex-lover was found, living nearby; after an examination and four hours under guard, she confessed: the coded letter had been written by Dr. Church.

Dr. Church was immediately arrested at his medical headquarters, across the road from General Washington's headquarters. Under interrogation, he admitted that the coded letter was his, but he said it was a family matter, sent to his brother-in-law. Unfortunately for Dr. Church, his story didn't jibe with the facts; when the letter was deciphered, it was addressed to a British Army officer and filled with confidential information about the Americans' military situation.

It did not help Dr. Church's case that the woman in question was known as "an infamous hussey," or that she was pregnant with his child. Other contemporary writers described the good doctor's mistress as "a Girl of Pleasure" and a "Concubine"; even Wenwood called her "a very lusty woman."

As word spread, other patriot leaders "could hardly conceive it possible." John Adams stood "astonished." "Our pride is sorely mortified when there are Grounds to suspect that so eminent a Countryman is become a Traitor," wrote Samuel Adams. But he added, "Before Church was detected, his Infidelity to his Wife had been notorious."

According to the official report of his trial on October 4, 1775, Dr. Church "explained his intention in writing said Letter, as calculated to impress the enemy with a strong idea of our strength and situation, in order to prevent an attack at a time when the Continental Army was in great want of ammunition." Still, the Council of War found Dr. Church guilty of carrying on a criminal correspondence with the enemy. He was stripped of his posts, both military and civilian. During the proceedings, he was held prisoner in his former headquarters, the Henry Vassall house in Cambridge, where he carved his name in a closet door: "B. Church jr." Later he was sent to jail in Norwich, Connecticut, "without the use of pen, ink and paper."

Henry Vassall House

In June of 1776, Dr. Church was sent back to Boston, which by then had been freed from British rule. Local residents felt so strongly about "that double damnable fellow," that "unprincipled wicked man," that he had to be kept in the town jail for his own safety. A prisoner exchange was attempted, trading Dr. Church for another surgeon who was being held by the British Army; but a rioting mob prevented Dr. Church's ship from leaving the dock.

Another mob destroyed the house where Mrs. Church was living; in her own words they "pillaged and destroyed every thing it contain'd, not leaving her a change of cloaths, nor even a bed for her and her children to lie on." Sarah Church fled to her native England, where she was granted a £150 annual pension, after she mentioned "certain services" that her husband had performed for the Crown.

In January 1778, Dr. Church was finally able to depart Massachusetts, where he was so detested. Permission was given for him to sail to the West Indies, "with orders never to return on pain of death" according to newspaper reports. His ship, the sloop *Welcome*, left Boston Harbor bound for Martinique. Lost at sea, neither the *Welcome* nor any of her passengers were ever heard from again.

To his end, Dr. Benjamin Church protested that he was innocent, a victim of circumstantial evidence. Yet time has proved him guilty. A full century and a half after Dr. Church's disappearance at sea, a wealthy collector from Michigan located the personal papers of British General Thomas Gage, purchased them from Gage's family, and brought them to America. When historians were at last able to go through General Gage's files, they found letters from Dr. Church, documenting that he'd been in the pay of His Majesty's government all along. America's first traitor, he was indeed.

His motive? We shall never know, but suspicion has long been that he did it for money, out of the need to support the "infamous hussey" with whom he had an affair.

The Death of General Warren at the Battle of Bunker Hill (detail), by John Trumbull

CHAPTER 9.

EVACUATION DAY

To Bostonians, March 17 is not St. Patrick's Day. The 17th marks Evacuation Day, a holiday to celebrate the liberation of the town from British rule in 1776. It was George Washington's first victory of the Revolution, won through the efforts of Henry Knox—a man with no formal military experience, who became one of Washington's closest advisers.

With the advent of war at Lexington and Concord on April 19, 1775, Boston remained under British control, but everything beyond the town limits was rebel territory. Boston was then a peninsula, linked to the mainland by a narrow neck of land (now Washington Street in the South End), and otherwise surrounded by water. Two other peninsulas overlooked Boston from either side of the harbor: Charlestown, with Bunker Hill, to the north; and Dorchester Heights, now South Boston, to the south.

At the Battle of Bunker Hill that June, the British forces gained Charlestown, but at a terrible cost; nearly half of His Majesty's men involved in that fight were killed or wounded. Dorchester Heights, to the south, remained unfortified rebel territory. A stalemate developed, with neither side feeling that it could profitably attack the other. And so it went,

‹ *George Washington at Dorchester Heights*, by Gilbert Stuart

no one willing to pick a fight with the other side, for nine months—through the summer, fall and winter.

Appointed commander-in-chief by the Continental Congress in Philadelphia, General Washington arrived in Cambridge to assume his command on July 2, just two weeks after the Bunker Hill battle. Three days after his arrival, Washington met 25-year-old Henry Knox, who impressed the general with his knowledge and engineering skills. They became friends; four months later, the commander-in-chief sent Knox on the mission that would ultimately win Boston.

As a teenager, Knox had been an apprentice at Daniel Henchman's bookshop on King Street, just a few doors away from the British Army's guardhouse, or military headquarters. Not long after the army entered Boston in 1768, officers started coming to Henchman to buy books on military subjects. When the books arrived from London, Knox read each volume before it was delivered to its purchaser. Through books, the young bookseller acquired much technical military knowledge, especially about artillery.

The mission entrusted to Knox was the retrieval of cannons from Fort Ticonderoga, a formerly British fort located near the southern end of Lake Champlain, on the New York–Vermont border. The previous May—after the fight at Lexington and Concord but before the Battle of Bunker Hill—Ethan Allen and his Green Mountain Boys had captured Ticonderoga for the American forces. Inside the fort was an arsenal of artillery. Those guns would be very useful to the American side, if somehow they could be transported back to the Boston area.

Dispatched from Cambridge in November, Knox arrived at Ticonderoga on December 5 and began moving the guns the same day. First the artillery pieces had to be barged down the length of Lake George before it froze over for the winter. One cannon fell into the Mohawk River (and was retrieved by historians decades later). From Albany, 60 tons of metal guns had to be brought overland on a narrow path—"rough, rocky, hilly, every way bad"—through the wilderness, crossing mountains, then down into river valleys.

To do the job, Knox hired 80 yoke of oxen and men to drive them. The muddy roads were unsuitable for such heavy loads, so they waited until

Hauling guns from Fort Ticonderoga, 1775

snow fell, then put the cannons onto 42 "exceeding strong sleds." At Springfield, Knox switched from oxen to horses. Heroic, nearly superhuman effort was needed; the 300-mile trip took seven weeks in the New England winter.

As they neared their destination, Knox rode ahead, reaching Cambridge on January 18, 1776. There he learned that, in his absence, he'd been commissioned a colonel, given command of all artillery for the newly created Continental Army.

The cannon followed, six days later. In all, Knox had brought 59 pieces of artillery—43 heavy brass and iron cannons, six cohorns, eight mortars and two howitzers—plus 23 boxes of leads and two barrels of flints. The stalemate was ended; the American army had a decisive edge for the first time since the war had begun the previous April.

General Washington proposed an invasion of Boston over the frozen Charles River, using the artillery to support the soldiers' march over the ice. Unanimously, his Council of War rejected that scheme. Instead, it was agreed to fortify the twin hilltops of Dorchester Heights, the peninsula overlooking Boston and its harbor from the south. Target date for the offensive was set for March 5, 1776, chosen since it would be the sixth anniversary of the Boston Massacre. Washington, Knox and their men had weeks to implement the plan. To be successful, they needed to surprise the Redcoats who were holed up in Boston.

The frozen soil would be impossible to dig by hand, so the fortifications were made off-site, then lugged in pieces to Dorchester Heights, where they were assembled in place. Some of the Ticonderoga cannons were carted up to the Heights; but some were placed in existing forts in Cambridge and Roxbury, along the Charles River. On the night of March 4, the guns by the river were fired almost continuously, both as a distraction and as a cover for noises coming from the Heights. But the cannons at Dorchester Heights never fired a shot.

On March 5, General Howe and his men awoke in Boston to see heavy guns pointed down at them from the peninsula to the south. Worse, the newly built forts were capable of firing on British ships coming into the harbor. The Redcoats' only access route for supplies and reinforcements had been cut off. Howe tried an amphibious assault on the American fort, but the weather didn't cooperate, and the British officers quickly realized that their position was no longer tenable. Departure from Boston was their only choice.

The exodus took a week to prepare. A flotilla of 120 ships, every vessel available, was used to evacuate some 11,000 people, including 8,900 soldiers and officers, 1,200 women and children, and 1,100 Massachusetts residents who remained loyal to the king. There was no room for possessions; even large quantities of military supplies had to be left behind, destroyed first if possible. With the evacuees were Henry Knox's in-laws, the loyalist parents of his wife Lucy. She never saw her family again.

An unwritten agreement was reached between the two sides: the British would not burn Boston if the Americans would guarantee them safe passage out of the harbor. On March 17, 1776, the ships cast off their lines and departed Boston's wharves; 145 years of British rule in Boston and Massachusetts came to an end. The fleet lingered a few days in the harbor, awaiting a fair breeze, and then sailed to Halifax, the closest port under British control. After dropping off their civilian passengers, the Army sailed to New York to begin the next phase of the war.

Accompanied by some aides, Washington entered the nearly deserted town on March 18. Within a few weeks he and his Continental Army, including Colonel Knox, departed Massachusetts for New York as well.

As the war progressed, Knox stayed at Washington's side, earning the commander's confidence in all matters military. By the time hostilities ended, he'd been promoted to Major General. When Washington was elected

President in 1789, he appointed Knox to be the nation's first Secretary of War. Knox is considered the founder of the U.S. Military Academy at West Point; Fort Knox in Kentucky and Knoxville in Tennessee are named in his honor. He retired with his wife to Maine in 1795 and died there 11 years later.

The peninsula around Dorchester Heights was renamed South Boston in 1806, and in the 20th century it became the city's largest Irish-American neighborhood. There, as in the rest of the city, true Bostonians enjoy celebrating Evacuation Day each March 17, the day that George Washington and Henry Knox drove the British government and military out of Boston.

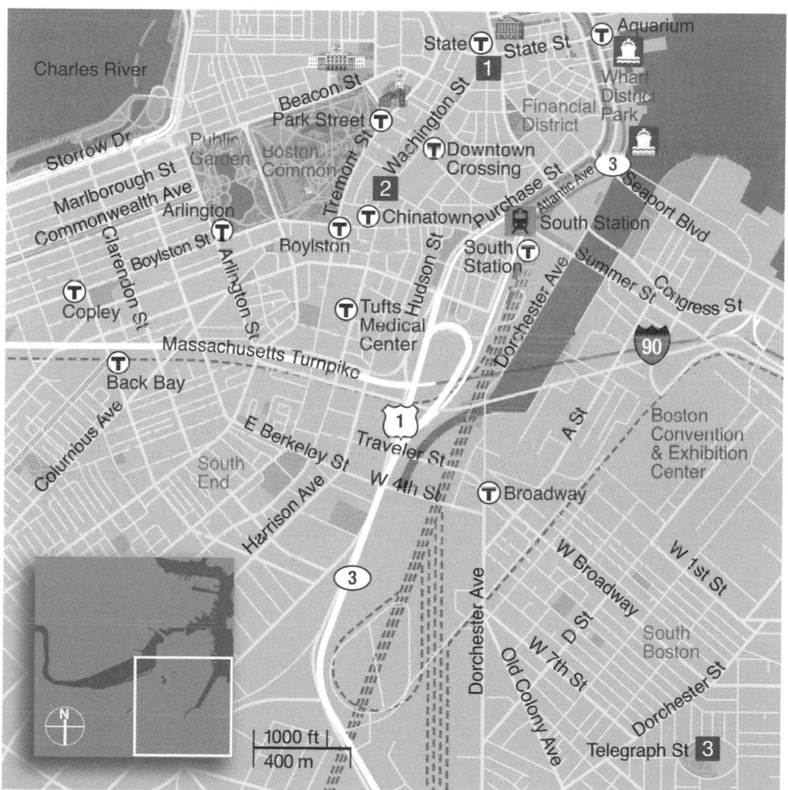

1 Daniel Henchman's bookshop: South corner of State and Washington streets
2 Washington Street
3 Dorchester Heights

CHAPTER 10.

THE HUB AT ITS PEAK

Of all the places in the Hub, there is one neighborhood that is quintessentially Boston. For two centuries, Beacon Hill has been the proper Bostonian's Boston, the epitome of elegance. Yet in the time of the Revolution, that hill was essentially undeveloped—so remote and rugged that no one would want to build a home there. Beacon Hill as we now know it was conceived in the era of prosperity that followed our independence from England.

Beacon Hill is one of the few surviving artifacts of Boston's ancient topography, although considerably altered over the centuries. Originally it had three peaks and was called the Tramountaine, Trimountain or simply Trimount. The central peak is the one that remains today, now 60 feet lower in height than it was in the colonial era.

The hill's name comes from the beacon, an alarm signal that was erected at its summit in 1634. Knowing the vulnerability of the town's situation at the end of a peninsula, early settlers placed this beacon at their community's highest point. It was a tall wooden pole with a pot of pitch hanging at its top. Should the town be attacked, someone would climb the pole and set the

‹ Beacon Hill from Mount Vernon Street, 1810

Charles Bulfinch

pitch afire, alerting nearby towns. When the original beacon blew down, the Sons of Liberty erected a replacement in 1768. Neither one was ever used.

By the time of the Revolution, there were just five houses on the south slope of Beacon Hill. Near the peak was John Hancock's grand mansion; further down Beacon Street was the home of artist John Singleton Copley, plus three smaller houses. Beyond these, Beacon Street led only to the mudflats of the Back Bay.

The far reaches of the hill were rather unsavory in the 1700s. Trimount's western peak gained its name from the ladies of the night who gathered there, in the town's most remote sector. "There's perhaps no town of its size could turn out more whores than this could," claimed Lieutenant Richard Williams, an engineer in His Majesty's Army during the occupation of Boston. And so the Lieutenant noted it on his map of the town: Mount Whoredom. He was not the only one to call it that.

As late as 1795, Beacon Hill was rough and remote from the rest of town. But in the decades after the Revolution, Boston prospered immensely from its sea trade; to reflect the town's newfound wealth, elegant houses, churches and public buildings were called for. Charles Bulfinch, the first person in the town to bill himself as an architect, became the tastemaker for the era.

Bulfinch lacked formal training in building design, but he'd shown an interest in the subject as a schoolchild. After graduating from Harvard, he took an extended visit to Europe, where he was inspired by the latest architectural fashions. Following his return to Boston in 1787, he embarked on a "season of leisure … giving gratuitous advice on Architecture." In the next eight years he designed a dozen structures scattered throughout Boston and New England.

Early in 1795, Bulfinch was selected as architect of the new Massachusetts State House, to be erected on the most conspicuous site in town—atop

Beacon Hill, facing the Common. Citizens wondered why such an important building was being erected "out of town," but the decision to put it there was the spark that led to the development of the rest of the hill.

Old Boston Day, Beacon Hill, 1925

Within months after a location for the State House was chosen, a group of investors bought 20 acres of land just to its west, including the peak of Mount Whoredom. With Boston running out of developable land, they would turn the "high, rough, broken & barren" soil of Beacon Hill into housing lots. But first they had to tame the topography, cutting the top off the ridge, smoothing the surface and carting the dirt downhill, filling more land at the riverbank.

Removing the upper strata of the soil, of course, would also remove the illicit activities that went on there. To further sanitize the neighborhood, Trimount's western summit was rechristened Mount Vernon, in honor of President Washington's home.

The Mount Vernon Proprietors, as the real estate investors called themselves, were led by two prominent lawyers, Harrison Gray Otis and Jonathan Mason. Other investors came and went; Charles Bulfinch was one of the original partners but had to sell out due to difficulties in his personal finances.

To cart the gravel down the hill, the first railroad in America was built. It was a double-tracked affair, a few hundred yards long, with ropes and pulleys so that the filled cars going downward would hoist the empty cars back up to the top. It attracted numerous spectators and became "a matter of public notoriety," observers noted later. "We boys used to run round that way to see what was going on," one local recalled.

Hoping to promote the sale of lots, both Otis and Mason engaged Bulfinch to design stately mansions for their own use. Set back 30 feet from Mount Vernon Street and boasting sprawling gardens, both houses were completed in 1802. Otis and Mason intended for the new neighborhood to be all freestanding residences. But it was not to be. Even in that era of prosperity, few Bostonians could afford such luxury.

Instead, the streets of Beacon Hill became lined with the attached rowhouses that we see today. Within two years after the Otis and Mason mansions were completed, Bulfinch was hired to design several sets of rowhouses along Chestnut and Mount Vernon streets. One of these, a group of four houses at 51–57 Mount Vernon Street, was built for Mason himself—legend has it for his daughters to occupy.

Bulfinch had introduced the rowhouse to Boston a decade earlier, with the Tontine Crescent development on Franklin Street in 1793. The concept came from examples he'd seen in England, such as the Royal Crescent in Bath; it didn't catch on in the United States until Beacon Hill was being built upon.

As demand for Boston real estate soared, Beacon Hill was developed almost exclusively as rowhouses. Just a handful of detached mansions were ever built; some of those were later taken down to make way for smaller rowhouses, and others became rowhouses when their gardens were sacrificed for new house lots. By 1855 there was just one detached house left on the hill: Charles Bulfinch's 1802 mansion for Harrison Gray Otis, at 85 Mount Vernon Street. It still stands apart today, a lone survivor, the most expensive piece of residential real estate in the city.

Bulfinch designed his last Beacon Hill house in 1805 and went on to bigger projects: banks, college buildings, entire streets of commercial structures. For a decade, he served as architect of the Capitol in Washington, D.C., finishing its initial construction.

Other designers, notably Asher Benjamin, Alexander Parris and Cornelius Coolidge, took Bulfinch's place on Beacon Hill, erecting the rows of attached houses that the hill has become known for. But they were largely copycats, gaining inspiration from the man who had first brought refined architectural tastes to Massachusetts.

Returning to Boston in 1830, after the Capitol was completed, Bulfinch retired at age 67 and reflected on his life. Architecture had never been lucrative for him; he'd been in and out of bankruptcy several times, relieved only by pay for municipal offices that were unrelated to his design work. Until he got his federal government post—and the salary that came with it—he'd never been financially secure. Once his children asked him if they should follow him into the architectural profession. According to his granddaughter, "he replied, with charming naiveté, that he did not think there would be much left for them to do. The States and prominent towns were already supplied with their chief buildings, and he hardly thought a young man could make a living as an architect."

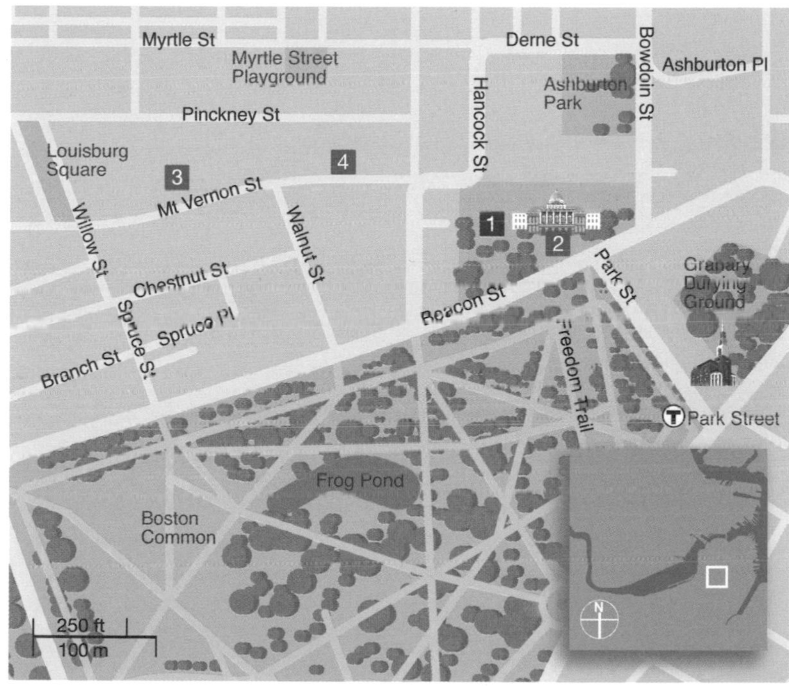

1 Hancock House: Beacon Street
2 Massachusetts State House: Beacon Street
3 Harrison Gray Otis Home: 85 Mount Vernon Street
4 Mason Rowhouses: 51-57 Mount Vernon Street

CHAPTER 11.

DEXTER'S FOLLY

It was the largest thing that most Bostonians had ever seen, the tallest building in the nation. And it collapsed twice. The first collapse was financial, and it brought down many of the city's craftsmen and shopowners. The second collapse was literal, and it happened in a blaze of glory.

Dexter's Folly, they called it. The Boston Exchange Coffee House was the dream of one man, Andrew Dexter, Jr. Most of Dexter's dreams were built on credit. Ultimately, most of them failed.

As a seaport and trading town, Boston needed a place to conduct its trade — a place where merchants could meet and make deals. A sea captain might have a shipful of goods to sell at wholesale. Or a ship owner might seek investors to buy shares in his next voyage. From the town's earliest days, the square by the first church became that trading place. A merchant could go there any day at noon and find a partner for whatever deal he had in mind.

When Boston's first public building, the Town House, was erected in that square in 1657, it was put on stilts so traders could meet beneath it. The Old State House of 1713 continued the practice; its enclosed first floor was

‹ *Conflagration of the Boston Exchange Coffee House*, by John Ritto Penniman, 1824

Andrew Dexter, by Gilbert Stuart

a large open room for the merchants' use. Yet as Boston prospered, the merchants gathering for the daily 'Change (short for "Exchange") routinely met outside, fair weather or no, precisely on the site where the Boston Massacre had occurred.

Andrew Dexter envisioned something grander, "an elegant Exchange room, furnished with every convenience for negotiation, and every facility for trade." There would be offices for brokers, rooms for private negotiations, and above all, a hotel, the first in the city. Dexter started buying land in spring of 1806; construction began a year later. The legislature chartered the venture, stipulating a cost not to exceed $200,000, not knowing that Dexter had already spent $110,000 on land alone. In August 1808 the first tenant moved in, even as workers were still erecting its upper floors.

But it was a house of paper. Dexter found few investors who shared his dream. With no one else to finance his enterprise, he simply printed the money himself. Gold and silver coins were the only legal tender then; there was no government-issued paper money. But privately-owned, state-chartered banks were allowed to issue paper notes. By 1806 there were dozens of banks across the country, each with its own money. These notes could be redeemed for gold and silver, if you went to the issuing bank.

Dexter chartered and acquired banks in remote locations, knowing that few people would travel hundreds of miles to redeem his paper money. Craftsmen and contractors working to build the Exchange Coffee House were paid with bills issued by banks in the Berkshires, in Maine, and in northern New Hampshire. One of Dexter's banks was in Michigan, a thousand miles away in the wilderness.

By the time it was done, $600,000 worth of Dexter's paper money had been paid out to erect and furnish the Exchange Coffee House—the equivalent of

Boston Exchange Coffee House, by Thomas Whitman, 1809

about $11 million today. In turn, the construction workers spent those notes at Boston's stores.

The collapse came just as construction was wrapping up. On February 28, 1809, the Farmers Exchange Bank in Gloucester, Rhode Island, stopped redeeming its currency. The first bank to fail in America, it had issued half a million dollars in bills in one year alone, backed by just $86.48 stored beneath a trap door in the bank's floor. Dexter's other banks, in Pittsfield, Detroit, Bucksport and more, followed in a cascade of failure.

Dexter escaped to rural Nova Scotia, one step ahead of the law and his creditors, ever on the move, even in another country. Back home, the Exchange Coffee House was auctioned to pay off the debts. Little was received; the town was awash in worthless paper scrip. But a succession of owners and managers did attempt a go at it, and after a few years the facility was attracting some business, even if the construction costs had been hopelessly written off.

Although some called it "a huge ill constructed edifice," others noted the "splendid charms the gazing eye beholds!" The seven-story structure covered a quarter acre of ground, its walls five feet thick and 90 feet in height. The main level was dominated by the 'Change Floor, 60 by 40 feet, overlooked by five galleries, each supported by 20 columns, the whole surmounted by an elliptical dome 95 feet above floor level. The Dining Hall seated 300, the 75-foot-long Ball Room had "superb" mirrors and "costly" chandeliers. A Reading Room, open to subscribers, was "filled with high tables and desks on which are laid the newspapers and public journals of this country and Europe." A four-story outhouse met patrons' sanitary needs.

While the Reading Room and the dining facilities eventually caught on, the 'Change Floor stayed deserted. Dexter had earned the disfavor of Boston's financial elite long before his paper money scheme collapsed, and they continued their habit of meeting outside. The 60 hotel rooms attracted few customers; they were on the sixth and seventh floors, decades before the elevator was invented—and the closest toilet facilities were on the fourth floor.

The end arrived on the evening of November 3, 1818. Around 7 o'clock, smoke was discovered in the seventh-floor Billiard Room. The first attempts to quell the flames seemed successful. But the fire was hidden inside the walls, perhaps sparked by a defective chimney. Soon the entire top floor was ablaze. The fate of Boston's tallest building was sealed: the town's fire engines could only spray water up to the fifth floor.

At about 9 p.m. the "noble dome" came down with a frightful crash. One by one, three of the brick walls fell. (The fourth was pulled down by workmen the next day.) By 10, "the whole of that magnificent, convenient and useful edifice … was reduced to a melancholy heap of smoking ruins," according to a newspaper report. The glow on the horizon was seen 60, even 100 miles away; the debris smoldered for months. The only human casualty came the next morning. "A promising lad, of about 10 years old," scavenging through the rubble, fell into a kettle of hot beer and was scalded to death.

Dexter wasn't around to see it. Unwelcome in Boston, always fleeing his creditors, he inherited shares in a long-forgotten Southern land venture. He was lucky to exchange his supposedly worthless scrip for some land on the Alabama River. There he's remembered as a founder of the city of Montgomery. But he died a pauper, some say in debtor's prison, buried in an unmarked grave in 1837.

The land where the Exchange Coffee House had stood was divided into smaller lots, and a street — now called Quaker Lane — was cut through it. A much smaller hotel, also called the Exchange Coffee House, was built on part of the site; it thrived for a few years.

As it's been since the 1650s, the area near the intersection of Congress and State streets remains the center of Boston's financial affairs. In 1834 Boston got a real stock exchange, which finally brought the traders indoors. Until it closed in 2007, the Boston Stock Exchange always kept its trading floor just a few steps away from the Old State House.

Today the block that was once the site of the Exchange Coffee House is occupied by some nondescript office buildings, erected about a century ago. Few people realize that they are the world headquarters of Fidelity Investments.

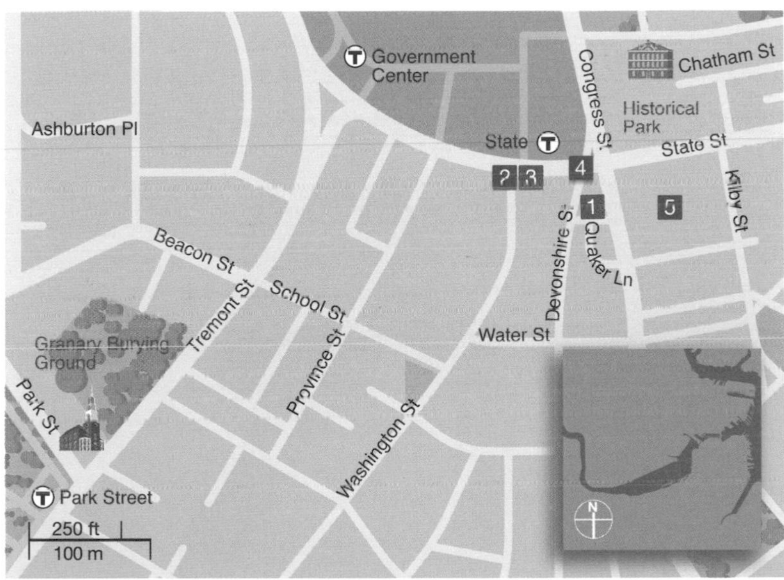

1 Boston Exchange Coffee House
2 Old State House: intersection of Washington and State streets
3 Town House: intersection of Washington and State streets
4 Boston Massacre Site: intersection of State and Devonshire Streets
5 Exchange Place: 53 State Street

A CORRECT LIKENESS OF DR. PARKMAN,

AS LAST SEEN PREVIOUS TO THE MURDER.

CHAPTER 12.

CRIME OF THE CENTURY

It was, without doubt, the crime of the century, an alleged murder that was shocking both for the prominence of its actors and for its gruesome circumstances. The victim's remains were never positively identified, although a few dismembered body parts matching his general appearance were found in a waste receptacle at Harvard Medical College. In the end, Dr. John White Webster was convicted and executed for the murder of Dr. George Parkman.

Dr. Webster's guilt is still debated by those who have studied the case. But guilty or not, most people agree that Dr. Webster never received a fair trial.

Edward Everett, the noted orator, called it "the most disgraceful event in our domestic history." At the trial, the president of Harvard University was a character witness for the defense. The Dean of the University's Medical College, Oliver Wendell Holmes, testified for the prosecution. Both witnesses knew the accused well; he was a professor at the Medical College. And both witnesses had known the victim well; he had been a major donor to the Medical College.

< Illustration of Doctor George Parkman in the *New York Daily Globe*, 1850

Doctor John White Webster

In 1849, Dr. George Parkman was 59 years old, one of the five or six wealthiest men in Boston. Behind his back, he was called "Old Chin" because of his protruding jaw. Trained as a doctor, he'd practiced medicine for a few years, but he spent most of his life managing real estate and lending out money. Indeed, he had given Harvard the land for its new Medical College, the very land where the human remains thought to be his would be found.

On Friday morning, November 23, 1849, Dr. Parkman left his Walnut Street house on Beacon Hill, as was his custom, to take care of business matters and errands. He met with his brother-in-law, Robert Gould Shaw, at Merchants' Bank on State Street, and then he went to Quincy Market where he purchased a head of lettuce, a rare delicacy at the time. Shortly after 1:00 he placed a grocery order at Holland's store on Blossom Street, with instructions that it be delivered to his home. Then he went to Harvard Medical College where he had business with Dr. Webster.

Dr. Webster was three years younger than Dr. Parkman. They'd known each other since college, but their lives had taken very different directions. Dr. Webster had suffered financial reversals; he was forced to sell his magnificent home in Cambridge just a year after he built it. For 13 years after that, his family lived in a small rented house near Harvard Square. His professor's salary of $1,900—about $54,000 today—didn't support his lifestyle; he was deeply in debt, including $2,432 owed to Dr. Parkman. At 1:45 that Friday afternoon, Dr. Parkman came, in a prearranged appointment, to collect part of that debt.

Several witnesses—including some who had known Dr. Parkman for years—testified that they saw him later that afternoon, and that "he appeared excited as if angry about some matter." But Dr. Parkman never came home that evening. Over the next few days, thousands of handbills were circulated, offering a reward of up to $3,000 for information relative to this "well known, and highly respected citizen of Boston."

left: Harvard Medical College, Grove St., circa 1840s; right: View of the interior of Prof. Webster's cell, *New York Daily Globe*, 1850

Exactly one week after the disappearance of Dr. Parkman, pieces of a human body were found in the Medical College building, in a privy vault underneath Dr. Webster's laboratory. The remains had been cut up; some pieces had been treated with chemicals, others had been burned in a furnace. The head, arms, hands and feet were never found. In an era before DNA testing, the body parts couldn't be positively identified; chemicals and heat had disfigured them beyond recognition. But the remains were consistent with Dr. Parkman's age and build.

That evening, the Friday after Thanksgiving, the professor was arrested at his home and charged with murder.

The wheels of justice spun quickly. The trial was held four months later, and newspapers from around the world sent reporters to observe it. Thousands of citizens queued up outside the courtroom to view the proceedings; every ten minutes, the marshals would clear the galleries and a new audience would file in. The police later estimated that at least 55,000 curiosity seekers had witnessed the 12-day trial.

Dr. Webster's case in court suffered from an inexperienced legal team, since few Boston lawyers were willing to argue his case. On August 30—nine months to the day after Dr. Parkman's body was found—Dr. John White Webster was hanged at the Leverett Street Jail. The *Evening Transcript* reported: "The body swayed slightly to and fro; and, in a few seconds after the fall, there was a spasmodic drawing-up of the legs, once or twice." Webster was left hanging for 30 minutes, after which two physicians examined him, and "informed the Sheriff that life was extinct."

Ephraim Littlefield

If the official record of the 19th century was grisly, more recent findings have been positively macabre. Unable to reconcile some aspects of the story, in the late 1960s a noted Massachusetts judge decided to delve more deeply into it. He discovered secret files kept by several of the *dramatis personae*, files that had been preserved for more than a century.

The pious Dr. Webster had professed his innocence to his end. Truth is, he may not have been guilty after all.

The culprit in this revisionist scenario is Ephraim Littlefield, the Medical College janitor, the man who told police that he had discovered the body. One of Littlefield's duties at the college was to procure cadavers for dissection in the anatomy classes, an activity entirely illegal at the time. Littlefield prowled the seedier areas of the city, buying bodies from anyone who offered them. The corpses might come from a grave robber or from a murderer seeking to cover up a crime. And besides his "official" acquisitions for the college, Littlefield had a side business, selling cadavers to students for $25 each (or roughly $700 today).

What if Littlefield had bought a corpse on the streets of the city, on the day after Dr. Parkman's disappearance? Perhaps Dr. Parkman had met with foul play after he left Dr. Webster's laboratory. Picture a scenario where Littlefield buys a body late at night, lugs it back to the college in a sack, and then sees to his horror that the body is Dr. Parkman! Littlefield's initial reaction is to try to destroy the evidence. Finding those efforts unsuccessful, he decides to plant the body parts in Dr. Webster's lab, to make it look like Dr. Webster had left them there…

That is exactly the scenario that Dr. Webster himself suggested, which he asked his defense attorneys to investigate. Instead, Dr. Webster's notes sat filed away, to be discovered by Judge Robert Sullivan when he was researching the case 120 years later.

Littlefield and Dr. Webster had both worked at the Medical College for years, but they were never close. Littlefield had keys to every room in the college building, including Dr. Webster's laboratory, and he had 24-hour access since he lived in an apartment on the premises.

While Dr. Webster was in prison awaiting execution, his wife and daughters visited him every day and they read Bible passages together. During this time, an alleged "confession" was circulated. But this confession was not in his handwriting, and Dr. Webster denied that he had dictated it; it turns out that the man who presented the document had connections with the prosecuting attorney. Yet it was—and remains—widely publicized as being the truth.

Following his execution, Dr. Webster's lawyers arranged for a middle of the night burial at Copp's Hill Burying Ground, in a grave marked by a flat, unlettered stone to prevent body-snatchers from finding his remains. Thousands of dollars were raised for the support of his widow, Harriet, who survived him but three years. Just days after Harriet's death, the family's grown daughters moved to the island of Faial, in the Azores, where they had relatives.

Dr. Parkman's son, George F. Parkman, never married; at his death many years later he bequeathed five million dollars (and a Beacon Hill mansion) to the city's Parks Department. Ephraim Littlefield, the janitor, reportedly collected the $3,000 reward offered for the discovery of Dr. Parkman's body and retired.

The case of *Commonwealth v. Webster* has had a lasting influence on American law. The instructions to the jury, delivered by Chief Justice Lemuel Shaw more than 160 years ago, remain a model for judges today, repeated on a daily basis in courtrooms across the country. Judge Shaw's definitions of many important legal terms have become accepted practice, and the trial remains one of the most often cited cases in the history of law.

CHAPTER 13.

FREEDOM'S BIRTHPLACE

Thousands of citizens gathered in protest as the soldiers marched along State Street. For the second time in Boston's history, troops had been sent from a distant capital to deprive free people of their liberty. Only this time—in 1854—the talk of slavery was literal; the men seized by those soldiers would be sent into servile bondage. And once again, the actions of Bostonians would ultimately be crucial in spreading liberty throughout the land.

For, just as Bostonians had helped spark the American Revolution, they played a key role in the effort to end slavery in our nation, four score years later.

Slavery was recorded in Boston as early as 1637. But New England was unsuited to plantation agriculture; black slaves here were generally household servants or perhaps groundskeepers on estates. During the Revolution, many slaves were left behind when loyalist masters fled; others were freed by patriot owners, supporters of "liberty," who realized the contradiction of seeking freedom while enslaving others. By 1778, relatively few slaves were left in Massachusetts.

"All men are born free and equal," declares the Massachusetts Constitution, adopted in 1780. Based on that language, some Massachusetts slaves sued for their freedom, and the commonwealth's Supreme Judicial Court ruled in 1783 that slavery was prohibited here—the first American state to outlaw that "peculiar institution."

Thus Boston gained an early reputation for being welcoming to African-Americans. In the early 1800s, the town had one of the nation's largest communities of free blacks—about 2,000 people, most living on the north slope of Beacon Hill. Many worked as household help, cooks, waiters, barbers and coachmen, and others started successful small businesses.

In 1831, William Lloyd Garrison chose Boston, "the birth place of liberty," for the headquarters of his anti-slavery newspaper *The Liberator*. Yet Boston's abolitionist movement was always a joint effort between white progressives, such as Garrison, and the city's black community. Still, sentiments weren't unanimous; there were some leading Bostonians who remained neutral on the issue and some who sided with slave owners.

As a center of anti-slavery activity, the city naturally attracted blacks who wanted to help others of their own race. One who came was Lewis Hayden.

Hayden was born into slavery in Kentucky, sometime between 1809 and 1815—no one knows for certain, since no records were kept. There he repeatedly saw his loved ones sold away from him—both his parents, all his siblings, his first wife and their only child—never to be seen or heard from again. Once he was traded for a pair of carriage horses. In 1844 Hayden, his second wife Harriet, and their son Joseph escaped to Ohio, and then to Canada. After six months in Canada, they returned to the United States to join the effort to end slavery. By May of 1846, Lewis and Harriet Hayden had moved to Massachusetts.

For a while Lewis was a traveling lecturer for the American Anti-Slavery Society. In 1849 he opened a store on Cambridge Street, advertising "a good assortment of men's and boy's clothing" as well as "little Knick Knacks," a store that eventually became the city's second-largest black-owned enterprise. And Lewis and Harriet began operating a boarding house in their home at 66 Southac (now Phillips) Street.

Escaping from slavery in wagons and on foot, following the Underground Railroad

But the boarding house was a subterfuge. The Haydens were actually the chief conductors for the Underground Railroad in Boston. Their house was the "Temple of Refuge," through which at least 75 former slaves—possibly dozens more—passed on their way to freedom in Canada or England. Harriet Beecher Stowe, the author of *Uncle Tom's Cabin*, visited the Haydens' home in 1853, where "thirteen newly-escaped slaves of all colors and sizes" were brought into one room for her to see.

One could flee the Hayden house through an underground passageway, several hundred yards long, "wet and barely high and wide enough to permit one person to crawl through it." Lewis Hayden's clothing store also provided garments to refugee slaves, and both sites were meeting places for Boston's abolitionists.

Everything changed with the passage of the Fugitive Slave Act in 1850. Until then, escaped slaves were generally safe once they reached a free state such as Massachusetts. But the new law required slaves to be returned to bondage, even from free states, on the testimony of an alleged owner's representative. There was no appeal; anyone who tried to interfere was subject to imprisonment and a stiff fine. Even blacks who had been born free in the North feared being kidnapped into Southern slavery.

Within weeks after the law's enactment, prominent Bostonians formed a biracial Committee of Vigilance to "protect the colored people of this city." Lewis Hayden served on its Executive Committee.

The committee's first test was Ellen and William Craft, a celebrated couple who'd escaped from slavery in Georgia in 1848. Because of the Crafts' fame, bounty hunters sought them out just a month after the Fugitive Slave Act became law. William Craft was in hiding at the Hayden home, where Lewis boasted that he had two kegs of gunpowder and a lighted torch ready to blow up the house and the entire neighborhood should the slave-catchers dare to approach. The Crafts were eventually spirited away to England and safety.

On February 15, 1851, waiter Shadrach Minkins was arrested at his job in the Cornhill Coffee House, accused of being a fugitive slave. Within four hours, a trial was underway, part of the efforts to return Minkins to Virginia. But just as a recess was called, "a crowd of sympathizing colored persons," allegedly led by Lewis Hayden, pressed into the courtroom, created a disturbance, and fled with Minkins to safety. By nightfall Minkins was 40 miles away, on his way to Montreal. Hayden and several other Boston men were arrested and charged with abetting Minkins's escape, but a hung jury refused to convict them—to the dismay of politicians from the slave states.

Not all were so lucky. Success eluded the Vigilance Committee in the cases of Thomas Sims and Anthony Burns, returned to slavery in April 1851 and June 1854, respectively. But it took an extreme effort for the federal government to enforce the detested law; the Burns case alone required 2,000 armed soldiers and Marines, and an estimated $40,000 in government expenditures. The cost was too great; never again were any attempts made to capture fugitive slaves in Boston.

Meanwhile, hundreds of other slaves passed through the city, and were assisted by the Committee, on their way to freedom. Committee members also raised $1,300 to buy Anthony Burns's freedom from his Virginia masters. With Burns's liberty regained, the Boston Vigilance Committee's

The 54th Massachusetts Regiment storming Fort Wagner

overall record came to more than 300 saved and only one lost.

Boston's resistance to the Fugitive Slave Act pushed the nation closer to Civil War—and closer to slavery's final end. When the war began, black citizens of Boston stood ready to fight for the rights of their Southern brethren.

Hayden became good friends with Massachusetts Governor John A. Andrew, who had also been a member of the Committee of Vigilance. Over Thanksgiving dinner at the Haydens' house in 1862, Governor Andrew and Lewis Hayden had discussions that led to the formation of the 54th Massachusetts Regiment, the first unit of African-Americans to serve in the Civil War.

Lewis Hayden's clothing store failed in the Panic of 1857; the next year he was appointed Messenger to the Massachusetts Secretary of State. It was the highest ranking government post ever held by an African-American to that date, and Hayden held the job for 30 years. Known at the State House as the "old philosopher," Lewis Hayden was also elected to the Massachusetts legislature for one term in 1873.

Active well into his 70s, Hayden's final victory was the erection of the Boston Massacre Monument on Boston Common, a project that he had promoted since the early 1850s. The monument was dedicated in November of 1888, less than five months before Hayden's death.

With 1,200 persons in attendance, Hayden's funeral was, the *Boston Globe* reported, "the greatest tribute of love, honor and respect ever shown any colored man in the United States." Born into slavery in Kentucky, he was a leader in the movement to end slavery—a movement with roots in Boston, the birthplace of freedom.

CHAPTER 14.

"THE ISLAND OF NORTH BOSTON"

The North End is not only Boston's oldest neighborhood, it's the oldest residential neighborhood in any major U.S. city. For nearly 400 years people have lived, worked, worshipped, walked in its narrow and curving streets. It's been home to the likes of Cotton Mather, Paul Revere, Sophie Tucker and Rose Kennedy. And it's still one of the liveliest places in the city.

Colonial Boston had three residential neighborhoods—the North End, South End and West End—fanning out like leaves of a clover from the hub at the Old State House and Faneuil Hall. Just as Boston was a peninsula, so the North End was a peninsula off the peninsula. Then in 1643 a canal was dug to connect the Mill Pond with the ocean. The canal, called Mill Creek, turned the North End into an island, linked to the rest of the town by two drawbridges.

By 1775 the North End was Boston's most populous neighborhood, with more than 6,000 residents and five houses of worship. First to build here was the Second Church, or Old North Meeting, organized in 1649 and rebuilt in 1677. Among its ministers were Increase, Cotton and Samuel Mather, father, son, and grandson, from a family that included several other prominent

‹ Statue of Paul Revere in front of Old North Church

preachers throughout Massachusetts. Increase and Cotton were both prolific and influential authors, whose writings played significant roles (on opposite sides) in the Salem witch trials of 1692.

North Street, 1881

Old North Meeting was followed by a Baptist congregation, then by the New North and New North Brick Meeting-Houses. Last of the Colonial parishes to settle here—and the only survivor—was Christ Church, in 1723. Later famous as Old North Church, it's not to be confused with the Old North Meeting-House that once stood in North Square.

Divisions of the congregations weren't always amicable. In 1719 dissenting members of the New North Meeting protested the installation of a new pastor by urinating (sprinkling "a liquor, which shall be nameless") from the balcony onto the celebrants below. "The filthy creatures entirely spoiled a new velvet hood which I had made for the occasion," complained one woman. The minority congregants then split off and built New North Brick a few blocks away. Their building was topped by a giant weathervane of a rooster, in allusion to Peter's betrayal of Christ at the crowing of the cock. (The detested pastor was named Peter.) At the dedication, a merry fellow straddled the weathervane and crowed three times. Forever after, the structure was known as the Cockerel Church or the Revenge Church of Christ.

Throughout the colonial era the North End was home to rich and poor alike. Craftsman Paul Revere lived just yards from Governor Thomas Hutchinson's elegant mansion. A small group of free blacks settled along Snow Hill Street, near Copp's Hill Burial Ground.

The post-Revolution surge in maritime trade meant intense activity on the wharves. At the end of a months-long voyage, sailors were discharged at the waterfront and paid their salary in cash. They sought the illicit pleasures of the harbor in the nearby North End; soon Richmond Street became known

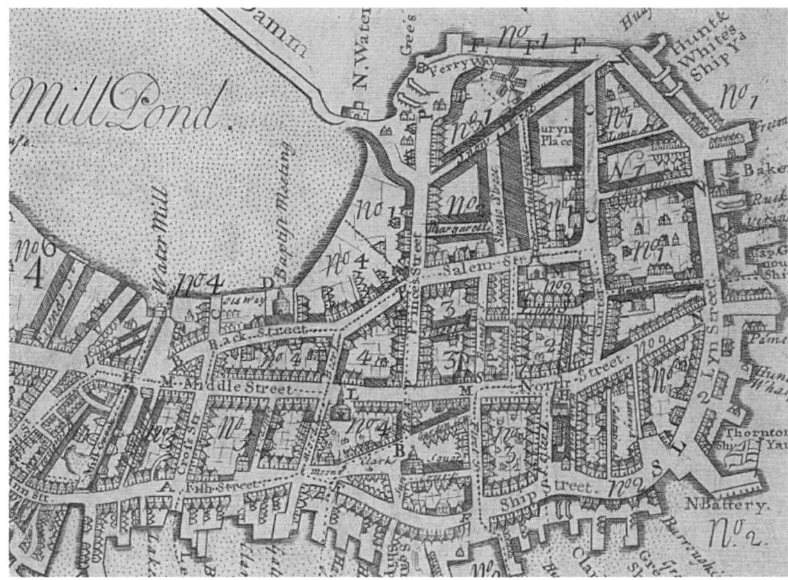

The North End, by William Price, 1743

as the Murder District. On April 23, 1851, police made the "great descent" on Ann Street, "capturing some one hundred and sixty bipeds"—over half of whom were females charged with prostitution. In another raid, 51 "nymphs of Ann Street" were arrested within half an hour. To relieve the stigma, the name of Ann Street was soon changed to North Street.

As respectable families fled to other neighborhoods, religious missions were formed to minister to the seamen. Most famous was the Boston Port Society, with Father Edward Taylor as its first pastor. Taylor, the "Sailor Preacher," was described by Walt Whitman as "the only essentially perfect orator." On his 1842 visit to Boston, Charles Dickens insisted on hearing Taylor preach; Dickens sat in a side pew next to a lame, one-eyed mariner, since center church was reserved for seamen. Today the Port Society still operates the Mariner's House overlooking North Square, a last survivor of several such missions that once served the North End.

The great emigration from Ireland after 1847 drew another group of residents. The North End's proximity to the waterfront made it a convenient

Boston Slums, by Thomas E. Marr, 1909

layover for new arrivals, many of whom settled in the area. The Irish who remained here were often the poorest of the poor, since the ones with a little bit of money could afford train fare out of Boston. Within a generation this was almost entirely an Irish neighborhood. It was in the North End where Mayor John F. Fitzgerald was born and raised, and where he settled on Garden Court Street with his bride after their 1889 marriage. Scarcely 10 months later, their first child was born, a daughter they named Rose.

A day after Rose Fitzgerald's birth, the infant girl was baptized at St. Stephen's Church on Hanover Street. Erected in 1804 for a Unitarian parish (successor to the New North Meeting), the building had been sold in 1862 to an Irish Roman Catholic congregation. The only Charles Bulfinch–designed house of worship remaining in Boston today, St. Stephen's was also the site of Rose Fitzgerald Kennedy's funeral in 1995.

Immigrants from other nations followed. The first Italians settled in North Square around 1870, followed by Jewish immigrants from Eastern Europe who found homes along Salem Street. The Jews bought the old Baptist church for use as a synagogue, and the Italians purchased Father Taylor's bethel from the Port Society. As the Irish prospered and moved to the suburbs, the Italians came to dominate the North End. A 1906 observer wrote that North Square was "swarming with Italians in every dirty nook and corner. In truth, it is hard to believe the evidence of our own senses, though the fumes of garlic are sufficiently convincing."

The Italian settlers were so many that they pushed the Jews out; most of them moved to the West End, including the area now called the "North

Slope" of Beacon Hill. (In so doing, they followed the steps of the free blacks a century earlier.) A few traces of the Jewish residents can be seen in today's North End, including an alley called Jerusalem Place and some Star of David motifs on nearby buildings.

Father Taylor's Bethel, North Square

But it was the Italians who stayed and gave the neighborhood its modern identity. Throughout the early years of the 20th century, it was Italian investors who erected the brick walk-up apartment buildings (once called "tenements") that now line the streets of the North End. It was the Italians who turned the neighborhood into a dining destination, starting with the European Restaurant, which opened in 1917 and lasted for 80 years.

In the 1950s the Central Artery was built along the route of the Mill Creek, once again isolating the North End, but also protecting it from the development that drastically altered so much of the city. Not long after the disastrous urban renewal project in the nearby (and similar) West End, Jane Jacobs' book *The Death and Life of Great American Cities* sang the praises of the North End. After two centuries of perceived decline, the North End again became desirable.

Today fewer and fewer North End residents have Italian roots; the walk-up flats are largely occupied by young professionals who work in the Financial District, and by college students. The great green wall of the Central Artery (officially the John F. Fitzgerald Expressway) is gone, replaced by the Rose Kennedy Greenway. Yet the North End is as lively as ever, as its crowded restaurants will attest. In an ironic twist, the "fumes of garlic" may be its biggest draw.

ARTHUR STOCKIN.
WOOD ENGRAVING
CLOTHES CLEANED PRESSED AND REPAIRED
BAY STATE LOAN CO.
LOANS AT TWO PER CENT PER MONTH
COLLATERAL LOANS
LOANS
OLD CORNER A.D. 1712. ENTRANCE 3 SCHOOL STREET
HAIR CUTTER
BOOKSELLERS.

CHAPTER 15.

HUB OF THE LITERARY SOLAR SYSTEM

Any shortlist of the greatest American authors would be top-heavy with Boston-based writers from the middle of the 19th century: Emerson, Hawthorne, Longfellow, Alcott, Whittier, Thoreau, Holmes, Howe. Many of these wordsmiths garnered their emotional and literary support from just one editor, a man who helped them craft their work. Yet James T. Fields was no ordinary editor; he was a marketing expert and businessman extraordinaire. It was Fields, and Fields alone, who turned the Old Corner Book Store into the literary hub of America.

The site at the corner of School and Washington streets was once home to Anne Hutchinson, before her banishment from the colony for religious dissent in 1637. Her house stood until the neighborhood was destroyed in a 1711 fire. The structure that currently occupies the site was built in 1718 by Thomas Crease, an apothecary. A century later, in 1829, it became the office of Richard Carter and Charles Hendee, book publishers who operated a retail shop on the first floor.

James Thomas Fields came to this bookshop in 1831, at the age of 14. Raised by his widowed mother in Portsmouth, New Hampshire, Fields was

‹ Old Corner Bookstore, circa 1900

James T. Fields

the son of a ship captain who had perished at sea. As a lad he loved books, so a family friend procured him an apprenticeship at Carter & Hendee's Bookstore. Fields settled in Boston and lived with the store's owners. Then, a year later, Carter & Hendee's shop was acquired by John Allen and William D. Ticknor. With the business came the apprenticeship contract for Jamie Fields—beginning a partnership that, over the next three decades, would change the American literary scene forever.

Young Fields proved an asset to the firm and was promoted to senior clerk in 1839, when he was 21. Always paying close attention to customers' requests, Fields convinced Ticknor that there was a demand for a long out-of-print volume of English poetry titled *Rejected Addresses*. Fields's hunch was right, and Ticknor's reprint of the book quickly sold out. After other, similar successes, Fields was promoted to junior partner at the firm, now called William D. Ticknor and Company, in 1843. (Allen had departed in 1834.)

Fields's next innovation was the payment of higher royalties to authors. He felt that fairer recompense for their creative efforts would encourage writers' loyalty to the publishing house, growing a profitable relationship over time. Again, his instincts proved right. In 1843, Fields persuaded Ticknor to offer Tennyson, the English poet, a 10 percent royalty on a new edition of his *Poems*; the following year the firm offered John Greenleaf Whittier a similar deal for a new volume of verses. Both Tennyson and Whittier became lifelong personal friends of Fields, and their subsequent writings were published exclusively with his firm.

His financial strategy a success, Fields cultivated personal relationships with local authors. With Longfellow, Fields offered an unheard-of 20 percent royalty, enticing the Cambridge poet to quit his earlier publisher. Issued by

Ticknor in 1849, Longfellow's *Evangeline* was another great success. Oliver Wendell Holmes, Ralph Waldo Emerson and Henry David Thoreau were among the other Boston writers whom Fields wooed, and won, for the firm.

After Nathaniel Hawthorne lost his job in the Salem Custom House, Fields traveled to that port city to encourage the despondent author, whose previous books had been issued by another publisher. At first Hawthorne denied having anything ready for publication, saying he was "the most unpopular writer in America." Spying a bureau in the room, Fields pointed to it, hinting that there was probably something in one of its drawers. "How in Heaven's name did you know this thing was in there?" Hawthorne exclaimed, handing Fields the manuscript of *The Scarlet Letter*. "Tell me, after you get home and have time to read it, if it is good for anything." Fields perused the novel on the train back to Boston and offered Hawthorne a contract the next day. Published a few months later, the book's title page was printed in red ink at Hawthorne's suggestion.

Fields was now a full partner, and in 1854 the name of the publishing house was changed to Ticknor and Fields, an imprint that has become immortal in literary history. Ticknor continued to run the financial and manufacturing aspects of the business, while Fields handled relationships with authors and marketing. In 10 years, Fields increased the company's advertising budget more than twentyfold. He cultivated friendships with newspaper and magazine editors to ensure prominent, positive reviews of the company's books; sometimes he even wrote reviews himself under an assumed name.

Thanks to Fields's high standards of quality, readers nationwide came to equate the firm's brown bindings with good literature, and new works by "the Boston authors" were eagerly sought out.

The year he became partner, Fields wed Annie Adams, 16 years his junior. Their home on Charles Street, overlooking the river and the Back Bay, became the social center for Boston's literati. To Henry James their house was a domestic "waterside museum," filled with artworks, books and literary mementos, a salon for intellectual discussions among friends.

Fields also socialized regularly at the Saturday Club, a gathering of friends—many of them authors—who met monthly for dinner at the

Interior of the Old Corner Book Store, 1891

Parker House hotel, at the far end of School Street from his office. The Parker House was also a sometime meeting place for the Atlantic Club, whose members planned issues of the *Atlantic Monthly*. Ticknor and Fields acquired that magazine in 1859; Fields was its editor for a decade.

The publisher's office on School Street doubled as a retail bookstore. "What a crowded, busy shop it was," wrote a contemporary observer, "with the shelves full of books, and piles of books upon the counters and tables, and loiterers tasting them with their eyes, and turning the glossy new pages ... You knew that you might be seeing there in the flesh and in common clothes the famous men and women" who had written the very books that were in those piles. From behind the green curtain in the corner could be heard the laughter and voices of Fields and the great authors who had been admitted to his inner sanctum.

Upon the death of his partner William Ticknor in 1864, Fields closed the retail store and moved the publishing business to 124 Tremont Street, across from Park Street Church. Citing health concerns, Fields retired from

Annie Adams Fields, 1861

publishing at the end of 1870; he continued to write and to lecture until shortly before his death in 1881. By that time, the publishing company he'd helped create had changed its name to Houghton, Mifflin, and Co., another legendary imprint—one that survives today.

After her husband passed away, Annie Adams Fields kept their Charles Street house as a literary salon where she entertained the couple's friends. She established a close relationship with Sarah Orne Jewett, a young Maine writer, who moved in with her. Annie and Sarah found friendship and literary encouragement in what Henry James termed a "Boston marriage": a long-term relationship, not uncommon in that era, between two unmarried women who shared a household. As her husband had done, Annie Fields wrote and published volumes of memoirs about the writers that the couple had known.

Following Annie's 1915 death, the house was demolished at her request—a parking garage was built on the site—but her garden, overlooking the river, miraculously survives to this day. The Old Corner building, meanwhile, remained a bookstore under different management until 1903. Since then it's served a variety of retail purposes, including another two-decade stint as a bookshop.

In addition to his memoirs, James Fields wrote just a few pieces of his own, mostly now forgotten. But many of his literary efforts survive, unremarked and anonymous, for his deft touch with an editor's pencil led to countless improvements in other author's works. He rewrote, for example, the final stanzas to Longfellow's "Paul Revere's Ride," crafting the poem into a much stronger lyric. As a friend recollected in the *Atlantic Monthly* after his death, he was "inflamed with a passionate love of literature and by a cordial admiration of men of letters." Characterized by a rare combination of business acumen and sound literary taste, James T. Fields shaped American literature.

CHAPTER 16.

CONFLAGRATION!

Fire was an ever-present danger in 19th-century cities, as it had been since the invention of the city. Flame, needed to provide heat and cook food, could quickly get out of control, destroying entire neighborhoods of flammable structures. Yet Bostonians, who were justifiably proud of their city, weren't really thinking about those dangers in the fall of 1872.

True, a disastrous conflagration had struck the city of Chicago just a year earlier, in October 1871. But Chicago had been a combustible city filled with wooden buildings. By contrast, Boston was a city of new granite warehouses that seemed indestructible. In the downtown district, especially, scores of fine commercial structures were sprouting on sites once occupied by houses, whose former residents had relocated to the new Back Bay neighborhood. The city's residents had "a feeling of pride and confidence in her fire department which had never been defeated."

John S. Damrell, Chief Engineer of the Boston Fire Department, thought otherwise. For years he had asked other city agencies to provide larger water mains downtown and to install more hydrants, with multiple hose connections. In reply, he was told, "Don't try to magnify the wants of

‹ Efforts to save Old South Church from the Great Boston Fire

The Great Fire at Boston, November 9th and 10th, 1872. Published By Haskell & Allen

your department or your office so much." Following the Chicago fire, Damrell had traveled to that city to learn what lessons he could.

The insurance underwriters of London shared Damrell's fears. On November 6, 1872, they described downtown Boston "as the next most likely place for a Chicago fire." Three days later that prediction came true.

November 9 was a Saturday; by evening the commercial district was emptying out. Shortly after 7 p.m., someone noted a flicker in basement windows at the corner of Summer and Kingston streets. The five-story granite building where the fire started was typical of the commercial structures in Boston's textile district; it housed a variety of dry-goods firms, including a hoop-skirt and corset factory on its highest floors.

It wasn't long before the flames traveled up the building's open elevator shaft and exploded into its top two floors. Onlookers gathered, wondering if the fire department had been notified. A mile and a half away, workers at a Charlestown drawbridge noted an orange glow on the horizon; it was 7:10 by the railroad clock. Finally, at 7:24, the alarm was received at the fire alarm office in Boston City Hall.

Why the delay? Twenty years earlier, Boston had established the world's first telegraphic fire alarm system, with alarm boxes at street corners across the city. But too many false alarms had been sounded. To prevent them, the city put locks on the alarm boxes and issued keys only to police officers and a few other "responsible" citizens. To send an alarm of fire, you had to find someone with a key.

On hearing the alarm bells, Chief Damrell ran from his Beacon Hill home to the scene of the fire. "The building was on fire from the basement to the top," he said later, "presenting, as it were, one large furnace." Flaming hoop-skirts were cascading out of the top floor windows. Pieces of granite were "flying in every direction, from pieces weighing one pound to 10 and 20." Adjacent buildings were already half consumed; those across the street were igniting. Damrell ordered a general alarm, bringing out the entire Boston Fire Department; then he ordered telegraph operators to notify every city within 50 miles, requesting help.

Yet there was a further delay in the response. That fall, a mysterious disease, an equine influenza called the epizootic, had stricken horses throughout the northeastern United States. Horses fell ill, unable to work for about 10 days. On November 9, it still affected many of the Fire Department's teams. Accordingly the department had hired 500 volunteers to pull the equipment by hand, at $1 per fire and 25¢ per hour.

When the flames arrived at the building known as Beebe's Block, in Winthrop Square, Boston suddenly realized her danger. "Iron melted; granite crumbled; brick and mortar fell away; and stout timbers glowed a moment, and then tumbled and crashed into the ash-heaps which seethed at the bottom of the fiery abyss ... Bales of shirts, boxes of dry goods, heaps of tailors' cloths, shelves of fancy goods, and costly stocks of hoop-skirts ... were charred to ashes, and sent off on the winds with every whiff of the rioting flames." The fire danced from one building to the next, spreading in every direction.

The fire traveled quickly. Boston's solid granite warehouses gave an illusion of indestructibility, but inside they were made of wood and filled with flammable merchandise. There were no firewalls, and open elevator shafts acted as massive chimneys. Surmounting it all were the fashionable—and combustible—mansard roofs, fanciful tops as much as 20 feet high, atop almost every new building in the city, nearly all of them wood-framed. Even the granite itself was not indestructible; heated enough, it would explode, shatter or simply crumble.

Water shortages were another problem. The water mains were adequate for the earlier residential neighborhood, but not for multistory commercial

The aftermath of the fire on Pearl Street, 1872

buildings. And since the hydrant fittings weren't standardized, fire engines from nearby towns couldn't easily connect to Boston's hydrants.

Amazingly, there was no easy way to shut off Boston's gas mains. Leaks from ruptured gas pipes fed the inferno until the gas company's entire supply had been used up. Then the gas system was shut down entirely, and all the city was without light for days.

Against the wishes of Chief Damrell, explosives were used in several locations to bring down buildings in the path of the advancing flames. But the blasts were unsuccessful; the fire simply leapt over the demolished heaps of rubble.

By daybreak Sunday, the fire had destroyed hundreds of buildings, dozens of acres. A turning point came at Old South Meeting-House, site of the Tea Meetings nearly a century earlier. When Old South's clock struck 6 a.m., the *Transcript* newspaper building across the street was aflame. "Dear old church," cried a bystander; "I'm afraid we shall never hear that bell again." Smoke started to issue from the steeple. Just then the Kearsarge No. 3 engine arrived from Portsmouth, New Hampshire, already in steam. The stream from Kearsarge's hose reached the belfry and cheers went up from the crowd. Old South was saved.

When the smoke cleared, the damage seemed astronomical: 776 buildings destroyed; 65 acres turned to "a desolate waste of trembling walls"; the total loss more than $75 million, or about $1.3 billion today—all in the space of just 15 hours. Eleven firemen were killed, another 17 injured. Civilian casualties were never accurately counted; 16 people were reported missing. Twenty thousand people were jobless; 22 fire insurance companies went bankrupt paying out claims. A charred piece of a $50 bill landed 20 miles away, in Abington.

The burnt district was shaped like a fan, bounded by Summer, Washington, Milk, State and Batterymarch Streets, and the waterfront. It was quickly rebuilt. Within six months, the city had completed plans to widen many streets and cut some new ones through—with new, larger water mains to be installed at the same time. Within two years, hundreds of replacement structures were erected, all meeting a rigorous new building code. Among other things, this code required mansard roofs to have iron or steel frames, rather than wood. A decade later, Mark Twain wrote, "there is no commercial district in any city in the world that can surpass it—or perhaps even rival it—in beauty, elegance and tastefulness."

John Damrell was severely interrogated about his actions before and during the fire; in 1874 he was relieved of his Chief Engineer position. His vindication came in 1877 when he was appointed Boston's first Building Commissioner, given the responsibility for enforcing the building codes that he had so long supported. He served for 25 years.

Saving Old South

Old South Meeting-House was rescued from the Great Fire of 1872, but it soon faced another threat—demolition.

Before the fire, Old South's congregation had made plans to move to the Back Bay and to sell the 140-year-old structure. Immediately after the fire, the meeting house was rented to the post office; when the mail workers moved out in 1876, the congregation auctioned off their old building to a demolition contractor for $1,350. As dismantling began, protests arose, spurred by memories of the loss of John Hancock's house 13 years earlier. Within a week, fundraising was underway to save Old South. A group of 20 "Women of Boston" bought the building for $3,500, but the congregation still wanted $425,000 for the land under it. Although a few major donors came forth, the women had to turn to fairs, theatricals, balls, crafts sales and the like to raise the needed funds.

One donor was Mary Tyler (née Sawyer), a Somerville resident. Six decades earlier, as a farm girl in Sterling, Mass., Mary had kept a pet lamb; one day the lamb followed her to school, inspiring the famous nursery rhyme. In 1878, Mary still had two pairs of stockings knit from the wool of her lamb's first fleece. To raise funds for Old South, she unraveled the stockings, clipped the yarn into short lengths and fastened the pieces to cards with her autograph, which were then sold. Thus Mary's Little Lamb helped save the Old South Meeting-House.

CHAPTER 17.

TRINITY CHURCH

Trinity Church is the jewel of the Back Bay, the greatest work of the greatest American architect of his century. And it figuratively set a foundation for American architecture, a design legacy for generations to follow.

Boston's Back Bay was once just that, a shallow bay of the ocean in back of the peninsula. At low tide it sometimes drained entirely, leaving only mud; at high tide it was navigable by rowboat. In 1821 a mill dam was built across the bay, along modern Beacon Street. But the dam restricted the tidal flow in and out of the bay. And as nearby neighborhoods were settled, their sewer lines dumped untreated filth into the bay.

In 1849 city officials declared the fetid Back Bay "nothing less than a great cesspool… Every west wind sends its pestilential exhalations across the entire City." With a growing city needing to expand, agreements were made to fill the bay. Work began in 1858. It took three decades to complete, creating more than 400 acres of new land. Soon, fine houses were being erected for the sons and daughters of Beacon Hill's families.

‹ Trinity Church from an etching by W. Harry Smith, 1929

Boston's churches followed the westward move of their parishioners. Among the religious bodies making an exodus from the old downtown was Trinity Church, the city's leading Episcopal congregation. In 1872, Trinity purchased a lot on Clarendon Street and invited six architects to submit entries for a design competition. Henry Hobson Richardson's design was chosen the winner.

Son of a wealthy New Orleans family, Richardson had come north to attend Harvard. After graduating in 1859, he sailed for Paris. There he became only the second American to enroll at the École des Beaux-Arts, the first school of architecture in the world. Returning to America in 1865, he set up practice in New York City. The young architect gained few commissions in New York; nearly all his jobs came from Massachusetts, often from his old classmates at Harvard. Those college connections undoubtedly helped Richardson win the Trinity job. Phillips Brooks and Robert Treat Paine, the parish rector and the chairman of the building committee respectively, had graduated Harvard four years before Richardson. Although they never met him at Harvard, they shared acquaintances and club memberships.

Before Trinity, Richardson had designed four other churches. The first three—two in Springfield and one in a Boston suburb—were unremarkable designs in the Gothic vernacular of that day. But in his fourth church project—the Brattle Square Church just two blocks from the Trinity site—Richardson had experimented with a new, Romanesque style. His first proposal for Trinity carried that experimentation further. With its massive stone arches and great rounded apse, it was a radical new direction for American architecture. His inspirations came from the south of France and from Spain, not from the English, Italian and Classical sources favored in America up to that point.

Yet the engineers said the watery soil couldn't support the tall stone tower of Richardson's design. The architect was also unhappy with the tower, which lacked the unity he desired. Browsing through photos, he saw the cathedral at Salamanca, in Spain. "This is what we want," he exclaimed. His new design was shorter, but the tower as built still weighs more than 9,000 tons.

The foundation consists of 4,500 wooden piles, driven into the muck of the Back Bay. On top of these sit granite blocks, some salvaged from the old Trinity building on Summer Street, destroyed in the Great Fire of 1872. The walls are rose-tinged Dedham granite, trimmed with brown Longmeadow freestone—their bold colors another radical change from the gray stone that had been the norm for New England architecture.

Trinity Church after the fire of November 1872

The true glory of Trinity is its decorated interior, described by the *Boston Evening Transcript* as having "a solidity and grandeur of effect not to be described, but to be seen and felt." The murals are by John La Farge, a New York artist and friend of Richardson's. They weren't in the original design; Richardson recommended La Farge to the building committee as construction was winding up. They're painted with encaustic, a medium of pigments mixed into hot wax and turpentine. A deep "Pompeian" red, the favorite color of both Richardson and Brooks, predominates. La Farge had just four months to create them.

Trinity Church was consecrated on February 9, 1877, eight days after La Farge completed the murals. Including the foundation, construction had taken nearly four years. Some details were still undone; the stained glass windows—many by La Farge—would be installed over a span of several years. An entrance porch, from plans suggested by Richardson, was added a decade after his death.

In Trinity, Richardson created an architectural style, Richardsonian Romanesque, that was fashionable in Boston and in America for a quarter of a century.

Trinity Church, Copley Square, 1895

With so many of his commissions originating in Boston, H. H. Richardson moved from New York to Brookline in 1874. Two years after Trinity was completed, the parish hired him to design a rectory on Clarendon Street. He did two other houses in the Back Bay, but much of his local work was in the suburbs. He created public libraries in Woburn, Malden, Quincy and Easton, and a string of stations for the Boston & Albany Railroad, whose vice president was an old Harvard pal. Further afield, his work took him to Chicago, Pittsburgh and Albany.

Richardson's personal appearance matched the solidity of his buildings, which are noted for their rounded bays. From his days at Harvard and Paris, he acquired an appreciation of fine clothing, food and companionship. "Fond of pleasure and society, and always ready for a dinner-party," as one friend from his student days remembered him, he enjoyed "the pleasures of art and appetite." His social abilities earned him jobs from wealthy clients, but cost him his health. At 345 pounds, his massive girth was both cause and symptom of numerous ailments. He died of kidney disease in 1886, at the prime of his career, 47 years old.

H. H. Richardson, by Sir Hubert von Herkomer, 1886

Beyond his own buildings, H. H. Richardson left another kind of legacy: he helped train a generation of architects. Among his assistants were the future designers of the Boston Public Library that would be built just across the square from Trinity Church; plus Symphony Hall, South Station, Cambridge's City Hall, M.I.T.'s new campus on the banks of the Charles, and many other Boston-area buildings. His descendants remained active in architecture for a century more.

Richardson also had a direct influence on two great architects of later eras; both Louis Sullivan and Frank Lloyd Wright described H. H. Richardson's designs as inspirations for their nascent careers. Sullivan enrolled in 1872 in the Massachusetts Institute of Technology's new School of Architecture, a block from the still-rising Brattle Square Church. Fourteen years later, as a leading architect in Chicago, Sullivan was a mentor for Wright, who began his architectural career in the Windy City just as two major Richardson projects were being completed there.

In 1885, eight years after Trinity Church was completed, *American Architect and Building News* asked its readers to list their favorite buildings. Trinity Church was the undisputed winner. A century later, in 1991, the American Institute of Architects made a similar poll of its members. Trinity ranked ninth. It was the only building from the original poll that still made the top ten.

CHAPTER 18.

WATSON, COME HERE!

"Mr. Watson, come here, I want to see you." With those legendary words, uttered in a Boston rooming house in 1876, the era of the telephone was born. It's a story that involves romance, luck and perhaps a little chicanery. Alexander Graham Bell won the patent for inventing the telephone. But he couldn't have done it — and it wouldn't have been such a financial success — without help from a young woman named Mabel Hubbard and her father, Gardiner Greene Hubbard.

Gardiner Hubbard was a Boston lawyer. In 1850 he built an elegant home on Cambridge's Brattle Street, where he was later described as "the prime mover in almost every project at the time for the practical benefit of the city." Within six years after moving across the river, Hubbard had organized companies to provide his new hometown with piped-in water and gas and horse-drawn street railway service.

Hubbard's civic activities were interrupted in 1862 when his 5-year-old daughter, Mabel, became permanently deaf from a bout with scarlet fever. Mabel's father then turned his focus to the education of deaf individuals; he helped found and became president of the Clarke School for the Deaf

‹ Alexander Graham Bell at the opening of the long-distance line from New York to Chicago, 1892

Alexander Graham Bell with his wife Mabel and daughters Elsie (left) and Marian (Daisy), circa 1885

in Northampton, Massachusetts.

Returning to his law practice, Hubbard grew interested in the communications needs of an expanding nation. He proposed a "U.S. Postal Telegraph Company" to compete with Western Union's effective monopoly on instantaneous, long-distance communications. Hubbard spent much time in Washington, lobbying Congress, where his proposal became known as the Hubbard Bill. Those efforts never succeeded, but for years Hubbard seemed fixated on his personal rivalry with the Western Union Telegraph Company.

Meanwhile, in Britain, Alexander Graham Bell was also becoming an expert on both the education of the deaf and on improvements to telegraphy. Bell's grandfather, Alexander Bell, taught elocution lessons in London; his father, Melville Bell, also gave speech lessons and was a pioneer in the scientific study of phonetics.

Aleck, as Bell was known in his youth, followed in the family profession, which by then had expanded into efforts to teach deaf people to speak, instead of using sign language. And he dabbled in science, too. While still a teenager, Aleck made an artificial speaking machine with his brother; at 20 he built a small telegraph system and exchanged messages with a friend. Soon he started experimenting with tuning forks, trying to create a "harmonic telegraph" that could relay multiple messages on one wire.

And someday, he thought, it might be possible to send voices over wires, too.

Alexander Graham Bell and Thomas Watson

By the early 1870s, both Aleck and his father were touring America, lecturing on their system of writing down vocal sounds using special symbols, known as "Visible Speech." In fall of 1873, Aleck was named a Professor of "Vocal Physiology and Elocution" at Boston University's School of Oratory. Chartered just four years earlier, the university was then at 18 Beacon Street, diagonally opposite the State House. Bell's university job required only five hours a week, and with it came a room he could use for private lessons.

One of his private students was Mabel Hubbard, not quite 16 years old, sent by her father for lessons. At first, she did not like her instructor, who was 10 years older than she. "He was tall and dark, with jet black hair and eyes, but dressed badly in an old-fashioned suit ... he seemed hardly a gentleman." But a month later, Mabel wrote to her mother, "I enjoy my lessons very much." And, she wrote in February, they "had a grand time running down hill through the deep snow" to the streetcar back to her Brattle Street home.

After a summer hiatus, Bell returned to Boston and his university classes, and to Mabel's lessons. Come October of 1874, Aleck Bell was invited to his pupil's home to meet her family.

It was a fortuitous encounter. After tea, Bell sat at the piano and played some pieces for the Hubbards. He then sang into the piano, to demonstrate how its strings would resonate with his voice, and he explained his work on the harmonic telegraph. Gardiner Hubbard's interest in telegraphy was known to Bell; but Hubbard had no reason to suspect that Bell shared that interest.

There, at the Hubbards' piano were the two people responsible for one of history's great technological breakthroughs: There was the inventor with

Bell Telephone Company, 1890

his scientific knowledge; and there was the entrepreneur with the business acumen and financial means needed to make the invention successful.

With money from Hubbard, and from the father of another pupil, Bell hired an assistant, Thomas Watson. Watson built various pieces of apparatus according to Bell's specifications, and they worked together on experiments, Bell squeezing the time in between his teaching and his courtship of Mabel. Whenever he was discouraged by his research, it was Mabel who urged him to press on. By June of 1875 he was able to send vocal sounds over wires, although the words were yet undistinguishable.

All the while, Bell was developing feelings for his young pupil. When Bell recognized it as love, he informed her parents, who thought her too young for romance (and him too old for her). Mabel, too, was unsure if she loved him or just liked him. Love did win out, and they were engaged on her 18th birthday, Thanksgiving Day, 1875. It was agreed that marriage needed to wait until Bell developed a steady source of income.

A rival inventor, Elisha Gray of Chicago, was making similar discoveries for Hubbard's old opponent, Western Union. On February 14, 1876, the U.S. Patent Office in Washington received paperwork from both Bell and Gray. To this day, historians debate which document arrived first; official records noted only the date, not the time. It's been speculated that Hubbard and his associates used their influence to win favorable treatment for Bell's application; an examiner handling the case for the patent office apparently owed money to one of Bell's attorneys. Just three weeks after his application was filed, Bell was awarded U.S. Patent 174,465 for an improvement in telegraphy—the patent on which the telephone was based.

On March 10, 1876, just three days after his patent was issued, Bell successfully transmitted intelligible human speech by wire for the first time. His request to "come here" was heard by Thomas Watson, two rooms away in Bell's rooming house at 5 Exeter Place in Boston's commercial district. (Once a dead-end off of Chauncy Street, Exeter Place is now part of the Avenue de Lafayette.)

On July 11, 1877, Alexander Graham Bell and Mabel Hubbard were wed at the Hubbard home in Cambridge. Bell gave his bride "an exquisite cross of eleven round pearls, the prettiest he could find in Boston," plus 1,487 shares in the newly founded Bell Telephone Company, organized just two days earlier. By then, more than 200 private line telephones had been installed. The first telephone exchange—which allowed a customer to call any other customer—began service the next winter.

As the man who created the telephone and developed it for commercial use, Bell essentially retired on earnings from his invention, although he remained prolific in other intellectual pursuits. He and Mabel divided their time between Washington, D.C., and Cape Breton, Nova Scotia, and they had a devoted marriage until his death in 1922.

Mabel's father, Gardiner Greene Hubbard, was the first president of the Bell Telephone Company, the company that later became American Telephone & Telegraph, or AT&T. He also founded the National Geographic Society in 1888. An energetic promoter, Gardiner Hubbard introduced many of the civic services now taken for granted. He brought water and gas service to the residents of Cambridge; he brought urban rail transit, the first predecessor of the MBTA, to greater Boston. He created the National Geographic Society and its beloved magazine. And through his son-in-law—and the inspiration provided by his daughter, Mabel—he brought the telephone to the world.

"WHERE ARE YOU GOING MY PRETTY MAID?"
"I'M GOING TO KEITH'S SIR", SHE SAID.

VAUDEVILLE

CHAPTER 19.

THE FATHER OF VAUDEVILLE

For three decades at the turn of the 20th century, the leading form of popular entertainment in America was a type of stage variety known as vaudeville. Its self-proclaimed "father," B. F. Keith, boasted that he'd "invented" the art form in Boston. Creator of vaudeville or not, Keith was certainly its greatest impresario, an entrepreneur who brought vaudeville to perfection on Washington Street. And it was on Washington Street where vaudeville's funeral was held—a funeral presided over by none other than Joseph P. Kennedy.

Benjamin Franklin Keith was a New England farm boy who ran away with the circus. As a young man he learned the art of entertainment on the road, a sideshow barker who hustled patrons into freak shows. Eventually he settled in Boston, in a time when "dime museums" were popular. These weren't museums at all, merely variants on circus sideshows that operated out of urban storefronts.

At the beginning of 1883 Keith and a partner rented an old candy store at 565 Washington Street for their New York Dime Museum. Upper Washington Street then was already the city's biggest entertainment district.

< Keith's Vaudeville advertisement, circa 1905

B.F. Keith

Keith's "museum" was nestled among some of Boston's largest theaters for live drama; it was on horse-drawn streetcar lines and at the edge of the retail district. Shoppers from nearby stores, such as the Jordan, Marsh emporium, might take a break to observe Keith's curiosities.

Keith's first exhibit was "Baby Alice, the Queen of Midgets," a tiny infant reputed to fit inside a milk bottle. But Baby Alice grew, to be replaced by a trained bear cub, a "chicken with a face of a dog," and other acts. The name of the establishment varied over the next year, as did Keith's partners. For the week of September 27, 1884, "Keith and Batcheller's Mamoth Museum" offered nine acts in its Curiosity Hall, among them The Three-Headed Songstress, Burnham's Colossal Tableaux of the American Rebellion, and Prof. S. K. Hodgson, who "will at short intervals deliver an interesting lecture." On the second floor was a stage program featuring comedians, singers and dancers.

The next year, Keith went into partnership with Edward F. Albee, an old circus friend (and grandfather of the like-named playwright). Down the street from their establishment, the authorized first run of Gilbert and Sullivan's *The Mikado* was playing to capacity audiences at $1.50 a seat. In the absence of international copyright laws, Albee decided to offer the "same show" for a quarter. With the profits from this venture, Keith and Albee leased the larger Bijou Theatre a few doors away from their first storefront.

American stage promoters had adopted the French term *vaudeville* a decade earlier, probably because it sounded vaguely exotic. (Vaudeville in this country was nothing like the French version, which referred to a light musical comedy or satire.) Keith popularized the name and pioneered the concept of continuous performances. His typical program consisted of eight stage acts, each act performing several times over the course of the 12-hour day. "It matters not at what hour of the day or evening you visit," Keith wrote, "the theatre is always occupied by more or less people, the show is in full swing, everything is bright, cheerful and inviting." When the acts started to repeat, you left.

Vaudeville was so successful that 1894 saw the opening of B. F. Keith's New Theatre, located directly behind the Bijou, seating nearly 1,800 patrons. Designed by the architect of New York's Metropolitan Opera House, this "dream palace of a theatre" offered splendor at a price that everyone could pay. As one critic noted, "It is almost incredible that all this elegance should be placed at the disposal of the public, the poor as well as the rich."

Vaudeville advertisement, 1894

Among the employees was a water boy whose sole duty was to course the aisles, offering free glasses of ice water from a silver tray. All this for a dime.

Keith and Albee moved beyond Boston to create an empire of nearly 400 theaters in cities small and large across the country. They ran a booking office too, contracting with thousands of performers who would travel the nation playing stages of the Keith-Albee Circuit. Although he always had his competitors, Keith was the undisputed king of the boards. His bookings office and blacklist could make or break an act—and did.

Above all, Keith envisioned vaudeville as family entertainment. A devout Catholic, he believed "the stage show must be free from vulgarisms and coarseness of any kind, so that the house and entertainment would directly appeal to the support of ladies and children." Players who uttered "son of a gun" or "hully gee" were not only subject to instant discharge, they "would never again be allowed to appear in a theatre where Mr. Keith is in authority." Actors sometimes called Keith's "the Sunday school circuit."

Even the audiences were expected to maintain decorum. Isabella Stewart Gardner, a regular patron at Keith's, was once ejected for refusing to remove her high-plumed hat.

B. F. Keith Memorial Theatre, 539 Washington Street

By 1909 Keith's business in Boston had grown enough that he leased the venerable Boston Theatre, adjacent to the two halls that he already controlled. Lobbies of the three theaters were connected, making a three-auditorium complex with nearly 7,000 seats, replete with a "crystal staircase" made of glass, with a waterfall beneath it, and a "crystal subway" lined with mirrors, allowing patrons to enter from Tremont Street.

Keith passed away in 1914. Ten years later, his partner Edward Albee announced plans to raze the Boston Theatre and build a magnificent memorial to the acknowledged "father of vaudeville." The B. F. Keith Memorial Theatre would be the "world's most beautiful playhouse." But by the time it was completed, vaudeville itself was exiting the stage.

B. F. Keith had introduced Boston's first moving pictures, the Vitascope, at Keith's New Theatre in 1896. Short subjects were presented three times a day, sandwiched among the vaudeville acts. In 1908, the Bijou—still

SOME COWARD CLOSED THE OLD HOWARD

If B. F. Keith's vaudeville was a variety show for family audiences, burlesque was the adult entertainment version. And Boston had America's most famous burlesque house: the Old Howard.

The Howard got its start as the Millerite Tabernacle, erected in 1843 by followers of Rev. William Miller. When the world did not end on March 21, 1844, as Miller had predicted, the Millerites recalculated their arithmetic. Soon the sect's remaining members sold the Tabernacle for use as a theater. When the original wooden building burned five months later, it was replaced by a new granite playhouse, its Gothic architecture resembling a church.

At its opening in 1846, the Howard Athenæum was the finest theater in Boston. But as newer, grander halls materialized, it started going downscale. By 1890 it was called the Old Howard and featured burlesque. That term originally referred to parodies of legitimate drama; but at the Howard it meant a mix of slapstick comedy, "living models," and something similar to a belly dance.

To meet competition from movies in the 1920s, the comedy got bawdier and the models' outfits got skimpier. The audiences famously included "bald headed men" along with Harvard students who came for an education of a different sort.

In 1933 the Old Howard was shut down for a month for presenting "raw filth." In 1953 the city again suspended its license, and the "Temple of Burlesque" sat vacant until a fire of undetermined origin struck in 1961. Not long afterwards, the neighborhood was cleared for Government Center.

Years later, a historic marker was placed on the site of the Old Howard's stage. It's in back of the Center Plaza building, just a few yards from the old Suffolk County Courthouse.

RKO Keith's Theater

under Keith's control—became the city's first theater to show nothing but movies, accompanied by an all-female orchestra. By the 1920s, films had eclipsed vaudeville as the main attraction. In 1926 there were only a dozen all-vaudeville houses left in the nation.

In the spring of 1928, as the Keith Memorial Theatre was under construction, Joseph P. Kennedy bought out the Keith-Albee Circuit. That fall, Kennedy sold it to RCA, the Radio Corporation of America, which sought a chain of performance halls that it could wire for talkies. The result was RKO. The *R* stood for *Radio*; the *K* for *Keith*; the *O* for *Orpheum*, another chain of theaters involved in the merger.

The Keith Memorial opened 11 days later, on October 29, 1928. It was the world's most beautiful playhouse, "a dazzling architectural dream in ivory and gold." But even as the audience was celebrating vaudeville, Kennedy had driven the nails into its coffin. On the bill that night, after the speeches and the live performers, was a movie. A block away, Al Jolson was "The Singing Fool" in a new "talking picture hit." Within a year, the Keith Memorial Theatre stopped presenting live acts.

Yet memories of vaudeville persist. Many vaudeville performers became movie stars: A 1902 program for Keith's New Theatre featured an "eccentric, juggling comedian" named W. C. Fields. The Marx Brothers, Fred Astaire, Jack Benny and Ethel Merman are among the artists who got their starts on the vaudeville stage. All of them passed through Boston many times in their early careers.

The B. F. Keith Memorial Theatre on Washington Street is now the Boston Opera House. It survived 50 years as a movie palace and a decade of abandonment, to be beautifully restored in 2004. Next door, the façade of the old Bijou Theatre still stands, although the auditorium was demolished decades ago. And a few blocks away is a statue of one of vaudeville's very earliest stars: the trained bear cub hired by B. F. Keith back in 1883. The bear was sold to a private men's club, the Tavern Club, and became their mascot. He's featured on a sculpted gateway at the entrance to Boylston Place.

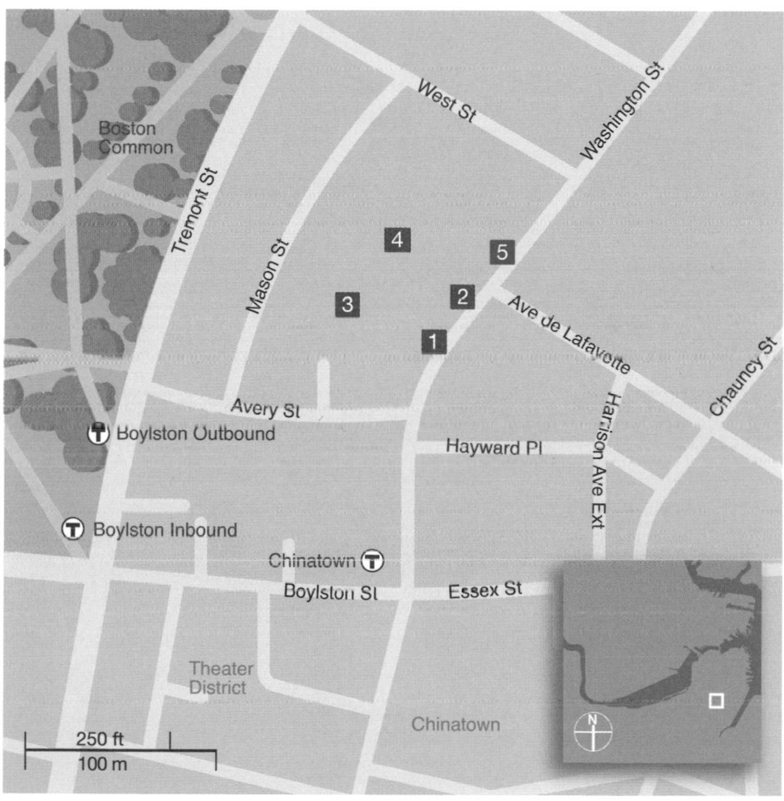

1 New York Dime Museum: 565 Washington Street
2 Bijou Theatre: 545 Washington Street
3 Keith's New Theatre: 547 Washington Street
4 Boston Theatre: 535 Washington Street
5 B. F. Keith Memorial Theatre: 539 Washington Street

CHAPTER 20.

MOVING BOSTON: HENRY M. WHITNEY AND THE DEVELOPMENT OF A MODERN TRANSIT SYSTEM

Great cities demand good transit. They need a speedy way to move masses of people or else they stagnate. Throughout the 19th century, Boston's unique topography—its bays, its hills, its crooked and narrow streets forced the city to be a transit pioneer.

Perhaps the man most responsible for the creation of Boston's modern transit system was Henry M. Whitney. In 1886, transit in Boston was typical of many cities: propelled by animals and fragmented in its management. It was Whitney who converted this into a mechanized, unified system. Yet Whitney's brief career in transit came by chance. He had no desire to revolutionize the transit industry worldwide; he merely wished to develop land that he and his neighbors owned in neighboring Brookline.

Transit in 1886 meant the horse-drawn street railway, with its rails in the middle of the public streets. Boston's first horsecar line opened on March 26, 1856, tracing much of the modern Red Line on its route to Cambridge. The Cambridge Railroad was the brainchild of Gardiner Greene Hubbard; one of its earliest lines conveniently passed Hubbard's own home on Brattle Street. Boston was just the fifth city in the world to have this innovative form of

< Subway construction, Park Street Station, 1896

transit, after New York, New Orleans, Paris and Brooklyn (then a separate municipality). The company was in such a rush to inaugurate the service that it used secondhand cars, still painted to advertise destinations in Brooklyn. Within four years, a score of horsecar lines were chartered in and around Boston.

Horsecars on the Cambridge Railroad, 1856

Affordable and relatively fast transit meant that, for the first time, large numbers of workers could commute into Boston from surrounding towns. The Streetcar Suburb had been invented. Between 1867 and 1874, Roxbury, Dorchester, Charlestown, West Roxbury and Brighton were all annexed into the City of Boston.

Yet Brookline bucked the trend. Its wealthy residents voted down a proposal to be absorbed into Boston, partly because they feared their tax money would be misused by the larger city. But their town was also poorly served by the existing street railways, since it was situated on the far side of the Back Bay, still being filled. Brookline's Beacon Street then was a narrow county road, lined with farms, inaccessible to much of Boston because of its lack of transit.

To Henry M. Whitney this was an opportunity. In 1886 Whitney was an established Boston businessman with an estate in Brookline, where he was active in civic affairs. He knew that the undeveloped land along Beacon Street could be converted into a fashionable residential neighborhood—but only if a transit line could be built to connect it with downtown Boston. When the existing transit companies showed no interest in his plans, Whitney chartered a new company, the West End Street Railway, to build and operate the line. Wanting nothing but the best, Whitney and his partners

Street views: Boylston Street, circa 1890

hired landscape architect Frederick Law Olmsted to plan the widening of Beacon Street into a 200-foot-wide boulevard.

Still, the four established street railway firms resisted Whitney's plans; they saw him as an interloper who would interfere with the status quo. Access to their tracks, needed for the West End's cars to reach downtown, was denied. Whitney and his partners responded in true capitalist fashion: they bought out their rivals. Whitney and his friends secretly bought up stock in each of the four existing companies that had tried to shut them out; in a few weeks, they owned controlling interests in all four firms. On November 12, 1887, all were merged into Whitney's company. Overnight, the West End Street Railway Co. metamorphosed from a paper company to the largest urban transit company in the world. It had 200 miles of track, 1,700 railway cars, 3,700 employees, and 8,400 horses—who ate 250,000 pounds of food and generated over 100 tons of manure each day.

Boston was thus the first major city in America to have a unified transit system. The amalgamated system allowed for much smoother operation, bitter rivalries were ended, and riders now paid a single flat fare, with free transfers, to travel almost anywhere in the metropolitan area.

Whitney could now turn his thoughts back to his proposed transit line on Beacon Street in Brookline. To build the first-class neighborhood that he desired, a horse-drawn line would not suffice. Some sort of mechanized transit line would be required. But what sort?

State-of-the-art transit in 1887 meant the cable car. Invented in San Francisco, cable car lines were running in a dozen U.S. cities and under construction in more. But cable technology was expensive and poorly

Trial run of car at the Public Garden entrance to the subway, 1897

suited to Boston's curving streets. More promising perhaps was the new electric railway technology, but it was still seen as experimental, and no large city had yet built a successful electric transit line. Early in 1888, Whitney traveled to Pittsburgh and to Richmond, Va., to see for himself. What he saw in Richmond convinced him. Henry Whitney's decision in July 1888, to build the Beacon Street line as an electric car line, was a turning point in the history of the transit industry. The cable car's future was dead; electric power would prevail.

The first trial runs into Park Square ran in the late hours of New Year's Eve, with holiday revelers invited aboard. Regular service began on January 3, 1889. Soon the company's directors voted to electrify the entire system as rapidly as possible. Other cities quickly followed. Electricity had indeed prevailed.

In Boston, the speedy electric trolley became a victim of its own success. Ridership grew, routes were extended, and soon traffic congestion on Tremont Street was so bad that you could walk from one end of the Common to the other faster than a trolley could take you. Few alternate routes were available, especially from the fast-growing districts to the west.

But Henry M. Whitney's tenure in the transit industry was short. He retired from the West End Street Railway in 1893, dismayed by the politics of transit expansion, finding that rival proposals were winning political favor over his own plans. And he disliked public scrutiny of his own motives and finances, so he removed himself from the limelight.

With Whitney no longer active in local transit affairs, a special state commission was created to study such options as laying tracks across Boston Common, erecting an elevated train line, or even tearing down blocks of buildings to construct a new street. Once again, Boston chose to be a pioneer: to alleviate the congestion, the city would build the first transit subway in America, and just the fourth in the world, after London, Budapest and Glasgow. The first segment, from the Public Garden to Park Street, opened on September 1, 1897.

The West End Street Railway became the Boston Elevated Railway, then the Metropolitan Transit Authority, and today the Massachusetts Bay Transportation Authority—still one of the largest transit systems in America, which now operates commuter rail and commuter boat routes, in addition to subways, streetcars and buses. The subway lines have been extended many times, and a few electric trolley lines survive—including the one on Beacon Street—although most of the old electric rail routes are now served by fossil-fueled, rubber-tired buses.

Henry M. Whitney, meanwhile, concentrated on businesses that were removed from the public view; in his lifetime he was president of the Dominion Coal Co., the Massachusetts Pipeline Gas Co., the Submarine Signal Co., the Never-Slip Horse Shoe Co., three steamship lines, and a host of other firms. Many of his new projects arose out of his already existing ventures. He needed coal, for example, to generate electricity for his streetcar lines, so he bought a coal mine in Canada and a steamship line to haul the coal to Boston. When the mine proved to have excess capacity, he built a steel mill next to it.

At his death in 1924, the *New York Times* called him "one of the greatest captains of industry of his time." A consummate capitalist, it was his vision that gave Boston a great transit system.

"LET US HAVE PEACE"

CHAPTER 21.

FROM CHERRY RIBBON TO CONCERT HALLS

It all began with a single yard of cherry-colored ribbon, sold over the counter to a friend, a simple transaction that was the genesis of New England's greatest store. But that cherry ribbon begat the grandest, most improbable concert extravaganzas ever heard in Boston—and it also led to the construction of some of the city's most beloved performance halls, for the founder of that store—and, later, his son—became leading benefactors of the musical arts in the Hub.

Born on a Maine farm in 1822, Eben D. Jordan came to Boston at age 14, an orphan with $1.25 in his pocket. Eventually he was hired on as an errand boy for a downtown dry goods store. In retail he found his true calling; when he was 19, a local merchant gave him money to open a store of his own. On his first day in business, a friend named Louisa Bareiss was waiting on the sidewalk for young Eben to unlock the door, so she could buy some ribbon.

Ten years later, Jordan became partners with Benjamin Marsh; the enterprise became known as Jordan and Marsh. Their motto was "The better you serve your customers, the better you serve yourself." In 1861, the Jordan, Marsh & Co. store moved to 450 Washington Street, its address for the next 135 years.

< The big drum, Boston Peace Jubilee, 1869

Jordan also “had the soul of an artist and a keen critical sense of musical ability,” according to one of his many newspaper obituaries. He assisted many music students and prominent artists, financially and otherwise.

One of America’s leading musicians was P. S. Gilmore, a bandleader who’d once worked with P. T. Barnum, and who’d learned some of Barnum’s techniques of self-promotion. (Gilmore is remembered today as the author of “When Johnny Comes Marching Home,” written under a pseudonym.) In 1867 Gilmore conceived a vision for a great National Peace Jubilee—“one of the most gigantic musical schemes in the world’s history,” as the *Boston Herald* called it—to celebrate the end of the Civil War and the restoration of peace throughout the land, to be held in Boston in the summer of 1869.

Gilmore was initially unsuccessful at raising funds for the mammoth event; but when Jordan agreed to be his Treasurer, it “gave fresh vigor to the whole undertaking,” as Gilmore later described it. Believing that the Jubilee would be good for Boston businesses, Jordan promoted the venture among the city’s merchants, and his support ensured that it would, indeed, come to fruition. Jordan also insisted that his friend Eben Tourjée, founder of the New England Conservatory of Music, should direct the Jubilee’s chorus.

Within three months an immense wooden “Temple of Peace” was erected in the just-filled (but still largely vacant) Back Bay, near where Trinity Church would later stand. It was 500 feet long, 300 feet wide, and 100 feet to the apex of its roof, seating 40,000 paying customers, plus a 10,000-voice chorus and a 1,000-piece orchestra. The Jubilee played to sold-out audiences for five days that June. The “striking” climax of each day’s performance was the anvil chorus from Verdi’s *Il Trovatore*, conducted by Gilmore himself, with a hundred Boston firemen beating hammers on anvils, accompanied by chimes, an organ with 1,011 pipes, “the world’s largest bass drum,” twelve cannons, and the church bells of the city.

The incredible affair actually covered its costs, netting a profit of $6,882.04 (about $110,000 today) after expenses were paid, out of a budget of nearly $300,000.00, or about $4.9 million dollars in today’s money.

Based on the success of the first Peace Jubilee, Gilmore and Jordan put on a more grandiose World Peace Jubilee in 1872, commemorating the end

Jordan, Marsh & Company, Washington Street

of the Franco-Prussian War. The second try was a flop. A new coliseum, designed for an audience of 100,000, collapsed during construction and had to be downsized to 60,000 seats. The drum, 21 feet in diameter, didn't vibrate right and couldn't be played. Instead of just five days of concerts, there were 16 this time—but the crowds didn't show. The World Peace Jubilee's only true success was the appearance of Johann Strauss, direct from Vienna, on his only trip to America.

In addition to his philanthropic and musical pursuits, Eben Jordan invested in a variety of businesses besides retail. He was a founding stockholder in the *Boston Globe* newspaper, and an early partner with Henry M. Whitney in the West End Street Railway; and he led efforts to develop the Corey Hill neighborhood of Brookline—served, of course, by the West End's Beacon Street streetcar line.

At Eben Jordan death in 1895, newspaper obituaries remembered him as "a splendid type of a self-made man" whose "name has been synonymous with integrity." Control of the department store passed to his son, Eben D. Jordan, Jr., who also inherited his father's passion for music. The younger Jordan had a special interest in vocal music; he'd wanted to be a professional singer but business obligations kept him from his dream. Instead, he became a patron, erecting halls for musical performances.

The son's earliest concert venue was the Majestic Theatre on Tremont Street. Opened February 16, 1903, it was designed for European operas. The first Boston auditorium with a cantilevered balcony—meaning no columns to obstruct sightlines—the Majestic was designed in the popular Beaux Arts style. Its ornate interior featured so much gold leaf that it was nicknamed the "House of Gold."

Next was a new building for the New England Conservatory of Music, continuing the Jordan family's longtime support for that institution. The junior Jordan purchased land on Huntington Avenue, diagonally opposite the newly opened Symphony Hall, then donated the money for the school's concert hall and its organ. In gratitude, the Conservatory named its new concert venue Jordan Hall.

Third of Eben Jordan's performance venues was the Boston Opera House, also on Huntington Avenue. (This shouldn't be confused with Boston's present Opera House, located on Washington Street; that was originally the Keith Memorial Theatre) Seating 2,700 people, with three balconies and three tiers of boxes, the Opera House had the largest stage in the nation. It opened November 8, 1909, with a performance of Ponchielli's *La Gioconda*.

And there was a fourth concert hall, a private one, in Jordan's own house, at 46 Beacon Street on Beacon Hill. The younger Jordan enlarged his father's home, combining it with the property next door, and built a music room that seated 170 people.

Just seven years after the opening of the Opera House, Eben D. Jordan, Jr., was dead. In failing health for some years, he passed away at a relatively young 59, leaving Boston a legacy in mercantilism and music. Of that heritage, some jewels still shine brightly today, but others have become tarnished, lost and forgotten.

For most of the last century Jordan, Marsh was New England's largest department store, at one point occupying two entire city blocks plus several suburban branches. But in 1996 it was merged into the Macy's chain, and the Jordan Marsh nameplate was erased from the retail scene.

Eben Jordan's own mansion on Beacon Hill, with its spectacular interior finishes, still stands, but is now deteriorating and neglected as the New England headquarters of Rev. Moon's Unification Church. And his Opera House on Huntington Avenue was demolished in 1958 to make way for a Northeastern University dormitory. Although the younger Jordan was lauded as "the father of grand opera in Boston," the reality was that opera never grew as fashionable here as it was elsewhere. The enormous hall soon became a white elephant, too large for Boston's tastes in music.

Yet Jordan's other two theaters not only survive, but they've been lovingly restored in recent years. After decades of decline as an increasingly seedy movie house, the Majestic Theatre was purchased by Emerson College in 1983. A grand restoration was completed in 2003, its centenary year, when it was rededicated as the Cutler Majestic Theatre.

Across town on Huntington Avenue, the New England Conservatory has always prized its elegant concert hall, named after the father and son who were the school's early benefactors. Its restoration was finished in 1995. Gian Carlo Menotti, the Italian composer, once called it "the most beautiful hall in the world ... it really is a gift from God."

Not bad for something that started with a yard of cherry ribbon.

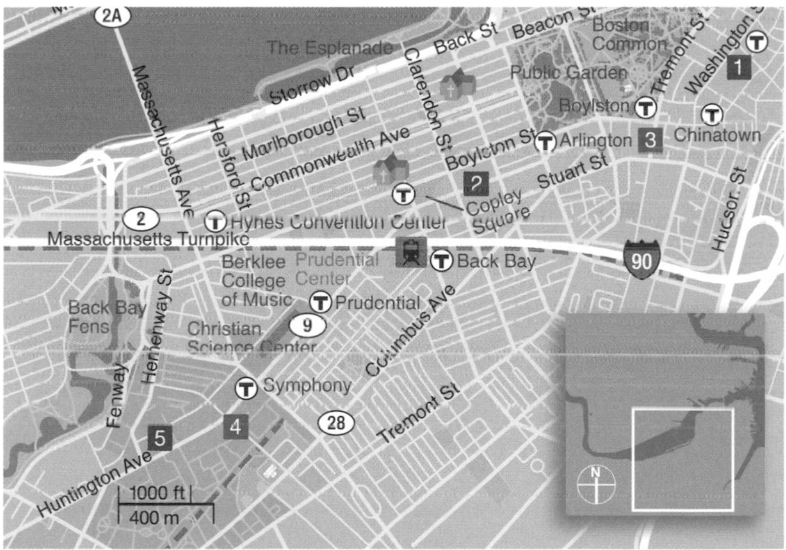

1 Jordan, Marsh & Co.: 450 Washington Street
2 Temple of Peace: Saint James Avenue
3 Majestic Theatre : 219 Tremont Street
4 New England Conservatory of Music Jordan Hall: 30 Gainsborough Street
5 Boston Opera House: 343 Huntington Avenue
6 Eben Jordan Home: 46 Beacon Street

CHAPTER 22.

QUEEN OF THE BACK BAY

Isabella Stewart Gardner was never really accepted in Boston. She was, after all, a transplanted New Yorker, even if she was a passionate Red Sox fan. Her passion for sports was, indeed, one reason why the Hub's society ladies thought her strange. Still, they attended her parties, if only to have something to gossip about afterwards. And she built the only palace ever erected in the city of Boston.

Isabella Stewart was born in 1840, the daughter of a self-made New York investor in coal and iron mining. Belle, as she was called, was a mischievous redhead, but her childhood was tinged with loss. Her dear sister, Adelia, two years younger, died suddenly a few days before she would have turned 12. To relieve Belle's sadness, her parents took her on an extended trip to Europe two years later. In Paris, she enrolled in a finishing school; in Italy, she saw her first palace. "If I ever have money of my own," 17-year-old Isabella Stewart told a friend, I want to "have a house … like the one in Milan, filled with beautiful pictures."

In Paris, the Stewarts met another visiting American family, the Gardners of Boston. Julia Gardner, a year younger than Belle, attended the same school,

‹ Isabella Stewart Gardner (center) and friends

Isabella Gardner, by John Singer Sargent, 1888

and the two girls became lifelong friends. After both families' return to America, Isabella was invited to visit Julia at her Boston home. On that visit, romance flourished between Belle and Julia's brother Jack.

A legend once circulated that "Belle Stewart jumped out of a boarding school window and eloped with Jack Gardner." That's a bit of an exaggeration; the couple likely met in Paris, and they cemented their relationship on her Boston visit in the winter of 1859. That February, Isabella Stewart and John L. Gardner, Jr., were formally engaged. They wed in April 1860. Isabella was four days shy of her 20th birthday; her new husband was 23.

Save for Julia and her sisters, the newlywed Isabella had no female friends in Boston. An outsider, she was resented for stealing away "Boston's most eligible bachelor." And she had a way with the men of the town that the ladies just didn't appreciate.

On Isabella's first visit to Boston, she and Jack often strolled to the edge of the Back Bay, to observe the landfill work that was just beginning. Here would be their new home. As a wedding gift, Isabella's father bought a choice lot on the water side of Beacon Street and had a house built there. But their dream home took years to erect, and the Gardners spent their first two married years as itinerants—first at his parents' house; then at the Hotel Pelham, the nation's first apartment building (as the wags said, for the "newly wed and the nearly dead").

In the summer of 1862, Jack and Isabella Gardner settled into their home at 152 Beacon Street. Scarcely a year later their only child was born, John L. Gardner, III. He lived less than two years. Six months after Jackie's passing, Isabella suffered a miscarriage that brought her near death; she could never have another child. Depression sank in again.

Once more, travel was prescribed to cheer her. In spring of 1867 Isabella's wheelchair was rolled aboard a steamer bound for Europe. She returned in exuberant spirits, walking off the ship with a stunning new wardrobe from Paris. Instead of the hoop skirts that were fashionable in America, she wore the latest European fashions, scandalously short gowns that were six inches above the ground, the better for dancing.

With no children, and with Jack's family business thriving, the couple explored far corners of the world in a day when few people could—Russia, Palestine, Japan, Java, India. She rode donkeys and camels in Egypt and an elephant in Cambodia. And there was always Europe.

On their European excursions, Isabella discovered her love for music and art. In 1880, Jack Gardner purchased the house at 150 Beacon Street, next door to their residence, for a music room. Contractors joined the two townhouses as one, even though the floor levels differed. Visiting musicians gave private concerts for the Gardners' guests; a society newspaper described an 1887 dance party at their home as "characteristic of its graceful hostess, gay, brilliant, magnificent," attracting "scores of pretty women" and "all the festive stags" alike.

For a decade the Gardners visited Europe at least every other year. Isabella's first acquisition of historic art was a painting bought in Spain in 1888. After her father died in 1891, Isabella used her $1.6 million inheritance (nearly $40 million today) to commence serious collecting—with encouragement from her husband.

Throughout her life, Gardner craved attention and never shied from scandal. She is reputed to have said, "Don't spoil a good story by telling the truth." She was known to borrow lion cubs from a zoo and bring them to her Beacon Street home; she was ejected from B. F. Keith's Boston Theatre for refusing to remove her tall, feathered hat. During the 1912 World Series, she shocked a Symphony Hall audience by wearing a headband with the words "Oh you Red Sox" on it. She socialized with Julia Ward Howe, Neville Chamberlain, John L. Sullivan, Henry James and T. S. Eliot. She even charmed the Pope into giving her a private audience at the Vatican–and she wasn't Roman Catholic.

Soon art filled every corner of the Gardners' paired houses on Beacon Street. By fall of 1896, Isabella was talking with an architect about enlarging the property to include a gallery or

Courtyard of the Isabella Stewart Gardner Museum

museum. Jack urged his wife to think grand, to "create a Venetian palace out of barren waste land" in a just-filled section of Boston called the Fenway. But Isabella loved the Beacon Street house and wanted to stay there.

Her mind suddenly changed when Jack died in December 1898. Within three weeks of her husband's passing, Isabella purchased a lot in the new district, and she instructed her architect to scrap the plans he'd just finished for the Beacon Street gallery, to draw up a design for the Fenway instead. Ground was broken six months later, and the Isabella Stewart Gardner Museum opened to invited guests at "nine o'clock punctually" on January 1, 1903.

To escape payment of import duties on the masterpieces she brought to America, Gardner chartered a nonprofit museum. Customs authorities questioned the arrangement; during her lifetime the public could visit only a few days each year, and she ended up paying the duties anyway. She kept an apartment on the top floor; the beloved Beacon Street house where she had lived with her husband was sold. Its new owner was required to demolish the existing structure and start anew. Even the street number had to be changed; no one will ever again live at 152 Beacon Street. .

Isabella Stewart Gardner devoted her final two decades to perfecting her creation. On her death in 1924, her will stipulated that the museum remain "for the education and enrichment of the public forever." No works of art could be sold, nor could "the general disposition or arrangement of any articles" be changed. Should those provisions be violated, the museum was to be dissolved, with everything sold in Paris, the money to benefit Harvard.

As in Mrs. Gardner's day, the museum features regular concerts by eminent musicians, and elaborate floral displays in its indoor courtyard.

The courtyard walls evoke a 15th-century Venetian palace, with fragments salvaged from real palaces—but turned inside-out as a gesture to the New England climate: its balconies face, not out over public streets, but inward to the covered, heated courtyard.

Few people are able to craft their own memorial, but that's what Isabella Stewart Gardner did. Fenway Court, the palace that she built in a barren section of the city, is now one of the world's great art museums, named after its benefactress. Inside are works by Titian, Rembrandt, Michelangelo, Whistler and her good friend John Singer Sargent, all selected by Mrs. Gardner herself, all placed exactly where she wanted them. Perhaps the world's only art museum to have been envisioned and created by just one woman, it remains the vision of a remarkable person, a lady who in her day was described by a newspaper columnist as "easily the brightest, breeziest woman in Boston."

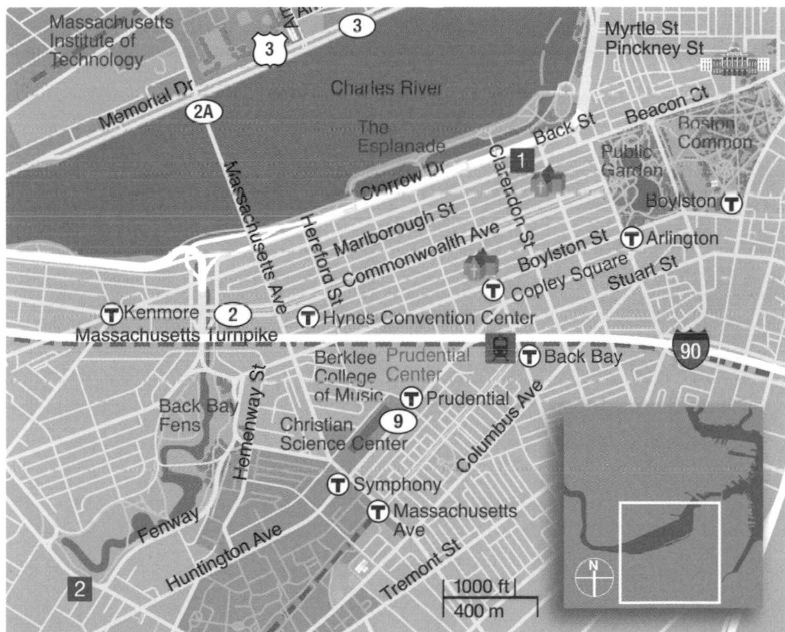

1 Gardner Manson: 152 Beacon Street
2 Isabella Stewart Gardner Museum: 280 The Fenway

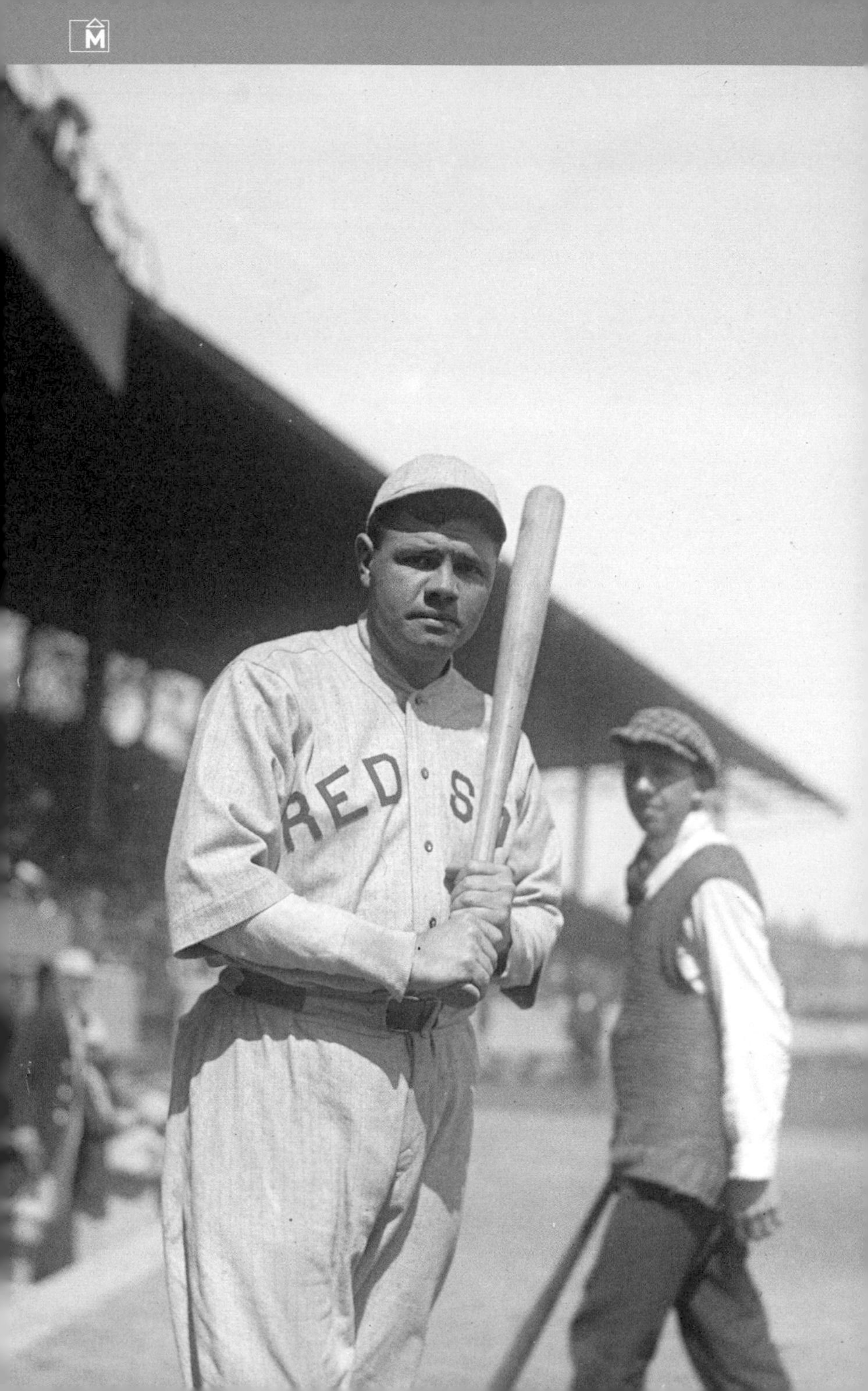
RED

CHAPTER 23.

BOSTON TERROR

He was Boston's star pitcher and a batting ace as well, yet his contract was sold to the New York Yankees, engendering one of the greatest rivalries in sport. Legend has it that he was sold, not for a song, but to finance a song, or rather a series of songs, in a Broadway musical. Like many legends, the truth is more complicated.

At the birth of professional baseball in the 1870s, the National League was the only "major" league, represented in Beantown by the team later known as the Boston Braves. The rival American League was organized in 1901 by Ban Johnson, an Ohio businessman; in a deliberate challenge to the older confederation, Boston was chosen as one of the new league's charter cities. The Hub's new ball club raided the best players from the city's older team and offered free passes to politicians and influential fans. The strategies paid off; in their first year, the Boston Americans outdrew the Nationals by large margins.

With their ownership changing five times in their first 16 seasons, Boston's American League team had a mixed record, winning four World Series, but just as often placing in the cellar. Notable among the club's early owners

‹ Babe Ruth, 1919

was John I. Taylor, known for making disastrous trades when a player somehow earned his disfavor. Meanwhile, League President Ban Johnson stood behind the scenes, trying to maintain strict control of all trades and ownership changes.

Johnson was particularly annoyed when Harry Harrison Frazee bought the Boston Red Sox just weeks after the team had won the 1916 World Series. Nicknamed "Handsome Harry" by the press, Frazee had a successful career in theatrical promotion; he then expanded into boxing matches, saying that drama and sports were both part of "the amusement business." Ownership of a baseball team had been his longtime dream, but Harry Frazee wasn't one of Ban Johnson's prescreened buyers and he wasn't going to be one of Johnson's puppets. That spelled trouble for the Red Sox, trouble which lasted generations after Frazee's departure.

Among the players on Frazee's newly acquired team was George Herman Ruth, Jr., known to all as the Babe. Just 21 years old, Babe Ruth was one of the game's best pitchers and had helped the Red Sox win two World Series championships in his two full seasons with the team.

Off the field, Babe Ruth was a hellion. The son of a Baltimore saloonkeeper, he'd spent most of his teenage years at St. Mary's Industrial School, a residential facility, where he'd been labeled "incorrigible." Yet the priests at the school had taught the boy baseball and helped him get a minor league contract in his hometown. After a few months there, the 19-year-old came to the Red Sox. Thrown into adulthood, he became famous for his indulgences with alcohol, women and fast cars—and his frequent auto accidents.

Four months after his arrival in Boston, Ruth married a coffee shop waitress whom he'd met here. Soon he bought a farm in Sudbury, 22 miles west of the city. While his wife stayed on the farm, Babe partied in Boston — where he kept an apartment in the red-light district—and on the team's many road trips. Often he was carousing at bars or brothels until almost daylight. Still, he usually performed well in the next afternoon's game.

In Harry Frazee's second season as Red Sox owner, the United States was at war. Conflict in Europe meant dwindling attendance at ballparks, and many ballplayers enlisted in the Army. With a shortage of players for fielding positions, the Red Sox asked Babe Ruth to play in the outfield or at first base on the days he didn't pitch. After all, the Babe's hitting was becoming just as good as his pitching; why not have his bat at the plate every day, not just on the days when his pitching arm was ready?

Entrance to Fenway Park, circa 1915

That 1918 season ended for the Red Sox with Babe Ruth as their winningest pitcher—with a 13–7 record—*and* their best hitter, with a .300 average. Plus, he led the American League in homers, with 11. The local press dubbed him "the Boston terror"; it's unclear if that was for his prowess on the field, for his antics off of it, or both. To climax the season, the Red Sox won the World Series, their fourth championship in seven years.

But the next year the team fell into a slump, experiencing its first sub-.500 season in a decade. And Frazee's continuing feud with Ban Johnson restricted his ability to trade for fresh talent, since most of the other team owners sided with the league's president. The team's only bright light was Babe Ruth. Although his pitching in 1919 was just average—and he refused to pitch at all for half the season—he smashed 29 home runs, then an all-time record for the sport.

Still, Frazee was tiring of his prima donna star, whose unpredictable behavior was hurting player morale. Twice, Ruth had skipped out on the team; before a crucial game, he'd gotten into a fight and injured his pitching hand. Now, at the end of the 1919 season, Ruth was demanding yet another pay increase. He wanted $20,000 to play the next year, double his previous salary and 33 percent more than more than any other player in the game. (Today that amount translates to about $220,000, less than half the major league minimum). If he didn't get it, the Babe said, he'd retire to his farm.

So, in December 1919, Harry Frazee sold Babe Ruth's contract to the New York Yankees.

Naming the Crimson Hose

John I. Taylor, son of the *Boston Globe's* publisher, owned Boston's American League baseball team for eight seasons in the early 1900s. Under his stewardship the team's performance was generally lackluster, but Red Sox fans are forever grateful to Taylor for three things: He named the Red Sox, and he built and named Fenway Park. The Red Sox moniker was selected by Taylor as the team's official name starting with the 1908 season. It harkens back to the city's first professional baseball club, the Boston Red Stockings of 1871. Many of that team's players had come from a defunct team in Cincinnati, so they brought the team name from Ohio to the Hub. When Taylor announced his club's new name in December 1907, the *Globe* suggested that it "will be a popular name with the Boston fans."

On building the club's new ballpark in 1912, Taylor famously said, "It's in the Fenway, isn't it? Then call it Fenway Park." A *fen* is a British term for a marshy area. When Frederick Law Olmsted laid out Boston's park system–the Emerald Necklace–in the 1880s, the landscaped marshes in that newly filled neighborhood were called the Back Bay Fens; and the adjacent parkway became the Fenway.

Historians still debate Frazee's true motives for the transaction. Some say that Frazee was in financial difficulty and needed cash; others say that he wanted money to invest in theatrical productions, including a play that later became the musical *No, No, Nanette*. Allegedly, Frazee once said, "the Ruth deal was the only way I could retain the Red Sox." But the source of that quote may be unreliable.

What's clear is that the personal relationship between Frazee and Ruth had deteriorated to a point of no return. And with Ban Johnson's ongoing vendetta against Harry Frazee, the Yankees were the only team that could possibly buy Ruth's contract from the Red Sox.

Disdained by the Boston fans for selling their favorite player, Harry Frazee also found himself increasingly isolated in the world of baseball—for Ban Johnson had many friends, especially among the media. Frazee held onto the Red Sox for another three and a half years, finally selling the club in the summer of 1923. Although a failure as a team owner, he cleared a nice profit from the sale and invested it in his successful theatrical ventures.

In New York, Babe Ruth found success far beyond what he'd experienced in Boston. The Yankees realized that his talents lay as a hitter, not as a pitcher; he threw just four innings for them in the 1920 season. But he bashed 54 home runs, nearly double his own record from the previous year.

Babe Ruth, Ernie Shore, Rube Foster, Del Gainer, Boston Red Sox, circa 1917

Yet in 1919, few people could have fully predicted Babe Ruth's success over the long term. His hitting style was foreign to the way that everyone else played the game, and many people thought his batting feats that season had been a fluke. No one realized that baseball itself was on the verge of a revolution.

For the sport, the sale of Babe Ruth marked the end of what's now called the "dead ball era" when home runs were a rarity; for the Yankees, it was the creation of a dynasty.

For the Red Sox, though, it was the beginning of one of the greatest slumps in sports history. After Frazee's departure, the team placed dead last in eight of the next 10 years. Even Tom Yawkey, who rebuilt Fenway Park in 1934, was unable to win a World Series in his four decades of ownership. In 1988 *Boston Globe* sportswriter Dan Shaughnessy coined the phrase "Curse of the Bambino" to explain why the Red Sox hadn't won a World Series since Babe Ruth had pitched for them in 1918.

It took a total lunar eclipse to reverse that curse. The next time the Boston Red Sox won the World Series was under a dusky full moon on a clear October night in 2004. After 86 long years, Red Sox Nation once again rejoiced as the winners of it all.

CHAPTER 24.

BOSTON'S SAPPHIRE JEWEL

Boston's Emerald Necklace—the string of parks designed by Frederick Law Olmsted—is well known; but for many people the city's greatest jewel is the Charles River Basin. Few other cities, if any, possess so grand a vista of their skyline. As poet David McCord said, it is "like a great mirror held to the city's most favoring profile."

The river was named by the future King Charles of England in 1615; the teenaged prince was handed a map of New England and given the opportunity to name any features he wanted. From the breadth of the river's mouth, as reported by explorers, he assumed that it was a very long river, so he named it after himself. From source to the sea, the Charles flows 80 miles; but it makes so many twists and turns that the distance is just 26½ miles as a crow flies.

In colonial days, the river opened into a great tidal bay behind the Boston peninsula: the Back Bay. It was from the foot of Boston Common, at the edge of the Back Bay, that British soldiers got in their rowboats to start their journey to Lexington and Concord. They crossed the Charles to Cambridge, landing near where the Cambridgeside Galleria mall is today.

‹ View of Boston from the Charles River

Charles River and the Back Bay, 1925

At low tide, the Back Bay became a mudflat. Early in the 19th century, investors concocted the idea of building a dam across this bay to harness the tidal power; in 1821 their Mill Dam was built along the line of modern Beacon Street, nearly a mile and a half from Charles Street to Kenmore Square. The dam didn't generate the desired power, but it did impede the water's flow, turning the bay into a fetid pool. Starting in 1857, the Back Bay was filled, becoming the desirable Back Bay neighborhood.

The Cambridge shore was also once marshes and mudflats; Massachusetts Avenue was a dead end known as the road to the oyster banks. In 1883, the Charles River Embankment Company began filling these lands, hoping to create an elegant neighborhood that would mirror the Back Bay across the river. But Cambridge's new territory was too remote, and only a handful of houses were ever built there. Much of this vacant land eventually became the M.I.T. campus.

To protect the filled land from tidal erosion, high granite seawalls were built on both shores. By 1900, these walls reached as far upstream as today's B.U. Bridge, where the river narrows and bends. In Boston, the seawall abutted the service alley ("Back Street") that adjoined the houses on the water side of Beacon Street.

At the time, strong tides discouraged any landscaping at the river's edges. The Charles was then an arm of the ocean, and the tides in Boston are especially high: roughly every 12 hours, the range between high and low water averages 9½ feet, even more during certain moon phases or in heavy storms. Damming the river was suggested, to keep its level constant, allowing parks to be placed along its banks. A dam might also reduce the foul emanations that emerged at low tide. "Under your nose," recalled

George Santayana, "rose now and then the stench from mudflats and sewage that the sluggish current ... did not avail to drain properly."

Closing of the dam gates, October 20, 1908

The proposed dam was controversial. Older residents recalled the Mill Dam of 1821, which had made the odor problems worse. And a few industries along the river still hauled goods by ship, and they worried about a dam's impact on navigation.

Chief advocate for the new dam was James Jackson Storrow, "the leading banker of the city." Just 36 years old, Storrow, along with his wife Helen, had become active in philanthropic causes; in 1901 he organized a new campaign to build a dam and to beautify the Charles River. He enlisted a covey of scientists and engineers to document the benefits of the proposed dam and used his social connections to win support from civic leaders. His efforts were successful; a commission was created in 1903 to design and build the new dam.

Unlike the old Mill Dam, which had tended to keep salt water *out* of the Back Bay, the new dam was designed to keep fresh water *in* the Charles River Basin. The new water surface would be seven feet above mean low tide, high enough to keep the flats fully submerged, but low enough to avoid flooding nearby basements.

Along with the dam, the commission was also instructed to build a park on the Boston side of the river. The Boston Embankment, as it was officially named, became popularly known as the Esplanade. It was 300 feet wide as it paralleled Charles Street at the bottom of Beacon Hill, and 100 feet wide near Beacon Street in the Back Bay. At the request of influential Beacon Street residents, the legislature specifically prohibited any roadways through the Back Bay section of the park.

Arthur Fiedler conducting the symphony on the Esplanade, Summer 1930

At the same time that these projects were being built, work was also underway on an ornamental bridge over the Charles River, later called the Longfellow Bridge. This grand arch bridge of steel and stone replaced a creaky wooden drawbridge on the main route between Boston and Cambridge, and included tracks for a new subway line linking the two cities.

Over time, various proposals surfaced to create islands in the middle of the river, but nothing ever came of them. At one point, it was even proposed to build M.I.T.'s new campus on a mid-river island.

The bridge opened in 1907; the dam and Esplanade were finished in 1910. With a steady water level, the riverbanks could now be formally landscaped; erosion was minimized and seawalls were no longer needed. Upstream industrial sites and "squalid hovels" were bought and demolished by the state, their sites converted into parks, reducing pollution in the downstream basin.

Sixteen years after the dam was completed, James J. Storrow passed away. In 1929 his widow, Helen Osborne Storrow, proposed to donate $1 million to double the width of the Esplanade, as a memorial to her late husband. It was her gift that created the wonderful park we know today, with lagoons, small decorative islands, boat landings, a concert oval and more. Completed in 1932, the enlarged park was officially renamed the Storrow Memorial Embankment, but most people still call it the Esplanade.

As Mrs. Storrow's donation was being discussed, state officials indicated their desire to include a roadway through the newly filled land parallel to Beacon Street. Strongly opposed to "invasion by automobile traffic," Helen Storrow stood her ground: The state would get her gift only if it eliminated the highway from its plans.

Unveiling the Storrow Memorial

Yet such agreements can be fickle. Helen Storrow died in 1944, and soon the highway scheme was revived. It was approved in 1949, completed in 1952, and widened in 1955. To compensate for the loss of green space, new land was created on the river side of the Esplanade, keeping the park's overall width the same. The highway was called James J. Storrow Memorial Drive, or Storrow Drive for short. Named, ironically, for the man who never wanted a road built along the river.

Today the Charles River Basin is about 2,000 feet wide as it skirts the Back Bay less than a quarter of its width before the Back Bay was filled, but wider than the Thames in London and the Seine in Paris combined. On summer days the Charles is filled with sailboats; the Esplanade is packed with joggers, strollers, skaters and sunbathers. It presents a glorious view to any Red Line rider who cares to look up from her newspaper. It's become the city's front door, the blue jewel in its crown. For all this, we must thank James and Helen Storrow, whose vision was responsible for its creation.

NEWTON
FRANKLIN

CHAPTER 25.

BUILDING THE NEW TECHNOLOGY

Merlin the Magician was the master of ceremonies. The Governor of Massachusetts came on horseback and sat in a throne. Other dignitaries arrived in a Venetian barge, captained by Christopher Columbus and propelled by a score of oarsmen. Ten thousand spectators viewed the pageant; the performers included "primitive men," gladiators, nymphs, fire dancers and a chorus of 500 voices. The Masque of Power, a one-night-only extravaganza, celebrated the completion of the new Cambridge campus of the Massachusetts Institute of Technology in 1916.

One of the greatest engineering and technical schools in the world, M.I.T. was the dream of one man, William Barton Rogers. As a professor at the University of Virginia, Rogers was distressed by what he perceived as a lack of support for serious academic programs there. After visits to Boston, he came to admire "the highly cultivated nature and society of glorious New England."

In 1846, while still teaching in Virginia, Rogers circulated "A Plan for a Polytechnic Institution in Boston." Seven years later, he gave up his professorship and moved north to make that plan into a reality. Gaining

< Massachusetts Institute of Technology, Rogers Building, Boston, between 1890 and 1901

William Barton Rogers

support from business and intellectual leaders, he applied to the Massachusetts legislature for a charter. The "Act to Incorporate the Massachusetts Institute of Technology" was enacted and signed by the governor on April 10, 1861. Along with the charter, the legislature also granted the Institute some land on Boylston Street in the newly filled Back Bay neighborhood, diagonally across from the site where Trinity Church stands today.

Classes were first held on February 20, 1865, in rented rooms on Summer Street in downtown; the next year, the Boylston Street building was completed. "Boston Tech," as it was nicknamed, grew and thrived. By 1907 the Institute had a total of 10 buildings and laboratories scattered around the Back Bay. Since there were no dormitories until 1902, students lived in nearby boarding houses.

Very quickly, M.I.T. found its autonomy challenged. Charles W. Eliot was the university's first professor of analytical chemistry in 1865, but four years later he was appointed the President of Harvard University. Within months of assuming the Harvard post, Eliot began to push for a merger of Harvard and the Institute. Of course, in Eliot's proposal, M.I.T. would have become part of Harvard, as the university's new engineering school. It was a recurring theme, proposed at least four times during Eliot's 40-year tenure at Harvard's helm.

By the turn of the century, M.I.T. was still growing, with about 1,500 full-time students, and it desperately needed to expand. Yet Back Bay real estate had become extraordinarily expensive and there were few vacant lots. So the Institute began to look elsewhere. Once again, Charles Eliot proposed a wedding with Harvard, even offering Tech a location for its new campus. Early in 1904, some friends of Harvard had purchased a large tract of land across the river from Harvard Square—where Harvard Business School stands today—intending that it would be M.I.T.'s new home after its merger with Harvard.

The Institute's alumni and professors were strongly against the plan, demanding that M.I.T. retain its independence. In one postcard poll, alumni voted 1,557 to 33 against a union with Harvard; the faculty opposed it by a vote of 56 to 7. Yet M.I.T.'s trustees—officially called the Corporation—went forward with the merger.

M.I.T., aerial view, circa 1920s

There was one catch: As a condition for consolidation, Harvard insisted that M.I.T. turn over the proceeds from the sale of its Copley Square campus—in essence, a dowry for the marriage. But the Boylston Street land had been granted to the Institute by the legislature, and in 1905 a court ruled that the lots couldn't be sold without permission from the legislature. There was no dowry, so no marriage could be consummated.

At this juncture, the Institute's Corporation sought new leadership; in 1908 Richard Cockburn Maclaurin was chosen M.I.T.'s sixth President. Just 39 years old when he took charge of the Institute, his mission was to find the land, and the money, for its new home.

On one of his earliest visits to Boston, Maclaurin visited a Tech alumnus who lived on the water side of Beacon Street. Looking out his host's window, the Institute's President-elect spied an immense vacant parcel on the Cambridge bank of the river. "The site is ideal for the Institute's purposes," he said later, "near to the heart of things, wonderfully accessible … and occupying a position that commands the public view." The Cambridge land had been filled, just like Boston's Back Bay; but dreams of turning it into an elegant residential neighborhood had not panned out.

Previous M.I.T. presidents had been reluctant to settle in Cambridge, fearful of opposition from Harvard, but Maclaurin accepted the challenge. With money from the du Pont family (of chemical factory fame) and other alumni,

Hacking the Dome

M.I.T. students have long loved pranks, especially if some sort of technical skill is involved in the escapade. These antics are known as "hacks", a term coined here in the 1950s, long before it was applied to computers. The most prominent point on the campus, the Great Dome, has been an irresistible venue for the hacker's art.

It has been decorated as the Great Pumpkin for Halloween, and as R2-D2 for the opening of a *Star Wars* movie. Snowmen have been erected on it in August (made of papier-mâché) and in February (made of real snow). An inflatable nipple was placed on its top, converting it into the "Giant Breast of Knowledge." And a life-size plastic cow, stolen from the lawn of the Hilltop Steak House in Saugus, was discovered atop the dome on Halloween 1979. No one would say how it got there; a crane was required to remove it.

The greatest dome hack to date is the police cruiser that was found, blue lights flashing, at its crest on May 9, 1994. Inside was a mannequin dressed as a police officer, with a toy gun, a cup of coffee and a box of donuts. The crew dispatched to dismantle the hack found only the sheet metal shell of a car–the fenders, hood, doors and other body parts had been mounted on plastic foam and cut into pieces that would fit through a 3-by-4-foot hatch leading to the dome's summit.

the Institute bought 50 acres of land on the Cambridge bank of the river, between Ames St. and Massachusetts Ave., in 1911. Now it was time to plan the buildings.

Maclaurin traveled the country meeting with alumni and friends, raising money for the campus. One day he met with George Eastman, founder of the Kodak Company. Although Eastman wasn't himself an alumnus, his company had hired many Tech graduates, and they had proven valuable to his business. At the end of their first meeting, after Maclaurin had described his plans, Eastman inquired, "What will it cost to put up the new buildings?"

"About two and a half millions," was Maclaurin's reply—nearly $60 million today.

Eastman's answer stunned Maclaurin: "I will send you a draft for that amount."

This $2.5 million gift was just the beginning; Eastman ultimately donated much more. He insisted that the gift be entirely secret. Maclaurin could tell his wife, and later his secretary, but no one else. To the rest of the world, the benefactor of the new Institute buildings was a mysterious "Mr. Smith." The donor's identity was eventually revealed in 1920.

The architect for the original campus was W. Welles Bosworth. As an M.I.T. architecture student in the 1880s, Bosworth had been a draftsman for H. H. Richardson; later he worked with Frederick Law Olmsted on his plan for Stanford University in California. At M.I.T., Bosworth followed ideas offered by Professor John Freeman, who suggested "architectural details and styles derived from the Greek Classic style, which have satisfied the human eye for 2,000 years," and demanded "functional buildings" with window light, ventilation and efficiency. He insisted that the buildings be connected, "avoiding to the maximum extent the need for men racing across lots, often scantily clad, from one building to another in Boston's raw climate." When completed, it was considered the largest monolithic structure in the world.

The focal point of the complex was the Great Dome, 150 feet high and 108 feet in diameter. It was inspired by the Pantheon in Rome as well as by the campus of the University of Virginia, where M.I.T. founder Rogers once taught.

The first concrete was poured in April 1913, and the dedication ceremonies were held on June 13 and 14, 1916. Ralph Adams Cram, an M.I.T. architecture professor, devised and planned the great dedication pageant, the Masque of Power, or more fully, the "Conquest of Chaos by Technology." It was held in the Great Court enclosed by Bosworth's new buildings, with Cram playing the starring role of Merlin. The following evening, a grand banquet was held at Symphony Hall, where the guests of honor included Alexander Graham Bell, Thomas Edison and Orville Wright.

The construction of Technology's new campus put a strain on Maclaurin's health. He died in 1920, at the age of 49, less than four years after the campus was dedicated. But his vision of a campus with room to expand has proven key to the Institute's success. The original 50-acre campus has grown to 168 acres; the 1,900 students of 1915 have become more than 10,500 today. Welles Bosworth's limestone and concrete buildings have proven remarkably adaptable to 21st-century needs. William Barton Rogers and Richard Cockburn Maclaurin would both be amazed at how "Boston Tech" has evolved.

22 Pages Today

The Boston Post

EXTRA

THURSDAY, JANUARY 16, 1919

HUGE MOLASSES TANK EXPLODES IN NORTH END; 11 DEAD, 50 HURT

Giant Wave of 2,300,000 Gallons of Molasses, 50 Feet High, Sweeps Everything Before It—100 Men, Women and Children Caught in Sticky Stream—Buildings, Vehicles and L Structure Crushed

35 STATES ON DRY LAW LIST

Amendment Ratified by Five Yesterday—One More Needed—Predict Nation Dry July 1

SECRECY IN PEACE CONGRESS

France, Italy and Japan Outvote U. S. and Britain

BOY'S STORY AID TO MRS. LEBAUDY

Messenger Left Mansion Before the Shooting—Life in Danger

KNOWN DEAD

MRS. BRIDGET CLOUGHERTY, 6 Copp's Hill terrace, North End.
WILLIAM A. DUFFEY, 67 Brighton street, West End.
ENGINEER GEORGE LAHEY, Engine 31, B. F. D., 401 Saratoga street, East Boston.
JAMES LENNON, 87 Brook avenue, Roxbury. Employee Public Works Department.
JOHN SEIBERLICH, 23 Fulda street, Roxbury. Employee Public Works Department.
PETER FRANCIS, 48 Monument street, Charlestown, employee Public Works Department.
JAMES J. KENNEALLY, 260 Bolton street, South Boston, employee Public Works Department.
THOMAS NOONAN.
MICHAEL SINNOTT, 78, 70 Bernard street, Dorchester.
WILLIAM BROGAN, 187 Webster street, East Boston.

UNIDENTIFIED DEAD

Girl about 14 years of age. She wore a gray jacket over a woolen middy blouse and carried a bag with an employment tag of the Revere Rubber Company.

SERIOUSLY INJURED

JOHN J. NOONE, 49, 41 Lawrence street, Charlestown. Employee Public Works Department. Fractured skull, fractures both legs. City Hospital; dangerous list.
ANTONIO DI STAZIO, 115 Charter street, North End. Compound fracture of skull. City Hospital; dangerous list.
OWEN GORMAN, 86 Trenton street, Charlestown. Employee Public Works Department. Injuries to chest, nose, left eye and fractures both legs. Haymarket Relief Station.

INJURED

JOSEPH BARRY, 9 Pine street, South End. City Hospital.
SAMUEL BLAIR, 4 Anderson street, West End. Haymarket Relief Station.
CHARLES BOWER, U. S. S. Starling, Navy Yard, Charlestown.
NATHANIEL BOWERING, Engine 31, B. F. D., 68 Decatur street, Charlestown.
PATRICK BREEN, 45 Fayette street, South End. Employee Public Works Department. Haymarket Relief Station.
CHARLES J. CASEY, 87 Dacia street, Roxbury. City Hospital.

Continued on Page 16—Seventh Col.

Search for More Victims During the Night

No Escape From Gigantic Wave of Fluid

INTERNAL EXPLOSION WAS CAUSE, SAYS STATE CHEMIST

It became known last night that W. L. Wedger, State police chemist in charge of explosives, had reached the positive conclusion that the disaster instead of being due to a collapse of the great tank was caused by an internal explosion. Mr. Wedger in his investigation is understood to have found that the tank was fitted with heating apparatus that connected with a boiler. This heating apparatus consisted of pipes inside the tank and its purpose was to make the molasses run freely into the tank carts that trucked it to the Cambridge distillery of the company.

Mr. Wedger after a careful study of the matter is reported to have reached the conclusion that in a great tank of molasses so heated there could be generated a mixture of air and gas that would be as explosive as the same amount of air and gasolene. That horses were blown about like chips, houses torn asunder, and the heavy section of the Elevated railroad structure smashed like an eggshell are other considerations linked with the conclusion of Mr. Wedger. That windows in the neighborhood remained intact is explained by the fact that the explosive waves in such a blowup would be decidedly different in their effect on surroundings than would be the case if dynamite exploded.

Thus it is understood that Mr. Wedger's formal report will be that the disaster was due to an internal explosion.

A 50-foot wave of molasses—2,300,000 gallons of it—released in some manner yet unexplained, from a giant tank, swept over Commercial street and its waterfront from Charter street to the southerly end of North End Park yesterday afternoon.

Ensnaring in its sticky flood more than 100 men, women and children; crushing buildings, teams, automobiles and street cars—everything in its path—the thick, reeking mass slapped against the side of the buildings facing Copp's Hill and then swished back towards the harbor.

Eleven persons—a woman, a girl and nine men—were the known dead at midnight. More than 50 injured were in hospitals and at their homes. Some of them may die. Dead horses, cats and dogs had been carted away in teams after team.

Boston's only trolley freight terminal was in ruins. Most of its big steel trolley-freight cars were destroyed.

Continued on Page 16—First Col.

News of North End disaster on pages 8, 14, 15 and 16

Real After-the-War News

CHAPTER 26.

THE GREAT MOLASSES FLOOD

When something is intractably slow, we say that it's "as slow as molasses in January." But Bostonians know that figure of speech isn't always accurate. On one January day in 1919, a huge molasses tank on Commercial Street burst, flooding the North End with 2,319,525 gallons of sticky goo, killing 20 people and innumerable horses. Some unfortunate souls perished because they couldn't run fast enough to outrace the speeding wave of molasses.

Boston's molasses trade dates back to colonial days. Lacking natural resources (furs, lumber, fish) or agricultural products (cotton, tobacco) to sell abroad, Bostonians turned to trade. Molasses was imported here from the West Indies and then distilled into rum, which could be exported. Profits from the sugar and rum trade were the engine of Boston's economy. In 1770 Boston had 36 distilleries, more than any other town in the 13 colonies. Massachusetts distilled two million gallons of rum a year, 40 percent of the total North American production, and nearly all of that came from Boston. Much was consumed locally, but nearly half was exported. Some of that exported rum was shipped to Africa, where it was exchanged for slaves, who were in turn transported to the West Indies and traded for more molasses—an infamous cycle later called the triangle trade.

‹ Front page of the *Boston Post*, January 16, 1919

Aftermath of the Molasses Disaster

The British government's efforts to tax, and to regulate, the molasses trade kindled some of the first sparks of the American Revolution. At least a third of the molasses imported into Massachusetts in the 1760s was smuggled—the Sugar Act of 1764 was an attempt to limit the smuggling, but it led to Faneuil Hall's earliest protests against taxation without representation. Molasses also became a staple of the New England diet, a key ingredient in baked beans, brown bread and Indian pudding.

For a century after the Revolution, Boston's molasses trade continued, as did the production and consumption of rum. Then, early in the 20th century, new techniques developed for the manufacture of smokeless powder and other explosives, requiring large amounts of alcohol as a raw material. To serve that market, a small distillery in Cambridge, Purity Distilling Company, was acquired by the United States Industrial Alcohol Company.

With the approach of the First World War, demand for explosives—and thus for alcohol—grew immensely. Purity Distilling and its parent company needed to expand, rapidly. They leased land on the North End waterfront for a new marine terminal. Molasses was offloaded from ships into an enormous new tank, 50 feet high by 90 feet in diameter; then stored there until it could be transported in tank cars over streetcar tracks in city streets to the distillery in Cambridge. Supervising every aspect of the plan was Arthur P. Jell, the treasurer and Boston manager of U.S. Industrial Alcohol. Jell had no engineering background or training.

The tank seemed star-crossed from the beginning. Although planning had begun a year in advance, it took nine months to negotiate the lease for the land, leaving just two months to lay a foundation and erect the tank. As the end of 1915 approached, Arthur Jell knew that his deadline was December 31. On that day a molasses tanker would arrive from the Caribbean. If the tank wasn't ready, he'd have to turn the ship, and its cargo, away.

The steel plates for the tank were delivered at the start of December, and the job was rushed to completion. Soon after the work began, a construction worker fell to his death. Weather caused more delays. The pressure was on Jell, who anticipated a promotion if he did the job right.

The contract with Hammond Iron Works called for the tank to be tested for leaks by filling it with water, all the way to the top. But the assembly wasn't completed in time, and so the leak test consisted of putting six inches of water into the 50-foot-high tank. Just a few days later, 700,000 gallons of molasses were pumped in, filling it to a depth of 14 feet.

From the beginning, the tank leaked. Syrupy goo oozed out of its rivet holes; drips leaked from its seams. Brown streaks stained its silver sides. The company's workers noticed it. The captain of a molasses ship noticed it. Neighbors sent their children over with buckets, to gather molasses for cooking. The company had the tank caulked a couple of times, then painted it brown, to hide the streaks.

The tank made noises as the heavy molasses strained its walls—sounds "like thunder, like rumbling … something inside of the molasses tank, bubbling and rolling," as a man who worked at a nearby city facility put it. The noises got worse as new shipments arrived, when the fresh molasses, still warm from the West Indies, mixed with the colder stuff that was

Lydia Marie Child's Indian Pudding

This recipe for boiled Indian pudding comes from the 12th edition of Mrs. Child's *The American Frugal Housewife*, published in 1833 by Carter, Hendee, and Co., at the corner of School and Washington Streets, in the building that would later be known as the Old Corner Book Store:

> "Indian pudding should be boiled four or five hours [in a double boiler]. Sifted Indian meal [*i.e.,* corn meal] and warm milk should be stirred together pretty stiff. A little salt, and two or three great spoonfuls of molasses, added; a spoonful of ginger, if you like that spice. Boil it in a tight covered pan, or a very thick cloth; if the water gets in, it will ruin it. Leave plenty of room; for Indian swells very much. The milk with which you mix it should be merely warm; if it be scalding, the pudding will break to pieces. Some people chop sweet suet fine, and warm in the milk; others warm thin slices of sweet apple to be stirred into the pudding. Water will answer instead of milk."

(Lydia Maria Child, a noted magazine editor and abolitionist, was also author of the poem that begins, "Over the river and through the woods, To grandfather's house we go....")

already inside. Experts later said this temperature mixing might have caused fermentation, yielding large gas bubbles inside the sticky liquid and increasing the pressure on the tank's walls.

The tank stood for three years. It received several shipments, but was never more than about four-fifths full. Then, on January 12, 1919, the ship *Miliero* delivered another 600,000 gallons. It took nearly 24 hours to pump its cargo into the bottom of the tank, pushing the existing contents up. For the first time, the tank was filled nearly to capacity, more than 97 percent full. The molasses inside weighed 13,000 tons, as much as a hundred steam locomotives. It stayed that way for just over two days—for precisely 50 hours.

At 12:40 p.m. on Wednesday, January 15, the tank burst.

"At first there was a low rumble," the *Boston Globe* reported, "not a sharp explosion, but a shaking. Then came the shower of molasses and the noise of smashing ... The wall of molasses, 50 feet high at the front, rolled over the ground with a seething, hissing sound."

One witness recalled later, "What looked like a moving wall of volcanic lava filled the street and was moving relentlessly towards me. Everything it overtook—horses, automobiles, people—disappeared."

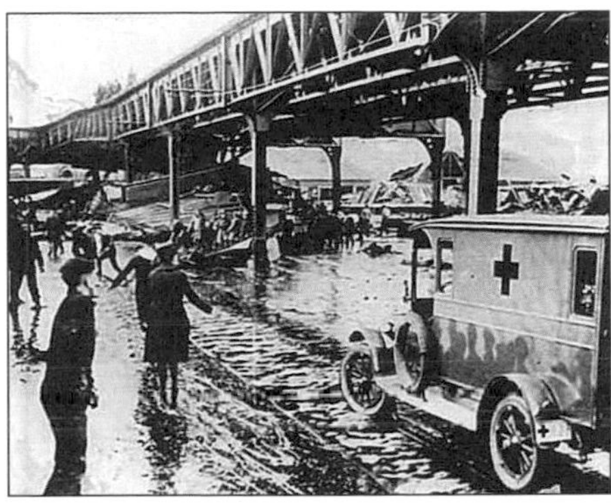
Molasses flood in 1919

A policeman reported a rat-tat-tat sound as rivets popped out of the tank. Another said he "beat it out in the race, for I rushed up a side street."

Across the street from the tank, a three-story house was shattered. The city fireboat station, Engine 31, was reduced from three stories to two. The upper floors collapsed into the demolished first story, trapping Third Engineer George Layhe, who drowned in molasses. Two children who had been picking up firewood and playing near the tank were killed; a third survived unharmed. A two-and-a-half-ton piece of the tank was found 180 feet away.

Arthur Jell and the lawyers for his company claimed that it had been a bomb. Anarchists had tried to blow up a police station a few blocks away just two years earlier, and a facility which helped make military supplies was a likely target for terrorists. But expert testimony proved without a doubt that the tank was poorly constructed. Neither Purity Distilling nor the Hammond Iron Works had hired an engineer to review the plans before the tank was built. After the disaster, investigators determined that the plans called for steel plates that were too thin to withstand the weight of the tank's contents—and the plates that were actually used were even thinner than the specifications. The tank's rivets were overstressed by a factor of 2.2, and may not have been heated properly before they were driven.

The damage claims took six years to settle. U.S. Industrial Alcohol paid a total of $628,000—about $7.9 million today—to 119 claimants. A few months after the disaster, the company closed its Purity Distilling plant in Cambridge. Arthur Jell was transferred back to the New York headquarters and eventually got his promotion.

How slow *is* molasses in January? On January 15, 1919, it's estimated that it was flowing at 35 miles an hour.

CHAPTER 27.

MARTIN AND CORETTA

He was the son of a minister from Atlanta, in Boston to work on his doctorate in Systematic Theology. She was the daughter of a farmer and small businessman from Alabama, a mezzo-soprano studying to become a concert singer. Besides their Southern roots, the two graduate students shared interests in progressive politics, pacifism, and the civil rights movement. They met and fell in love in Boston. Together they changed the world.

While Martin Luther King, Jr., is best known for his work in Montgomery, Washington, D.C., and Memphis, it was the lessons he learned in Boston—and the life partner that he found here—that made those later achievements possible.

As a boy, King knew that he was destined for the pulpit. He didn't have much choice: his father, both of his grandfathers, his great-grandfather, his brother and an uncle were all preachers. Ordained a minister at the age of 19, while he was still a college senior, he then went to a seminary to further his training.

< President Lyndon B. Johnson and Rev. Dr. Martin Luther King, Jr., meet at the White House, 1966

Dr. and Mrs. Martin Luther King, Jr., 1964

Like John Winthrop and the Puritans, he was wary of "unlettered," or poorly trained, clergy. And so he began, as he put it later, a "serious intellectual quest for a method to eliminate social evil." As an undergraduate at Morehouse College in his hometown of Atlanta, he read Henry David Thoreau's essay *On Civil Disobedience*; at seminary in Pennsylvania he was introduced to the work of Mohandas Gandhi. He also became familiar with the work of Dr. Edgar S. Brightman, then a professor at Boston University, and decided to study with the theologian. So, as he neared the end of his seminary studies, Martin Luther King, Jr., applied to a Ph.D. program at B.U.

King arrived in Boston in September 1951, just 22 years old. Immediately he had problems finding a place to live. "I went into place after place where there were signs that rooms were for rent," he recalled later. "They were for rent until they found that I was a Negro, and suddenly they had just been rented." Finally, he found a room in a boarding house on Saint Botolph Street for his first semester.

In January, King and a friend rented an apartment together at 397 Massachusetts Avenue. Although it was only a block from Saint Botolph Street, the new place was literally on the other side of the tracks, in the South End instead of the Back Bay—and at the focus of Boston's black community. African-Americans had settled along Columbus Avenue in the early 1900s because of its proximity to the railroad yards, which once took up the site now occupied by the Prudential Center. Many black men worked for the railroads as Pullman porters, one of the best opportunities available to blacks in a segregated society.

By 1950 the corner of Massachusetts and Columbus Avenues was an African-American cultural center known for its nightclubs and cafés; some called it a miniature version of Harlem. A dozen venues such as the Hi-Hat, the Savoy, the Rainbow Club and Wally's Paradise attracted a racially mixed clientele to hear the likes of Count Basie, Charlie Mingus and Buddy Rich, plus small jazz combos.

But King was not in Boston to hear jazz; he had come here for more studious matters. He and his roommate organized a Philosophical Club of black college students, who gathered once or twice a month to discuss scholarly subjects.

Even though King was new to Boston, he did not lack for acquaintances. Several friends from his undergraduate days were in town for graduate school, including his roommate in the Mass. Ave. apartment. King's father had made arrangements for his son, too. As a preacher at a prominent black congregation in Atlanta, Martin Sr. belonged to an informal social network of Baptist clergymen across the country. "Daddy King had called ahead," one of Martin's friends later reminisced, "and asked Rev. [William] Hester to look after Martin."

So the young minister in training joined Rev. Hester's congregation the Twelfth Baptist Church in nearby Roxbury—and started preaching at the evening services. Martin was aware of, and awed by, the Twelfth Baptist's history; as the second-oldest black church in Boston, its members had led the struggle against slavery a century earlier. Then the parish had been located on the back of Beacon Hill, near Lewis Hayden's house.

Yet there was one thing missing in King's life. Coming from a family of preachers, he knew firsthand that the pastor's wife was the key to the pastor's own success or failure. Ministry without a wife was simply not acceptable in the black churches of the day. So he sought a suitable companion. In February 1952 he asked Mary Powell, another friend from Atlanta, who was studying at the New England Conservatory of Music, and a part time secretary at Twelfth Baptist, if she knew of "any nice, attractive young ladies." Mary immediately thought of another Conservatory student: Coretta Scott.

Coretta Scott had grown up in rural Alabama, then attended Antioch College in Ohio, where she became interested in social justice issues. Following Antioch, she enrolled on a scholarship at the New England Conservatory, to train for a career as a singer. She had been youth choir director at her church when she was just 15 years old; and, in an America that was still largely segregated, music seemed to be one of the few careers where people of color could really be accepted.

Playing the role of matchmaker, Mary Powell described "M. L. King" (as he was known then) to Coretta Scott. Scott, at this point in her life, was dissatisfied with organized religion; as she wrote years later: "The moment Mary told me the young man was a minister I lost interest, for I began to think of the stereotypes of ministers I had known."

A few days later Martin called Coretta. "A mutual friend of ours told me about you," he said. "She said some very wonderful things about you and I'd like very much to meet you and talk to you." After a long conversation, they agreed on a lunchtime date for the next day. He drove his new green Chevy from B.U. to the Conservatory, where she was waiting for him on the steps. Lunch was at Sharaf's, a cafeteria on Massachusetts Avenue. They talked about issues such as racial and economic justice, communism and capitalism, and the question of peace; both seemed hungry for intellectual stimulation. One hour after they first met, King said, "You have everything I have ever wanted in a wife ... I want to see you again. When can I?"

Dexter Avenue King Memorial Baptist Church, Montgomery

It was a shock to Scott, who didn't want to stop her career. But she finally opened herself to the relationship. Sixteen months later they were married.

The wedding was at her brother's house in Marion, Alabama, officiated by M. L. King, Sr., on June 18, 1953. In September they returned to Boston and settled into an apartment at 396 Northampton Street, just around the block from King's old apartment. They lived there while finishing their studies in Boston.

The following spring, Martin Luther King, Jr., was invited to be the new minister of the Dexter Avenue Baptist Church in Montgomery, Alabama. He took the post in September 1954; although his classes in Boston had ended, he was still writing his dissertation and had to commute regularly between Massachusetts and Alabama. He received his degree from Boston University on June 5, 1955.

Exactly six months later, the Montgomery bus boycott began.

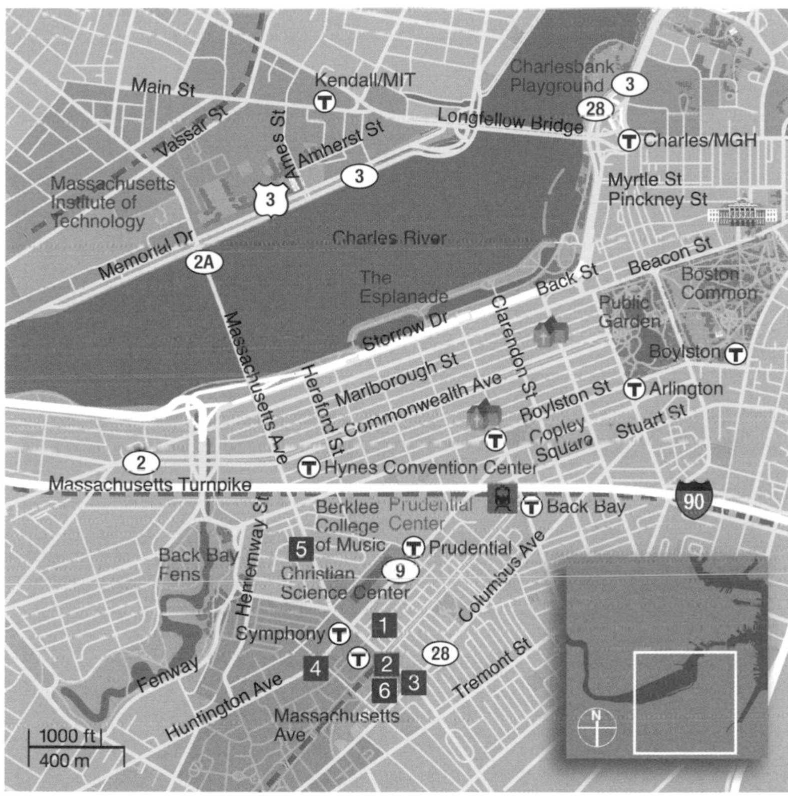

1 MLK Boarding House: 170 Saint Botolph Street
2 MLK Apartment: 397 Massachusetts Avenue
3 Jazz Clubs: Intersection of Massachusetts and Columbus avenues
4 New England Conservatory: Huntington Ave. and Gainsborough Street
5 Sharaf's Cafeteria: 187 Massachusetts Avenue
6 Martin Luther and Coretta Scott King Apartment: 396 Northampton Street.

CHAPTER 28.

THE NEW BOSTON

By 1969, many Bostonians were probably feeling like the two women portrayed that April in a *New Yorker* cartoon. "I feel I should warn you," said one lady to her seatmate on a train, "they've taken down most of Boston and they're putting up something else." In less than two decades, five major projects had resulted in demolition of large swaths of the city's fabric—after nearly half a century when little had been built in central Boston.

John B. Hynes coined the term "New Boston" as a campaign slogan in the 1949 mayoral contest. After defeating longtime incumbent James Michael Curley that November, it was Mayor Hynes who brought large-scale urban renewal to Boston in the 1950s. Highway projects, on the other hand, were the province of the state government, where William F. Callahan was the chief roadbuilder, first as Commissioner of Public Works, then as Chairman of the Massachusetts Turnpike Authority.

In 1948 a state Highway Master Plan proposed a "Central Artery"—an elevated, six-lane highway through downtown. Under Callahan's direction, demolition began in fall of 1951 and required removal of a 250-foot-wide corridor nearly two miles long. The first section opened from the Mystic

‹ View of the Prudential Center and the Back Bay

River Bridge to Dock Square in fall 1954. By then, the ugliness of the massive steel structure was undeniable, and a decision was made to put the southern part of the highway underground. The entire roadway opened on June 25, 1959, enabling motorists to go from Peabody to Braintree without encountering a stoplight.

Gov. Peabody, Mayor Collins and Cardinal Cushing at groundbreaking for the new City Hall

Officially, the new highway became the John F. Fitzgerald Expressway, in honor of the former mayor (and grandfather of then U.S. Senator John F. Kennedy). A few years later, the nearby street of "Honey Fitz"'s birth was wiped off the map for another of Callahan's projects, a new tunnel under Boston Harbor. That was named for Callahan's son, a World War II hero: the William F. Callahan Jr. Tunnel.

While Callahan's agency was at work on the highway, Mayor Hynes assembled a coalition of bankers, businessmen, religious leaders, even blacks and Republicans—all groups who'd felt neglected in Curley's administration—to make his "New Boston" a reality.

Hynes then focused on what city planners had called an "obsolete" neighborhood. The West End was akin to the North End, dominated by four- and five-story walkups, many with stores on the first floor. It was a working-class mix of mostly Italians and Jews. Its community was an extension of what is now called the "north slope" of Beacon Hill. But the neighborhood lacked political clout, and it lacked the history of Paul Revere.

Plans to redevelop the West End surfaced in 1950, and Hynes got funding from the federal Urban Renewal Administration. There was no stopping the so-called progress. The first wrecking ball struck late in 1958. Just two churches, a rectory, and a historic mansion were spared. By summer 1960, only rubble was left on the 48-acre site. What had been home to 2,700 families was now a wasteland. Even the city streets were gone.

Early on, it was assumed that the cleared land would be used for low-rent housing to accommodate displaced residents. But as the buildings were coming down, the Boston Redevelopment Authority signed a contract with Jerome Rappoport, a former Hynes campaign manager who wanted to build luxury apartments. As a final indignity, the project's giant billboard proclaimed: "If you lived here... You'd be home now."

It was an era when civic protests were rare. Chan Rogers, a Central Artery road designer, recalled years later that "In those days, people more or less accepted public improvements. They just accepted them—as opposed to voicing opinions in opposition." No public hearings on the West End project were held until fall of 1957; by then, planners were ready to issue their final approvals, and they thought it was too late to reverse years of work. Bankers, newspaper editors and the Roman Catholic archdiocese all supported the neighborhood's removal.

After a decade in office, Mayor Hynes chose not to run for re-election in 1959, with two major projects still on the drawing boards. Although Hynes had eagerly promoted Government Center and the Prudential Center, he'd been unable to finalize their arrangements. His successor, Mayor John F. Collins, would have to oversee their completion.

Government Center would replace Scollay Square, once an area of fine theaters and hotels. Over time, the theaters had become burlesque houses and the hotels flophouses; by World War II, good old Scollay Square was known far and wide as the place where Sailor Johnny or Soldier Billy could have a fun time while on leave in Boston. College students, too, were eager customers for an education that their parents never imagined. In the eyes of the city fathers, Scollay had to go.

Demolition started early in 1962. The sleazy bars and burleys would be replaced by new offices for city, state and federal agencies. The greatest architects and planners of the era, I. M. Pei and Kevin Lynch, created the master plan, which reduced 22 narrow streets to six broad avenues. The centerpiece would be the new City Hall. Architects worldwide were invited to submit their designs. Winners of the competition were Kallman, McKinnell, and Knowles, three young professors at Columbia University who had never designed a major structure that had actually been built.

Described as an "exciting and monumental" structure with "Mycenaean or Aztec overtones," the Brutalist design for City Hall stunned many. Even Mayor Collins looked surprised when he unveiled a mockup of the building in 1962. Five years later, it neared completion as Collins was finishing his term, and he promised to spend his last two weeks as Mayor working from his new office in "the most exciting public building in America." On December 18, 1967, he greeted visitors in his unfinished suite. Alas, the heating system wasn't yet functioning. Collins caught pneumonia on that chilly day and was bedridden for the rest of his term.

On the map, Government Center abutted both the West End project and the Central Artery, creating three linked areas of the city that were totally cleansed of their past—or, as one observer said, "a devastation here unmatched since that of the fire of 1872."

To the west, the Back Bay wasn't spared either. With Victorian architecture out of favor, many of its once-elegant mansions had become rooming houses. There was some discussion of clearing it as well, but those thoughts never came to fruition.

At Back Bay's edge were the tracks of the Boston & Albany Railroad, a straight line leading west out of the city. The rail right-of-way was selected as the route for Callahan's Massachusetts Turnpike, an express toll road. Acres of unneeded rail yards were transferred to the Prudential Insurance Company for a new development along the lines of New York's Rockefeller Center. Other properties, adjoining the rail facilities, came down as well. The Prudential Tower opened in 1964; the Turnpike followed the next February.

The "New Boston" did put a modern face on much of the city, but it has been rightfully criticized. The West End's demolition shocked Bostonians, and soon the project was seen as a lesson in the failures of urban renewal. Jane Jacobs' seminal book *The Death and Life of Great American Cities* appeared even before its replacement buildings were completed; in the wake of her writings, no one would ever dream of a similar project today.

The highway planning process has seen a similar change to greater public involvement. Within a decade after William Callahan passed away in 1964, proposed expressways through Jamaica Plain, the Fenway and Cambridge were cancelled as neighborhood residents arose in protest. By then, plans were already being offered to put the Central Artery underground; its subterranean replacement, the "Big Dig," opened in 2003. Just one steel post remains today, kept as a historic monument next to Quincy Market.

Until they were redesigned, the Prudential Center's shopping arcades went virtually empty, and there have been decades of debate about how to revitalize Government Center's stark brick plaza. Perhaps the ultimate insult to Mayor Hynes' vision came in 2008, when an internet poll selected Boston City Hall as the ugliest building in the world.

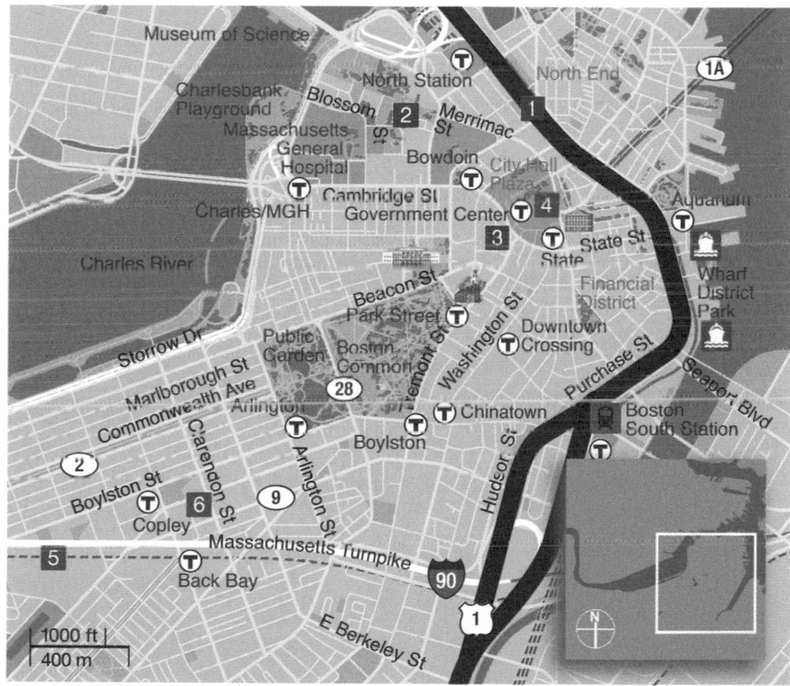

1 Central Artery
2 West End
3 Scollay Square
4 City Hall
5 Prudential Tower: 800 Boylston Street
6 John Hancock Tower: 200 Clarendon St.

CHAPTER 29.

FOR ONE BRIEF SHINING MOMENT

Boston's proudest moment came on January 20, 1961, when John Fitzgerald Kennedy was inaugurated President of the United States of America. The leader of the free world was a son and grandson of Boston, and a great-grandson of Ireland. To the residents of America's most Irish city, it was the American dream come true, a saga of the generations.

It took just over a century and three generations for the Kennedy family to rise from immigrant to president. All eight of JFK's great-grandparents were born in Ireland and emigrated to Massachusetts as young adults following the Irish Potato Famine of 1845–47. They were among some 50,000 Irish nationals who came to Boston in that decade, increasing the city's population by half.

The Kennedy family settled in East Boston, across the harbor from Boston proper, where Patrick J. Kennedy—the president's grandfather—was born in 1858. At 14 he quit school to support his widowed mother and three sisters. After a stint loading cargo at the docks, he became a successful business owner, with taverns and a liquor importing business. In 1892 he helped found a bank, the Columbia Trust Company.

‹ President John F. Kennedy sailing aboard the U. S. Coast Guard yacht *Manitou*, 1962

The Kennedy family in Hyannis Port, 1931

Across the harbor, the Fitzgeralds—JFK's maternal ancestors—moved to Boston's poorest district, the North End. Born in 1863, John Francis Fitzgerald also left school at age 14 and hawked newspapers on the street. Short in stature, he was picked on by bigger boys; he responded by organizing young hawkers against the older newsboys' attempts at extortion. He did go back to school, but his father's sudden death dashed his hopes for higher education. Matthew Keany, the North End's ward boss, took young Fitzgerald under his wing and got him a government job. From there, "Honey Fitz" went into politics full time, eventually becoming a Congressman and, later, Mayor of Boston.

It was politics that brought the two families together. Fitzgerald, running for Congress in 1894, sought support from Kennedy, then the East Boston ward boss. They became friends, and their families took vacations together. Rose Fitzgerald and Joseph P. Kennedy first met at Old Orchard Beach in the summer of 1895. She was 5; he was 7 years old. Romance had to wait until they were teenagers, 11 summers later.

Rose had her heart set on prestigious Wellesley College, but her father forbade her to attend a Protestant school; instead she studied at the Convent of the Sacred Heart in Boston, following the recommendation of Archbishop William O'Connell. Joe Kennedy graduated from Harvard in 1912; but as an Irish Catholic, he never felt fully accepted by the university's Protestant social elite, a slight that rankled him for the rest of his life.

Yet Joseph P. Kennedy had a charming personality and a thorough knowledge of finance. In 1914, at the age of 25, he rescued his father's bank from a takeover and was rewarded with the bank's presidency. "The youngest man to hold the presidency of a banking house in the state of

Massachusetts," the newspapers hailed him.

John F. Kennedy home, Brookline, Massachusetts

Now that Joe had suitable employment, Mayor Fitzgerald finally considered him worthy of his daughter's hand. In a ceremony seen as the union of the city's two most prominent Roman Catholic families, the couple was wed that October by Cardinal O'Connell himself.

After their honeymoon, Joseph and Rose Kennedy settled in the largely Protestant suburb of Brookline. Their first son, Joseph Jr., was born nine months after their marriage; a second son, named John Fitzgerald Kennedy in honor of Rose's father, followed in May 1917. In all, the couple had four sons and five daughters. Despite his wealth, however, Joseph P. Kennedy said he never felt welcome among Boston's Protestant business community. In 1927, when son John was just 10, Joseph moved his family to New York City.

To keep Massachusetts ties, the family bought a summer estate at Hyannis, on Cape Cod. And all four sons—Joe Jr., Jack, Bobby and Teddy—attended Harvard, with John graduating in 1940.

Joseph P. Kennedy, the President's father, was a master at making money for himself, by investing other people's assets. Using borrowed funds—a good deal of them from his father's Columbia Trust Company—he earned hundreds of millions of dollars in industries such as real estate, film production, shipbuilding and liquor importing. In 1957, at age 69, *Fortune* magazine ranked him among America's 16 wealthiest individuals.

Yet the flamboyant Joe Kennedy had become a lightning rod for public controversy—both as a financier and as an official in Franklin Roosevelt's

Senator John F. Kennedy and Jacqueline Bouvier Kennedy on their wedding day, September 12, 1953

administration—and he realized that he could never be elected president himself. Instead, he groomed his sons to go into politics. Eldest son, Joseph P. Kennedy, Jr., was the one who was supposed to be a politician, but Joe Jr. died in World War II. Thus the second son, John Fitzgerald Kennedy, was first to seek a political career.

When the war ended, JFK came to Boston, the city of his family's roots, where a Congressional seat had opened up. The district included heavily Democratic, working-class neighborhoods like Charlestown and Cambridge, and the energetic Jack Kennedy won his first race easily. Flashing a big smile, he was an unusual face in Massachusetts politics of that era: like many voters, he was of Irish ancestry, but he was also a Harvard graduate, intelligent and literate. And although he was a Democrat, he wasn't part of the established political machines. It was 1946, and he was just 29 years old.

After three terms in the House, JFK ran for a Senate seat. By narrowly defeating the incumbent Republican, Henry Cabot Lodge, in 1952, the young, charismatic Kennedy became a rising star in the national Democratic Party. It was only natural that he would decide to run for President in 1960.

John Kennedy loved Boston, and the city loved him back. Until he became president, he kept an apartment on Bowdoin Street, across from the State House, as his voting residence, even though he had a house in the family compound at Hyannis Port. And on the eve of his election, he returned to Boston to campaign one last time. An estimated 20,000 people—well over the official capacity—attended a massive rally at Boston Garden, the city's indoor sports arena, on Monday night, November 7, 1960. Thousands more lined the motorcade route; newspapers reported that it took 90 minutes for his limousine to travel the mile and a half from his hotel to the Garden. After the Garden rally, JFK went to Faneuil Hall, the "cradle of liberty," to give a final campaign speech for national television. The next morning, Election Day, Jack and Jackie Kennedy cast their ballots at the Old West Church (at that time a library) before flying to Hyannis to await the results.

Senator John F. Kennedy stops in a diner in Nashua, New Hampshire, during the 1960 primary campaign

Like other members of his family, John Kennedy knew and loved the city's history. His father, Joe, and his grandfather, Honey Fitz, had each been tour guides in their youth; his mother Rose instilled an appreciation of Boston's heritage in all of her children. (JFK's brother, Senator Edward Kennedy, once narrated a recording of Longfellow's poem "Paul Revere's Ride.")

On January 9, 1961, just 11 days before his inauguration as President, John Fitzgerald Kennedy addressed the Great and General Court, the state legislature of Massachusetts, in the State House on Beacon Hill. He spoke of the contributions that his home state had made "to our national greatness" over three centuries; he spoke of "the common threads woven by the Pilgrim and the Puritan, the fisherman and the farmer, the Yankee and the immigrant." And he vowed that he was still guided by John Winthrop's words, 331 years after they were uttered: "For we must consider that we shall be as a City upon a Hill; the eyes of all people are upon Us."

Despite his hopes, John Kennedy did not survive to return to Massachusetts after his presidency. But like John Winthrop before him, the young

Inaugural Address of John F. Kennedy, 35th President of the United States, Washington, D.C., January 20, 1961

Irish-American President continues to guide and inspire new generations of Boston residents, Yankees and immigrants alike. To borrow the words of the musical *Camelot*—reportedly a personal favorite of the President, as well as an oft-cited metaphor for his term in office—his administration was, "for one brief shining moment," an era of idealism and optimism for Boston and America.

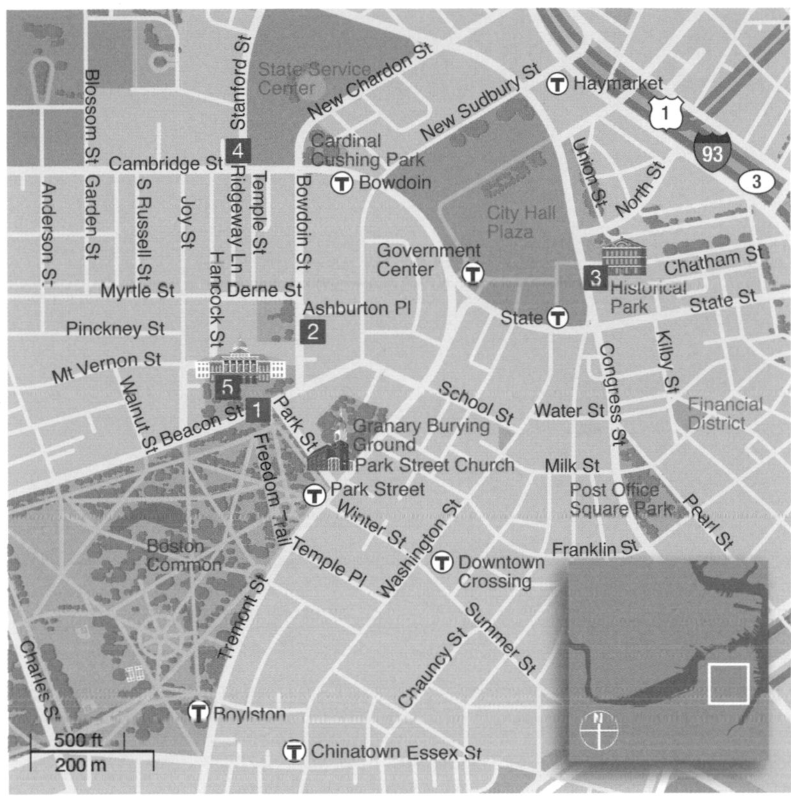

1 John Francis Fitzgerald Sold Newspapers
2 JFK Apartment: 122 Bowdoin Street
3 Faneuil Hall
4 Old West Church: 131 Cambridge Street
5 Massachusetts State House: Beacon Street

BOSTON WALKING TOURS

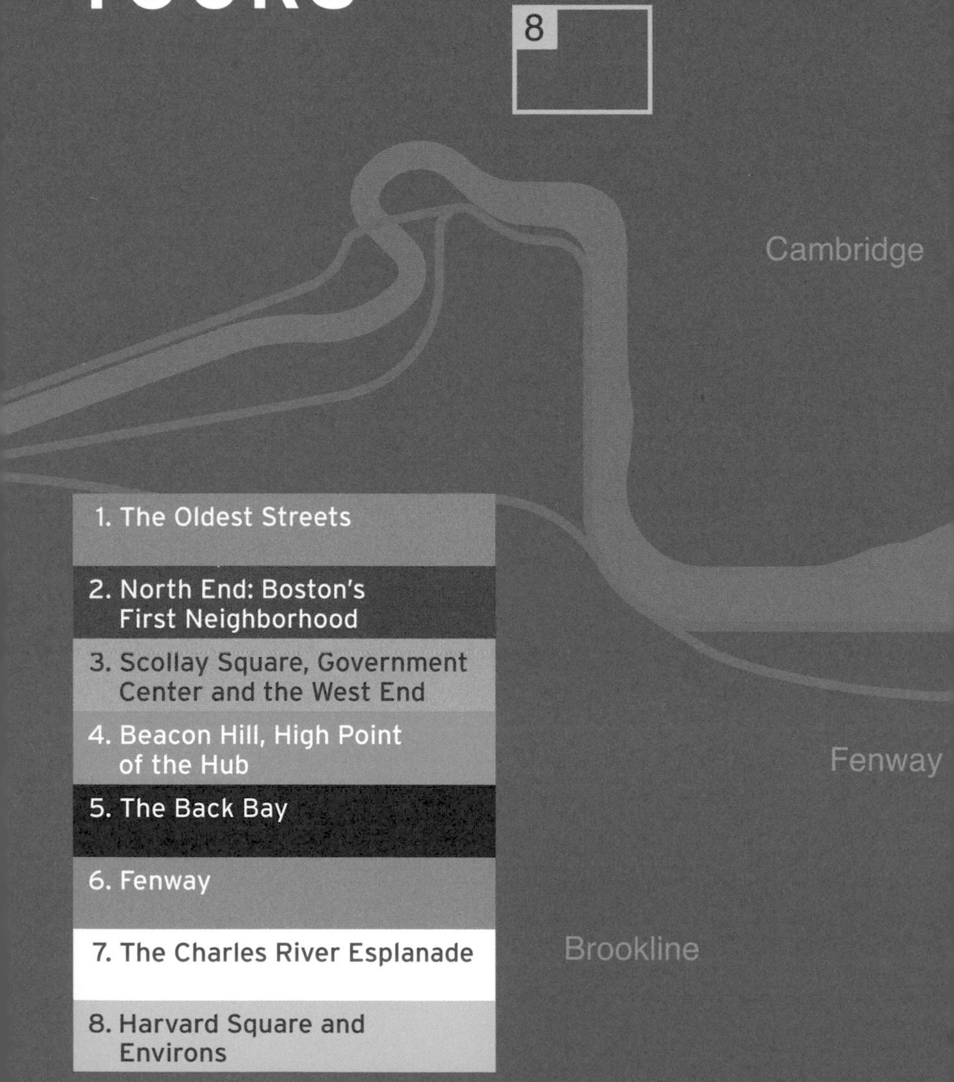

8

Cambridge

Fenway

Brookline

1. The Oldest Streets
2. North End: Boston's First Neighborhood
3. Scollay Square, Government Center and the West End
4. Beacon Hill, High Point of the Hub
5. The Back Bay
6. Fenway
7. The Charles River Esplanade
8. Harvard Square and Environs

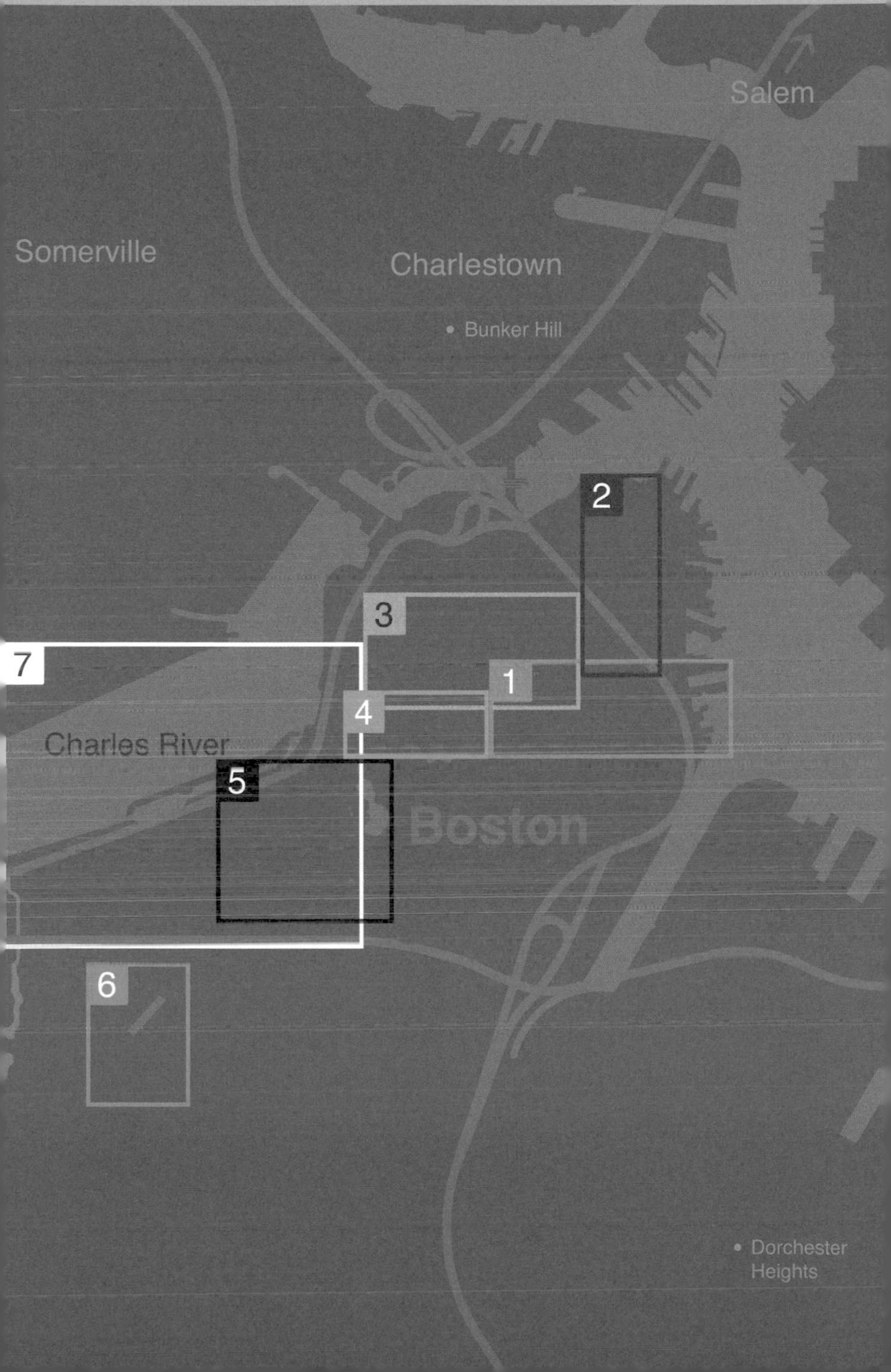

Salem

Somerville

Charlestown

Bunker Hill

2

3

7

1

4

Charles River

5

Boston

6

Dorchester Heights

THE OLDEST STREETS

1 Park Street Station
2 Park Street Church
3 Granary Burying Ground
4 Tremont Temple Baptist Church
5 Parker House
6 King's Chapel
7 Boston Latin School
8 Old City Hall
9 Province Steps
10 Transcript Building
11 Old South Meeting House
12 Old Corner Book Store
13 Winthrop Building
14 Spring Lane
15 Post Office Square
16 Exchange Coffee House
17 Boston Massacre Site
18 Old State House
19 Exchange Place
20 Original Shoreline
21 Richards Building
22 Cunard Building
23 150 State Street
24 Custom House
25 State Street Block
26 Long Wharf
27 Chart House Restaurant

Above: View of Boston, 1727

 ■ Exisiting Building or Reconstruction ■ Building No Longer Exists

Boston North Station
North Station
Rose Kennedy Greenway
Causeway St
Canal St
N Washington St
Endicott St
N Margin St
Prince St
Charter St
Salem St
N Bennet St
Commercial St
North St
1A
Pilot House Park
North End
Cross St
Merrimac St
New Chardon St
Hanover St
North St
Atlantic Ave
Congress St
Haymarket
Surface Rd
93
Christopher Columbus Waterfront Park
Bowdoin
Cambridge St
City Hall Plaza
Government Center
Clinton St
Waterfront
Bowdoin St
Somerset St
Derne St
Ashburton Pl
Historical Park
Chatham St
State St
Aquarium
State
Kilby St
Milk St
India St
E India Row
Beacon St
Park St
Water St
Wharf District Park
Boston Common
Freedom Trail
Province St
Milk St
Financial District
Post Office Square Park
Oliver St
Winter St
Washington St
Downtown Crossing
Franklin St
Congress St
Pearl St
Purchase St
Atlantic Ave
Seaport Blvd
Tremont St
Summer St
Chauncy St
Boston Opera House
Fort Point Channel
Boylston
Essex St
Boston South Station
Chinatown
Theater District
Chinatown
South Station
Beach St
Leather District
Lagrange St
Kneeland St
Dorchester Ave
Hudson St
500 ft
200 m

START:
Boston Common, corner of Tremont and Park Streets

METRO:
Green and Red Lines to Park Street

END:
Long Wharf

METRO:
Blue Line at Aquarium

Freedom Trail

The paths from Boston Common to the waterfront have borne the footsteps of Bostonians for nearly four centuries now. Along these thoroughfares you'll find the city's most significant landmarks: centers of commerce, politics and religion from 1630 to the present.

1 When "the crooked but narrow streets of Boston" proved unsuited for heavy volumes of streetcar traffic, Bostonians went underground, putting their transit lines in America's first subway—and the fourth in the world, after London, Budapest and Glasgow. Park Street station was one of the first two to open, on September 1, 1897.

2 Across from the subway station is Park Street Church, erected in 1809 as a response by

Congregational Trinitarians to the newly popular doctrine of Unitarianism. Site of the first public singing of the hymn "America" and William Lloyd Garrison's first antislavery speech, the building is also revered for its elegant design and prominent location.

3 Granary Burying Ground (1661) is neither the city's oldest nor its largest colonial graveyard, but it contains the remains of most of the well-known Bostonians from the Revolutionary era, including Paul Revere and John Hancock. Its name comes from the old town granary, a barn for storing wheat and other grains, that once stood on the site of Park Street Church.

4 Walk past the graveyard and look across the street to find Tremont Temple Baptist Church at 88 Tremont St. Organized in 1843 as a response to the segregation that was enforced in other parishes, it was the first American church to allow blacks and whites to sit together in the same pews. The present building (1896) is the congregation's fourth, following fires in its first three structures, all on this site. Its architect was Clarence Blackall, designer of many Boston theaters.

5 Established in October 1855 by Harvey D. Parker, the Parker House is America's oldest continuously operating hotel (as opposed to an inn). The current building, at the corner of School Street, dates from 1927, although an older annex survives. The hotel's innovations include Boston cream pie and Parker House rolls; its employees over the years have included Ho Chi Minh (a pastry chef in 1912) and Malcolm X (a busboy in the early 1940s).

Park Street Church, 1904

6 In 1687, King James II ordered construction of an Anglican church in Boston, over objections of town residents, whose Puritan ancestors had emigrated to America to get away from the Church of England. That first King's Chapel was erected on a corner of the town's oldest burying ground, a "bare-faced squat" on land taken from the dead, when no living person would sell to the hated church. This stone building at what is now the corner of Tremont and School streets, the parish's third, was completed in 1754 and became the primary house of worship for pre-Revolutionary royal officials. In 1785 the parish became America's first Unitarian congregation.

7 School Street was the site of the first permanent building of America's first public school, the Boston Latin School. A statue of Benjamin Franklin, the school's most famous dropout, stands on the site where Boston boys studied for more than a century.

8 The "granite granny of School Street," Old City Hall was the seat of Boston municipal government from 1864 until 1968, after which it was sold to a private owner. The donkey sculpture was installed in 2000, in honor of the many Democratic mayors who served here including John F. Fitzgerald and James Michael Curley.

9 Make a right on Province Street. On your right, just before the Café Marliave, the Province Steps are all that remain of the Province House, the 17th-century dwelling of Massachusetts's royal governors. Erected as an elegant private home in the late 1600s, it became the governor's mansion in 1716; within its walls General Gage planned the British soldiers' march to Lexington and Concord. After being converted for commercial uses, the building burned in 1864; a few remnants survived

until 1922. Turn left on Bromfield Street and again on Washington; across from the intersection of Milk and Washington Streets, a plaque shows what the grand house once looked like.

10 Look to your right to see the Transcript Building, which was erected in 1874 to house the *Boston Evening Transcript* newspaper, replacing a new structure of an almost identical design that had been destroyed in the Great Boston Fire of 1872.

11 On December 16, 1773, thousands of Bostonians met in Old South Meeting House at the corner of Washington and Milk Streets to demand that the hated tea, that worst of plagues, be returned to England without being unloaded from the ships that had borne it to Boston. After their demands were refused by Governor Hutchinson, the meeting broke up after nightfall; the crowds then moved to Griffin's Wharf to watch (and cheer on) as a small group of disguised "Mohawks" destroyed the accursed herb, dumping 46 tons of tea leaves into the salt water of Boston Harbor. Today Old South, "Nursery and Sanctuary of Freedom," is a museum and historic site.

12 The redbrick building at the corner of Washington and School Streets was once the Old Corner Book Store, the literary hub of Boston—and of America—from 1833 to 1864, when it housed the office of Ticknor and Fields, publishers. The building was erected around 1712 as a home and shop for Thomas Crease, an apothecary. It stands on the site of what was Anne Hutchinson's home before she was banished from Massachusetts for preaching her unorthodox religious views in 1638.

Province House

Exchange Coffee House

13 As leader of the Massachusetts Bay Colony, Governor John Winthrop got first choice of house lots and picked the one next to the town spring. At the corner of Washington Street and Spring Lane, the yellow-brick Winthrop Building, Boston's first steel-framed skyscraper (1893), marks the site.

14 Turn down Spring Lane, a pedestrian walkway that recalls the narrow thoroughfares of old Boston. Halfway down on the left, a plaque marks the site of the Great Spring, which furnished much of the town's water in colonial days. At the end of the lane turn left, then right onto Water Street.

15 At the intersection of Water and Congress Streets, look to your right. Here you will see Post Office Square, dating from 1874, when the triangle in front of the new Post Office building was dedicated as a public way; the fountain in its middle (1912) was originally a watering trough for horses. All of the buildings in this area were destroyed in the 1872 fire.

16 Turn left onto Congress Street. The two arms of U-shaped Quaker Lane embrace the former site of the Exchange Coffee House. The vision of Andrew Dexter, the coffee house was erected in 1809 at a cost of $600,000, nearly all of that financed by worthless paper money printed by Dexter and his associates. Two stories taller than any of the town's fire engines could pump water, the grandiose structure burned and collapsed just nine years after it was built.

17 The intersection of State and Congress streets was the site of the Boston Massacre, when five residents of Boston were killed by British soldiers on the evening of March 5, 1770. In the extended sidewalk in front of the Old State House, a circle of paving stones supposedly marks the Massacre site; but that circle of stones has been moved three times since it was first installed in 1887. The actual site was literally in the middle of the intersection, where cars and trucks now whiz over it.

18 Beyond the Massacre site you will see the balcony of the Old State House, used for proclamations by the royal governor; from it, the Declaration of Independence was first publicly read in Boston on July 18, 1776. On hearing that their bonds with Great Britain were dissolved, joyous Bostonians then burned the original lion and unicorn, symbols of the Crown. A new lion and unicorn were installed when the building opened as a museum in 1882.

Old State House, circa 1900

19 Turn right onto State Street, Boston's financial center; at one point, 22 banks had their headquarters on it. At 53 State Street, the Exchange Building was built in 1896 to house the Boston Stock Exchange; today its granite walls and grand lobby staircase have been incorporated into a 40-story glass skyscraper called Exchange Place.

Then & Now

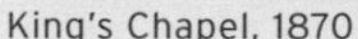

King's Chapel, 1870

20 The obvious avenue to "the part of the world that really mattered," as Walter Muir Whitehill called it, colonial Boston's King Street led to Long Wharf (26), and thus to continents across the sea. After independence its name was changed to State Street. The original 17th-century shoreline was roughly at modern Kilby Street.

21 Boston has only a few buildings with cast-iron façades, assembled from mass-produced parts that could be ordered out of a catalog. One of the finest is the Richards Building at 114 State St., erected around 1867, with the top two stories added in 1889.

22 Next to the Richards Building, the Cunard Building at No. 120 housed the local office of the famed British steamship company. Nautical motifs, including anchors, dolphins, Neptunes and a ship's prow, decorate its façade.

23 The tiny building at 150 State Street is one of the financial district's oldest structures, a warehouse dating from the 18th century. But its "Elizabethan" façade is a much later invention, added in 1911 when this building housed the British consulate.

24 On your right in McKinley Square, the Custom House is actually two buildings: a four-story granite base completed in 1849, and a 25-story steel-framed tower added atop it in 1917. As a federal government building, the tower was exempt from city ordinances restricting height, and so it became Boston's tallest building for three decades. It was converted to a hotel in 1997. Inquire inside about visiting its open-air observation deck.

25 The Custom House was built on newly filled land at the water's edge, but within a decade its view of the ocean was blocked by the massive State Street Block (1858). This granite row was originally 15 bays long, but its eastern half was demolished in the early 1950s to make way for the original elevated Central Artery.

26 Continue across the Greenway to Long Wharf (1711), Boston's first deep-water pier, originally extending a third of a mile into the ocean. Its waterside end is at its original location, but the wharf lost half its length as new land was filled at the town end. Here the British soldiers landed on October 1, 1768, troops that would be involved in the horrid Boston Massacre just 17 months later.

27 In colonial days, Long Wharf was lined with brick warehouses, of which one remains: the Chart House restaurant occupies a circa 1763 structure once owned by John Hancock.

Before returning to land, stroll to the wharf's end to admire the view of Boston Harbor, for centuries the city's primary link with the rest of the world.

24

25

26

27

Then & Now

City Hall, circa 1920

NORTH END: BOSTON'S FIRST NEIGHBORHOOD

1 Samuel Adams Statue
2 Kevin H. White Statue
3 Faneuil Hall
4 Quincy Market
5 Mayor Curley Statue
6 New England Holocaust Memorial
7 Union Oyster House
8 Green Dragon Tavern
9 Ebenezer Hancock House
10 Boston Stone
11 Blackstone Street
12 Asaroton
13 Mill Creek
14 Rose Kennedy Greenway
15 North End
16 Cockerel Hall
17 Richmond Street
18 North Street
19 Pierce-Hichborn House
20 Paul Revere House
21 Mariners House
22 Sacred Heart Italian Church
23 Garden Court Street
24 Fitzgerald Home
25 St. Stephen's Church
26 Paul Revere Statue
27 Christs Church (Old North Church)
28 Copp's Hill Burying Ground
29 44 Hull Street
30 Copp's Hill Terraces
31 Clougherty Home
32 Purity Distilling Company Molasses Tank
33 Langone Park

Above: North Square, circa 1909

 ■ Exisiting Building or Reconstruction ■ Building No Longer Exists

Charlestown Bridge
Langone Park
Andrew P. Puopolo Jr. Athletic Field
Commercial St
N Hudson St
Copp's Hill Terrace
Foster St
N Washington Street
Copp's Hill Burying Ground
Hull St
Charter St
Snow Hill St
Beverly St
Causeway St
N Washington St
Prince St
Old North Church
Unity St
Battery St
Sheafe St
Paul Revere Mall
Salutation St
Boston North Station
Cleveland Pl
DeFilippo Playground
Margaret St
Hanover Ave
Medford St
Salem St
Tileston St
N Bennet St
North Station
Thatcher St
Rose Kennedy Greenway
Polcari Playground
North St
Lynn St
Endicott St
N Margin St
Fleet St
North End
Canal St
Hanover St
Sumner Traffic Tunnel
Callahan Traffic Tunnel
Lewis St
Salem St
Cross St
Surface Rd
Haymarket
Fulton St
Richmond St
North St
New Sudbury St
North End Park
Congress St
Union St
Blackstone St
Commercial St
Christopher Columbus Waterfront Park
Union Street Park
City Hall Plaza
North St
Clinton St
Durgin Park
Cambridge St
City Hall
Faneuil Hall
S Market St
Government Center
Cornhill St
Historical Park
Chatham St
Aquarium
State St
Wharf District Park
250 ft
100 m

START:
Faneuil Hall

METRO:
Orange and Blue Lines to State; Green Line to Government Center

END:
North End Park on Commercial Street

METRO:
Walk to Green and Orange Lines at North Station

Boston's most colorful neighborhood is also its oldest, the only survivor of the colonial town's three residential "ends"—North, South and West. Once home to Paul Revere and Thomas Hutchinson, throughout the 1800s the North End was overrun with raucous sailors and impoverished immigrants. Today it's been revitalized thanks to the hard work of Italian immigrants and their descendants over the past century.

1 With its arms crossed, Ann Whitney's statue of Samuel Adams (1880) surveys passersby. The "man of the town meeting" wasn't known for his oratory—he suffered from a palsy, which gave him a halting, stuttered speech—but he was unrivaled with the pen. When neighbors spied candlelight in his study into the wee hours of the morning, they knew that he was writing letters and newspaper columns to advance the cause of the colonists' rights.

2 To the left of Adams, a larger-than-life bronze statue of Kevin H. White strides towards Faneuil Hall. Boston's Mayor from 1968 to 1984, White was responsible for the restoration of Quincy Market **4**.

3 Faneuil Hall (1742; 1805) was the gift of colonial merchant Peter Faneuil, a combined food market and town meeting hall. The ground floor is now a visitor center for Boston National Historical Park; the upstairs remains the Cradle of Liberty where Bostonians have for 270 years debated the political issues of the day.

4 Directly opposite, Quincy Market, also known as Faneuil Hall Marketplace (1826; 1976), was an extension of the food markets under Faneuil Hall, erected during the administration of Mayor Josiah Quincy. After a century and a half, it was restored as a shopping mall to commemorate the American Bicentennial—one of Boston's few truly successful urban renewal projects.

Then & Now

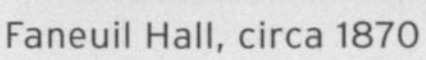

Faneuil Hall, circa 1870

5 Return to North Street and cross to Carmen Park at the corner of Congress Street. Lloyd Lillie's double statue of Mayor James Michael Curley (1980) recalls two aspects of the Irish politician's personality: He was a great orator, yet quite approachable if you wanted to sit down for a chat. (Cynics would say that his willingness to chat might depend on how much you were willing to give him in exchange.) The great rival of John F. Fitzgerald, Curley served four non-consecutive terms as mayor between 1914 and 1949, one term as Governor, parts of four terms in Congress, and two terms in federal prison on fraud convictions.

6 Continue through the park to the New England Holocaust Memorial (1995), created by architect Stanley Saitowitz. Its six glass towers recall the six death camps in Europe where millions of Jews were murdered by the Nazis.

7 Across the street at the Union Oyster House (1826), you can still sit at the half-round oyster bar where Daniel Webster gorged himself on shellfish and brandy, or dine in the booth where John F. Kennedy enjoyed lobster stew on Sunday afternoons. The structure was built around 1714 and housed offices of the radical pre-revolutionary *Massachusetts Spy* newspaper.

8 Turn down tiny Marshall Street to find the Green Dragon Tavern, which takes its name from the historic drinking place where patriots made plans to dump the hated tea in Boston Harbor in 1773. The old tavern stood around the corner, near the present subway entrance on Congress Street.

9 Set at an angle to Marshall Street is the Ebenezer Hancock house (1767), home of John Hancock's

younger brother. Ebenezer was Deputy-Paymaster-general of the Continental Army, and his house once held 2½ million crowns in gleaming silver coins, sent by the French king Louis XVI to pay the American soldiers.

10 Low in the wall of a brick building is the Boston Stone. Imported from England before 1700 as a millstone to grind paint pigments, it was placed in front of a tavern near here in 1737, to protect the building from carriage wheels. It became known as the Boston Stone because of its resemblance to the famed London Stone, but unlike its British counterpart, the stone here was never used as a distance marker.

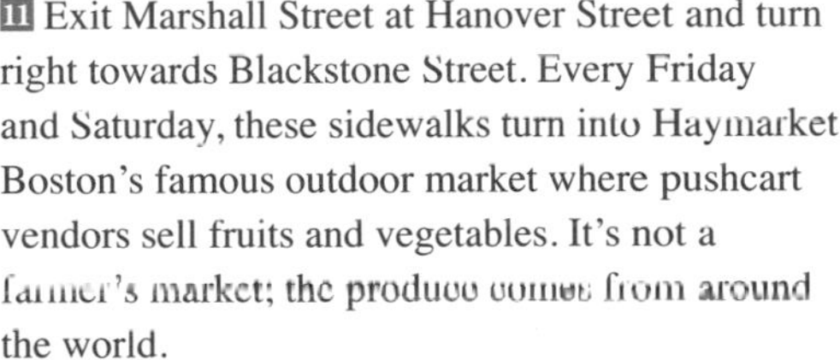
11 Exit Marshall Street at Hanover Street and turn right towards Blackstone Street. Every Friday and Saturday, these sidewalks turn into Haymarket, Boston's famous outdoor market where pushcart vendors sell fruits and vegetables. It's not a farmer's market; the produce comes from around the world.

Haymarket, 1973

12 Embedded in the pavement of two crosswalks are pieces of bronze "garbage" recalling the clutter of market day. It's a sculpture called *Asaroton*, by Mags Harries (1976; enlarged and reinstalled in 2005).

13 Blackstone Street runs parallel to the place where a ditch or canal was dug in 1643 connecting Mill Cove and Town Cove. In 1666, the town declared that the canal—called Mill Creek—was the only place in town where butchers could dispose of "garbidge, beast entrails, &c." Although garbage disposal regulations were soon changed, and the canal was filled around 1830, some butchers remain here nearly 3 ½ centuries later.

Lime Alley and Charter St., circa 1893

14 Boston's elevated Central Artery expressway opened in 1954; today's underground highway opened on the same route in 2003. The original aboveground road was named for Mayor John F. Fitzgerald; the park above its replacement tunnel is dedicated to his daughter, Rose Kennedy.

15 On the far side of the Greenway, enter the North End neighborhood, called in colonial times "the island of North Boston."

16 "Cockerel Hall" at 287 Hanover St. was erected in the 1870s on the site once occupied by the Cockerel Church. This was the parish whose members had seceded from nearby New North Meeting over their disagreement with Rev. Peter Thacher in 1719. They adorned their building with a rooster weathervane, an allusion to Peter's betrayal of Christ upon the crowing of the cock. The

weathervane is now atop a church in Cambridge [see Tour 8]; the brick Gothic building here is now condos and a branch bank.

17 Turn back and make a left down Richmond Street, known in the 19th century as the "Black Sea" or the "Murder District," because of its many taverns, boarding houses, brothels and gambling dens.

18 Turn left on North Street, once known as Ann Street, site of the infamous "Ann Street descent" vice raid of April 23, 1851. Above the liquor store, notice the carved stone sign on the third floor corner. The letters $_{T}W_{S}$ refer to Timothy and Susannah Wadsworth, proprietors of the Red Lyon Inn at this corner in 1694. When the historic inn was demolished, the sign was re-created on the 1850 building that replaced it.

19 At North Square, look through the iron gate on your left to see the front of the Pierce-Hichborn House (circa 1711), erected for Moses Pierce, a glazier or glass merchant. Pierce's profession explains the house's many large windows, which were unusual for its day. In 1948, the house was occupied by a barbershop with a bookie joint in its back room; when the cops raided it, a picture of its interior appeared in a local newspaper. The photo focused attention on the fine quality of the house's woodwork and the building was turned into a house museum. (To visit it, inquire next door at the Paul Revere House.)

20 The oldest house in historic Boston is known not for its age, but for the silversmith who lived in it nearly a century after it was built. One of a row of three houses erected in 1680, it was considered

small and outdated when Paul Revere bought it in 1770. Revere settled here with his wife, his mother, five children and a dog. It was here that Revere was living when he departed Boston on his famous midnight ride on the night of April 18, 1775.

21 Next door, an anchor hangs from the façade of the Mariners House (1847), still operated as a mission to seamen by the Boston Port Society.

22 Across the square, the Sacred Heart Italian Church was originally the bethel, or chapel, of the Boston Port Society (1833). Here was the "quaint, ship-cabin-looking church" where Father Edward Taylor preached to seamen; where Dickens, Longfellow and Walt Whitman all came to hear the "Sailor Preacher." "I set my bethel in North Square," said Father Taylor, "because I learned to set my net where the fish ran." In 1888 the Port Society sold the building to an Italian Catholic congregation, which altered its exterior. A plaque on the building shows its original appearance.

23 At the end of the square, follow Garden Court Street. A bronze plaque on the left depicts the stately home of Governor Thomas Hutchinson. During protests against the Stamp Act, a mob ransacked Hutchinson's house on the night of August 26, 1765, leaving "nothing remaining but the bare walls and floors." Hutchinson rebuilt, but the elegant mansion was demolished in 1834 for a street-widening project.

24 In September 1889, John F. Fitzgerald and his bride, Josie Hannon, moved into an apartment at number 4 Garden Court St.; 10 months later, their first daughter was born in that apartment:

Rose Fitzgerald, later to become the mother of President John F. Kennedy. No longer standing, her birthplace was a twin to the bowfronted, black-shuttered house next door at No. 6.

25 At the end of Garden Court, make a left, then a quick right onto Hanover Street. The land at Hanover and Clark Streets has been used for religious purposes since 1714. The first house of worship on this site was the New North Meeting; the parish's 1719 decision to hire Rev. Peter Thacher led to a nasty split. In 1804 the parishioners of New North Meeting erected the present brick building to replace their earlier wooden one; of the four Boston churches designed by architect Charles Bulfinch, this is the only one surviving today. In 1862 the New North, then a Unitarian parish, sold the building to an Irish Catholic congregation for $35,000. Ever since, it's been known as St. Stephen's Church. Here Rose Fitzgerald was baptized on the day after her birth in 1890, and here her funeral service was held 104 years later, in 1995.

26 Across the street, in one of the city's most photographed scenes, a statue of Paul Revere gallops away from the Old North Church, with the church steeple looming over the midnight rider's shoulder. The sculpture is the work of Cyrus Dallin, a Utah native who came to Boston to study art. Dallin was a young man when he started work on his statue honoring Revere, in response to an 1882 competition organized by the city. (It was originally supposed to be placed in Copley Square, near Trinity Church.) By the time the statue was finally cast and installed on its pedestal here, some 58 years had elapsed and the sculptor was a few weeks shy of his 79th birthday.

Paul Revere statue and Old North Church, circa 1970

Old North Church

27 Continue through the Paul Revere Mall and up the steps to the church. Officially it's Christ Church, but thanks to poet Henry Wadsworth Longfellow, the world knows it as Old North Church. Erected in 1723 to a design by bookseller William Price and built by mason Ebenezer Clough and his partner, its walls comprise 513,654 bricks made in nearby Medford. The church's fame comes from the two lanterns hung in its steeple on the night of April 18, 1775, to warn residents across the Charles River that His Majesty's troops were commencing their expedition (by water) to Lexington and Concord. That original steeple blew down in 1804, and a second steeple blew over in 1954; the present steeple is a replica of the first. As a bellringer, 15-year-old Paul Revere pulled the ropes here.

28 At the top of the hill, Copp's Hill Burying Ground (1660) is the second oldest graveyard in the city. His Majesty's soldiers camped here during the Revolution and used some gravestones for target practice. Local legend also says that this is where Dr. John White Webster was buried in an unmarked grave, after his execution for the murder of Dr. George Parkman.

29 Across the street, the tiny residence at 44 Hull St. is the narrowest house in Boston, only 10 feet 5 inches wide at the front, and just 6 feet 2 inches deep in some interior rooms. It has 964 square feet, spread out over four floors.

30 Make a right on Snow Hill Street and another on Charter Street. The Copps Hill Terraces offer an impressive view of the Charles River and Boston Harbor, in a park laid out by landscape architect Frederick Law Olmsted. Follow the stone steps down and turn left.

31 Next to the steps, a lot at 534 Commercial St. provides off-street parking for two cars. Here stood Bridget Clougherty's three-story wooden house. On the afternoon of January 15, 1919, Mrs. Clougherty was taking a nap when the molasses tank across the street burst. She died instantly when the upper floors of the house collapsed onto the bed where she was sleeping.

32 The 2.3-million-gallon tank of the Purity Distilling Company stood almost exactly where the pitcher's mound and home plate of the softball field are today.

33 Walk through Langone Park to the banks of the Charles River. Near here was where Paul Revere and his friends crossed in their rowboat on the evening of April 18, 1775. He landed in Charlestown, near U.S.S. *Constitution*'s present-day berth, where he "got a Horse of Deacon Larkin" and began his famous midnight ride.

Admire the view of Charlestown, including U.S.S. *Constitution* and the Bunker Hill Monument; then follow the path westward along the river. At the tennis courts, turn inland; beyond them, the waterside path leads only to a dead end. North Station, on the Green and Orange Lines, is a few short blocks west of here on Causeway Street.

30

31

32

33

Then & Now

Paul Revere House

SCOLLAY SQUARE, GOVERNMENT CENTER AND THE WEST END

1 Old State House
2 Ames Building
3 Franklin Printshop
4 26 Court St.
5 Steaming Kettle
6 Scollay Square
7 Sears' Crescent
8 City Hall
9 Williams Workshop
10 Center Plaza
11 Pemberton Square
12 Old Howard
13 Ashburton Park
14 Kennedy Apartment
15 Red Hat Tavern
16 State Service Center
17 Old West Church
18 First Otis House
19 West End Neighborhood
20 Abiel Smith School
21 African Meeting House
22 Holmes Alley
23 34 Myrtle St.
24 Rollins Place
25 Coburn's Gaming House
26 Vilna Shul
27 Hayden Home
28 25 North Anderson St.
29 Massachusetts General Hospital
30 Harvard Medical School
31 Resident Physician's House
32 Liberty Hotel

Above: Scollay Square, 1910

 ■ Exisiting Building or Reconstruction ■ Building No Longer Exists

Museum Way
Education Street
North Point Park
Charles River Bridge
Paul Revere Park
Charlestown Bridge
Langone Park
Nashua Street Park
Museum of Science
Science Park
Boston North Station
Rose Kennedy Greenway
N Washington St
Prince St
Endicott St
N Margin St
North Station
Causeway St
Canal St
Emerson Pl
Charles St
Charlesbank Playground
Massachusetts General Hospital
Merrimac St
Cross St
New Chardon St
Congress St
Haymarket
Parkman St
N Grove St
N Anderson St
Blossom St
S Russell St
Bowdoin
City Hall Plaza
Government Center
Historical Park
Cambridge St
Charles/MGH
Phillips St
Grove St
Garden St
Joy St
Hancock St
Bowdoin St
Somerset St
Revere St
Myrtle St
Pinckney St
Derne St
Ashburton Pl
State
State St
W Cedar St
David G Mugar Way
Beacon Hill
Mt Vernon St
Chestnut St
Lime St
Beacon St
Park St
School St
Water St
Milk St
Freedom Trail
Park Street
Winter St
Washington St
Downtown Crossing
Franklin St
Arlington St
Public Garden
Boston Common
Tremont St
Boston Opera House
Chauncy St
Boylston
Essex St
Arlington
Theater District
Chinatown
Park Plaza
Lagrange St
Kneeland St
Leather District
500 ft
200 m
N

START:
Old State House, Washington and State Streets

METRO:
Orange and Blue Lines to State; Green Line to Government Center

END:
Charles Circle

METRO:
Red Line at Charles/MGH

Scollay Square and the West End no longer exist as neighborhoods. They were eradicated so thoroughly by urban renewal that even their streets have disappeared. But if you look carefully, you can find a few signs of the past, from the Steaming Kettle of the Oriental Tea Company to the stage door of the Old Howard; from reminders of Alexander Graham Bell and John F. Kennedy to the alleged site of the gruesome murder of Dr. George Parkman.

1 The oldest surviving government building in British America, the Old State House was erected in 1713 and was headquarters for the government of Massachusetts until the new State House on Beacon Hill opened in 1798. In the years leading up to the Revolution, both the Assembly—the elected representatives of the people—and the Governor—the appointed representative of the king—met here. The building was the focus for almost-constant disputes between the two sides. It's been a museum since 1882.

2 Cross to Court Street to view Boston's first skyscraper. For 22 years after its 1893 construction, the Ames Building at No. 1 was the tallest in Boston, with 13 stories (though technically, the steeple of the Church of the Covenant was higher). Unlike modern skyscrapers, it lacks a steel frame; the granite exterior walls carry the weight of the entire structure. In 2009 it was converted to a hotel.

3 On the side of the Center for Homeless Veterans, a plaque marks the site of the printing shop where Benjamin Franklin was apprenticed to his older brother James in 1718–23. Later it was the printing office of Benjamin Edes and John Gill, publishers of the *Boston Gazette*, one of the most radical and influential newspapers in the decade before the Revolution. Above the shop was the "Long Room," site of many meetings of the Sons of Liberty.

4 The lot across the street has been used for government purposes since the earliest days of English settlement. Here stood the old prison where Captain Kidd, the pirate, was detained—some say unjustly—in 1699, before being sent to London for trial and execution. Courthouses stood here for much of the 19th century; at an 1851 trial, a mob of abolitionists rescued Shadrach Minkins, preventing his return to slavery in Virginia. Today, 26 Court St. is home to offices for the public school system.

5 Follow Court Street as it veers to the right. The Steaming Kettle was installed in front of the Oriental Tea Company's store, a few doors away from here, in 1873. A contest was held to guess the kettle's capacity, and 15,000 people gathered in the square to observe its official measurement: 227 gallons, 2 quarts, 1 pint and 3 gills. (A gill is half a cup.)

Oriental Tea Company

Scollay Square, circa 1906

6 The intersection here is called Scollay Square, after Scollay's Buildings, a row of structures bought by William Scollay in 1790, removed from the center of the "square" in the 1800s. By World War II this had become an entertainment district for sailors and soldiers, known for its bars, tattoo parlors and burlesque houses. All was demolished to make way for Government Center in the 1960s, replacing one kind of sleaze with another.

7 Just two buildings were deemed historic enough to be saved when the bulldozers of urban renewal tore through this area: the brick Sears' Crescent (1816) and the stone Sears' Block (1848), both erected by David Sears.

8 The focal point of the Government Center project was Boston's new City Hall (1968), designed by Kallmann, McKinnell & Knowles. The Brutalist building makes frequent appearances on

ugly-building lists; some say that it looks like an Aztec pyramid turned upside-down. Plans to add life to its vast, desert-like brick plaza have been circulating ever since it was completed.

9 Follow the plaza along Cambridge Street. Near the John F. Kennedy Federal Office Building, a stone marker proclaims the "birthplace of the telephone." Here at 109 Court Street was the workshop of Charles Williams, where Alexander Graham Bell and Thomas Watson conducted their initial experiments in 1875. Perfection of the device occurred later, at Bell's rooming house on Exeter Place.

10 Across the street, the curving Center Plaza building is one of Boston's largest office buildings, making up in length what it lacks in height. Cross the street via the traffic island opposite the Steaming Kettle and take the stairs up to the other side of Center Plaza.

11 Laid out in 1835, Pemberton Square was once a garden square lined with gracious townhouses. Commercial buildings began to encroach on it in the late 19th century; Suffolk County Courthouse was erected here in 1894. In 2002 the restored building was renamed the John Adams Courthouse; it now houses the state's highest tribunals.

12 A reminder of Scollay Square's boisterous days can be found just to the north of the courthouse complex, near the rear entrance to 1 Center Plaza: a plaque marking the site of the stage of the Old Howard, the most famous burlesque theater in Boston. The stage door to the notorious performance place was just a few yards from the new (1937) wing of the courthouse.

13 Walk back past the courthouse and exit the plaza to the right. Turn right on Somerset Street and then left on Ashburton Place. At Bowdoin Street, Ashburton Park is part of the grounds of the Massachusetts State House, framing the capitol's 1898 yellow-brick extension. At its center is a copy of Charles Bulfinch's 1790 monument, the first memorial anywhere to the American Revolution. When the town's beacon (a pole for sending warning signals) blew over in 1789, Bulfinch was commissioned to design this memorial column for the summit of Beacon Hill. Twenty years later, the monument had to be removed when the top of the hill was cut down by 60 feet. The replica column, which includes some pieces salvaged from Bulfinch's original, dates from 1898.

14 While serving in office in Washington, John F. Kennedy maintained his local residence in Apartment 36 at 122 Bowdoin Street—the red brick building at the corner of Ashburton Place, overlooking the State House.

15 At the bottom of Bowdoin Street's steep hill, The Red Hat tavern claims to be one of Boston's oldest drinking establishments, a last vestige of old Scollay Square.

Boston Common, May 30, 1844

2 Walk through the park to the corner of Park and Beacon streets, where John F. Fitzgerald, grandfather of President John F. Kennedy, hawked newspapers as a boy.

3 To the left sits one of the finest war memorials in America, the Robert Gould Shaw/54th Regiment Memorial, which honors the first black soldiers to fight in the Civil War. Shaw, the son of a prominent white family, volunteered to lead the segregated regiment, since blacks weren't allowed to serve as officers. Dedicated in 1897, the bronze sculpture is by Augustus Saint-Gaudens.

4 Across the street looms the grand Massachusetts State House. Designed by architect Charles Bulfinch, its cornerstone was laid by Samuel Adams and Paul Revere on July 4, 1795. Revere also supplied copper for the building's dome in 1802, replacing wooden shingles that leaked. Bulfinch's

Hancock House, 1850

original structure, just 60 feet deep, is now dwarfed by wings to the sides and an "extension" at the rear. It is open for tours on weekdays.

5 John Hancock's fine granite mansion stood on what's now the west lawn of the State House. Taken down in 1863, it was replaced by a pair of townhouses, now also gone.

6 Looking like a taller triplet to its two adjacent rowhouses, the building at 25 Beacon St. was built a century later than its mates, which were erected in 1825. When the American Unitarian Association moved here from the corner of Bowdoin Street, they brought their street number with them.

7 Parkman House (33 Beacon St.) was bequeathed to the city by George Francis Parkman, son of murder victim Dr. George Parkman. Three years after his father's unseemly demise, the younger Parkman sold the family house on Walnut Street and moved here with his mother and sister. He never married and lived in near seclusion, leaving all he owned to the Boston Parks Department.

8 One of the earliest apartment buildings on Beacon Hill, the Tudor (1886), at the corner of Beacon and Joy Streets, is an exuberant example of Victorian architecture. Its name comes not from its style, but from the man who lived on this site before: Frederic Tudor, the "Ice King," who made a fortune harvesting ice from New England ponds and shipping it to tropical destinations such as Jamaica and India.

9 The ivy-covered houses at 39–40 Beacon St. are an 1820 design by Alexander Parris. The purple windowpanes are original, from a shipment of imported glass with extra manganese in its composition. Perfectly clear on its arrival from Germany, the glass turned violet after exposure to sunlight. The second-floor parlor on the right was locale for the "quietly sumptuous" 1843 wedding of Henry Wadsworth Longfellow and Fanny Appleton, daughter of textile mill owner Nathan Appleton.

10 Alexander Parris also designed 42 Beacon Street (1819) for Colonel David Sears. Originally a two-story residence with one rounded bay, Sears extended it to the west and added a second swell front in 1832. Four decades later, it became headquarters of the Somerset Club, which added the third floor and the rusticated stone wall along the sidewalk. The magnificent studded doors, with lion's head doorknockers, are the service entrance, leading to the kitchen.

11 Harrison Gray Otis, one of the Mount Vernon Proprietors, built three houses on Beacon Hill, all designed by Charles Bulfinch within a span of 10 years. Apparently dissatisfied with the first two, he liked this third one (45 Beacon Street, 1806), and lived here the rest of his life. Its original carriage house survives at the rear. While a resident here, Otis served as a state senator, U.S. Senator and Mayor of Boston. His house is now headquarters of the American Meteorological Society.

12 Eben Jordan, Jr.—department store magnate and musical patron—took his father's house (46 Beacon) and joined it with its neighbor (47 Beacon) in 1913, turning the combined dwelling into Beacon Hill's most palatial residence. (Notice how the windows of the two halves don't quite line up.) It featured gold-plated hardware, enameled woodwork and an acoustically perfect music room seating 170.

13

14

15

After an appearance in the 1968 film *The Thomas Crown Affair*, the building is now the Boston office of Rev. Sun Myung Moon's Unification Church.

13 A plaque on the façade of 50 Beacon Street says it was the site of William Blackstone's (spelled here "Blaxton") home in the 1620s. No one knows its true location; this is as good a guess as any. Across the street is the Founder's Memorial, erected in the Common for Boston's tercentennial in 1930.

14 Turn onto Spruce Street and make a right onto Chestnut Street. One of the oldest houses on Beacon Hill (1802), 29A Chestnut Street. had its bowfront added around 1820—hence the lavender glass, part of the same shipment seen on Beacon Street. Its side garden is a rare feature on Beacon Hill. Next door is a Gothic edifice, originally a chapel for Boston University's School of Theology and now condos.

15 Few women were allowed to make their own real estate investments in the early 1800s; Hepzibah Swan did so because her husband James was incarcerated in Paris by his political enemies. With her husband in enforced absentia, Swan became one of the Mount Vernon Proprietors. At 13–17 Chestnut Street she had Charles Bulfinch erect three houses, which she gave to her three daughters, specifying in the deeds that they were to be "free and exempt from control of husband."

16 At 6–8 Chestnut Street are another pair of Bulfinch designs, now a meetinghouse for the Society of Friends (Quakers).

17 Arriving in Boston as a grad student in 1951, Coretta Scott boarded at 1 Chestnut Street in the "big old house" of Mrs. Charlotte Bartol. A patron

of Antioch College (where Scott had been an undergraduate), the widowed Bartol rented rooms to college women and was active in the World Peace Foundation. Normal rent for a fifth-floor room and breakfast was $7 a week, but Coretta worked out a deal to scrub floors and wash pillowcases instead.

18 Look across the intersection with Walnut Street. On the morning of November 23, 1849, Dr. George Parkman left his house at 8 Walnut St. on what he thought were a normal day's errands. He strolled past the Doric columns that flanked his recessed entry door and down the steps, never to return. His dismembered body was discovered a few days later at the Harvard Medical School. Turn left and continue up Walnut Street to Mount Vernon Street.

19 The Mount Vernon Proprietors' effort to turn old "Mount Whoredom" into a more genteel "Mount Vernon" was led by two lawyer-investors, Jonathan Mason and Harrison Gray Otis, who were in turn among the first residents of the neighborhood. In 1802, Charles Bulfinch designed freestanding mansions for both men. Mason's house, long demolished, stood at present-day numbers 61–65 Mount Vernon St.

20 Turn right onto Mount Vernon Street. Two years after settling into his own detached house nearby, Jonathan Mason hired Bulfinch to design a row of four houses—one of the first rowhouse groupings on the hill—at 51–57 Mount Vernon Street. Legend, unproven, says that they were built for his daughters. The westernmost two houses looked over Mason's garden. The Rose Nichols House, at No. 55, is open for tours. Turn around and begin walking downhill along Mount Vernon Street.

16

17

18

19

20

Acorn Street

21 The Greek Revival house at 59 Mount Vernon St. was erected in 1837, blocking the garden view from the front (western) windows of No. 57. The owners of the latter then extended their house by eight feet to fill the gap left between the two houses.

22 The three low buildings on the left hand side of the street were once occupied by stables for the three houses erected for Mrs. Swan's daughters, on the Chestnut Street side of the block (15). Deed restrictions limit their height to 13 feet and require that the double doorway be wide enough for a cow to enter.

23 Harrison Gray Otis only lived in it for four years, but his second house by Bulfinch (85 Mount Vernon Street; 1802) is now Boston's grandest

and most expensive single-family residence. It's also Beacon Hill's only remaining freestanding home. The entrance porch at the rear driveway corner was added in the 1850s by the three Pratt sisters, who moved it here from their old house on Summer Street.

23

24 In 1805 Charles Bulfinch designed two houses at 87–89 Mount Vernon St. The one to the right was supposed to be Bulfinch's own, but financial reversals forced him to sell it before it was completed. The leftmost one, damaged in a fire, has been replaced by a 20th-century residence.

24

25 Long the epitome of Beacon Hill elegance, Louisburg Square was laid out in 1826 by S. P. Fuller, its concept copied from Bulfinch's Tontine Crescent on Franklin Street. In 1844 the abutting homeowners agreed to share responsibility for maintenance of the street and garden; six years later, resident Joseph Iasigi donated the Italian marble statues of Christopher Columbus and Aristides the Just as "embellishments." One advantage of living on a private street: each house comes with deeded parking spaces, a rarity on Beacon Hill.

25

26 Turn left down Willow Street to reach cobblestoned Acorn Street (1823), reputedly the most-photographed street in Boston. Coachmen's houses were originally on the left, stables on the right. At the bottom of Acorn Street turn right on West Cedar Street, then left to rejoin Mount Vernon Street.

26

27 At the corner of Charles and Mount Vernon Streets, the Charles Street Meeting House (1807) was built on the riverbank for the Third Baptist Church; in 1876 it was sold to an African Methodist

Episcopal congregation whose black members resided on Beacon Hill's northern slope. Since 1939 it's been an Albanian Orthodox church, a Universalist house of worship and now stores and offices.

28 On the left is "Sunflower Castle," as Oliver Wendell Holmes called it, an early example (circa 1870) of Queen Anne architecture, perhaps the work of artist Frank Hill Smith, who resided here.

29 For a behind-the-scenes view of Beacon Hill, turn right and stroll up the lane beside the old firehouse. Within one block, the alleyway changes its name from River Street to River Street Place to Mount Vernon Square and finally to Public Alley No. 301. At the end of the alley make a right and follow Pinckney Street back to Louisburg Square.

30 Behind No. 74 Pinckney is one of Beacon Hill's "hidden houses," a four-story, seven-room residence accessed only by the gated passageway to the left of the green-shuttered window.

31 A "scholar of elegance and taste," George Hillard was Charles Sumner's law partner, as well as an author and political official; his wife Susan was an ardent abolitionist. Years after their deaths, workers renovating their house at 62 Pinckney St. found evidence that it had been a station on the Underground Railroad.

32 Erected in 1824 as English High School, this building became the Phillips School in 1844. For the next decade it was the focus of the city's fight over school segregation and became Boston's first racially integrated public school in 1855. It's now condos.

33 A "high-grade sailors' boarding place" when it was constructed in the early 1800s, the house at the east corner of Pinckney and Anderson streets was still a rooming house until the early 1980s, when it too was converted to condos.

34 The "house of odd windows" at 24 Pinckney St. was originally the stable (1802) for Jonathan Mason's house on the other side of the block (19). In 1884 architect William Ralph Emerson (a cousin of Ralph Waldo Emerson) remodeled it as his own home. Two doors down, No. 20 Pinckney was one of many homes rented briefly by Bronson Alcott and his family, including daughter Louisa May Alcott.

35 The oldest house on Beacon Hill is the wooden residence at 5–7 Pinckney St., erected before 1795 for two African-American bachelors, George Middleton and Louis Glapion. Middleton, a black "horsebreaker" or jockey, had commanded an all-black unit known as the "Bucks of America" in the Revolution; Glapion, a French mulatto, was a hairdresser and barber.

36 Look east on Mount Vernon Street to see the yellow-brick "extension" of the State House, added in 1898. The original summit of Beacon Hill was near where that extension now stands, and 60 feet higher than present ground level.

Follow Joy Street downhill to return to Boston Common and Park Street subway station.

32

33

34

35

36

THE BACK BAY

1 Public Garden
2 Duckling Sculpture
3 Swan Boats
4 George Washington Statue
5 Arlington Street Church
6 Commonwealth Avenue Mall
7 Alexander Hamilton Statue
8 20-36 Commonwealth Ave.
9 Lothrop Home
10 Haddon Hall
11 First Lutheran Church
12 First and Second Church
13 Mill Dam
14 Gibson House Museum
15 Isabella Stewart Home
16 180 Beacon Street
17 First Baptist Church
18 Trinity Church Rectory
19 Newbury Street
20 Hotel Vendome
21 Hotel Vendome Fire Monument
22 Ames Home
23 Victorian Homes (1878-1883)
24 First Spiritualist Temple
25 Boylston Street
26 Boston Marathon Finish Line
27 Old South Church
28 Boston Public Library
29 Library Courtyard
30 Copley Square
31 Museum of Fine Arts
32 Trinity Church
33 John Hancock Tower
34 Tortoise and Hare Sculpture

 ■ Exisiting Building or Reconstruction ■ Building No Longer Exists

Charlesbank Playground
Massachusetts General Hospital
Broad Canal St
Wadsworth St
Longfellow Bridge
Memorial Dr
N Grove St
N Anderson St
Charles/MGH
Phillips St
Garden St
Revere St
Grove St
Myrtle St
W Cedar St
Pinckney St
Charles River
David G Mugar Way
Beacon Hill
Charles St
Lime St
Chestnut St
River St
The Esplanade
Beaver Pl
Beacon St
Boston Common
Public Garden
Arlington St
Berkeley St
Storrow Dr
Back St
Beacon St
Dartmouth St
Clarendon Street Play Lot
Commonwealth Ave
Fairfield St
Marlborough St
Clarendon St
Boylston St
Arlington
Park Plaza
Commonwealth Ave
Exeter St
St.James Ave
Newbury St
Copley
Stuart St
Columbus Ave
Isabella St
Cortes St
Boston Back Bay Station
Back Bay
Huntington Ave
St Botolph St
SW Corridor Path
Chandler St
Belvidere St
Prudential
Appleton St
Christian Science Center
W Newton St
Dartmouth Square
Tremont St
500 ft
200 m

START:
Corner of Beacon and Charles streets

METRO:
Green Line to Arlington, or Red Line to Charles

END:
Copley Square

METRO:
Green Line at Copley

It came from the swamp. In 1855, the Back Bay was literally a bay, a tidal pool whose natural drainage had been blocked by dams and railroad trestles. It was a fetid repository of raw sewage that sent pestilential exhalations over the city with every western breeze. But a growing and prosperous Boston needed land for expansion. The transformation of this public health hazard into an elegant residential area was a miracle of Victorian technology.

1 The oldest publicly owned botanical garden in the world, the Public Garden dates to 1837; the present plan, with its lagoon and suspension bridge, is from 1861.

2 Nancy Schön's 1987 sculpture tells us that this was the route taken by Mrs. Mallard and her eight ducklings—Jack, Kack, Lack, Mack, Nack, Ouack, Pack and Quack—as they waddled to the lagoon in Robert McCloskey's 1941 children's book *Make Way for Ducklings*.

3 The fleet of pedal-powered swan boats have been plying the waters of the lagoon since they were invented by Robert Paget in 1877, inspired by the opera *Lohengrin*. Paget's descendants still operate the swan boats today.

4 Cross the bridge and walk toward the equestrian statue of George Washington, sculpted by Thomas Ball in 1869. Washington's horse is modeled after Black Prince, ridden by the Prince of Wales on his visit to Boston that year—an American President astride the horse of a future King of England.

Swan Boats, 1883

5 Exit the park and make a left on Arlington Street. After years of political debate, work to fill the Back Bay commenced in 1857. The gridded street plan, laid out by Arthur Gilman, was in sharp contrast to the legendary "cowpaths" elsewhere in central Boston. And unlike the city's earlier neighborhoods, all houses had to be set back 20 feet from the sidewalk.

Even before residential construction began, Boston's churches were eager to move to the Back Bay; their former locations downtown were no longer convenient for parishioners. The first building erected in the Back Bay was Arlington Street Church (1858), at the corner of Boylston Street, designed by the same Arthur Gilman who'd laid out the neighborhood's streets. The sanctuary is noted for its Tiffany stained-glass windows, installed starting in 1898.

6 Before shopping center developers stole the word, a *mall* was a formal, tree-lined walkway, a fashionable promenade. Commonwealth Avenue, the broad boulevard at the center of Gilman's plan for the Back Bay, features such a mall, 100 feet

wide. The street name honors the state government, the Commonwealth of Massachusetts, which sponsored the project to fill the Back Bay. The neighborhood's cross streets are named alphabetically: Arlington, Berkeley, Clarendon, Dartmouth, Exeter, Fairfield, Gloucester and Hereford.

7 Each block of the Commonwealth Avenue Mall is ornamented with a sculpture. Setting the precedent was this granite statue of Alexander Hamilton, installed in the initial block in 1865.

8 Many Back Bay houses were designed in the newly fashionable French Mansard style, such as the impressive grouping of nine rowhouses on your left at numbers 20–36 Commonwealth Avenue, designed by Gridley J. F. Bryant and Arthur Gilman in 1861.

9 Exactly one Back Bay house has a side yard: Thornton Lothrop's 1861 residence at 27 Commonwealth Avenue. Purchase of a second lot to use solely as open space was an extremely expensive proposition.

10 Looking a bit out of place is Haddon Hall, a 10-story, 10-unit luxury apartment tower erected at the corner of Berkeley Street and Commonwealth Avenue in 1894. Its 125-foot height spurred efforts, which were partly successful, to enact height restrictions in the residential section of the Back Bay.

11 Turn right on Berkeley Street to discover one of the Back Bay's more successful attempts at modern architecture: Pietro Belluschi's First Lutheran Church (1959), at the corner of Marlborough Street.

12 Across the street is another church to make the exodus from downtown to the Back Bay: the First Church in Boston, built at the corner of Berkeley and Marlborough streets in 1868. Following a 1968 fire, the church tower and one wall were salvaged and grafted onto a modern sanctuary in the Brutalist style, by architect Paul Rudolph. After a merger, the congregation is now called First and Second Church.

First Church, 1920

13 Continue walking towards Beacon Street, which marks the 1821 site of the Mill Dam. The 1½-mile-long dam was intended to harness tidal power, but the projected mills were unsuccessful. Instead, the dam restricted the cleansing flow of water in and out of the Back Bay, turning it into a reeking basin of filth—leading to the bay's filling four decades later.

14 Make a right on Beacon Street to visit the Gibson House Museum (137 Beacon Street), a window into Back Bay townhouse life in Victorian days. Three generations of Gibsons rarely threw anything out and preserved their house as it was in the 19th century. It's been a museum since 1957.

15 Walk back past Berkeley Street and continue up Beacon Street. The home of John L. Gardner, Jr., and his wife Isabella Stewart Gardner once stood on 152 Beacon St.—but there's nothing numbered 152 on the street today. The Gardners had number 152 built for them shortly after their marriage in 1860; 20 years later, they purchased the adjacent house at 150 Beacon and connected it to their original house as their music room and art gallery. When Mrs. Gardner built her museum in the Fenway, she sold the Beacon Street residence, specifying that the new owners had to tear it down—and that they couldn't even reuse her house number. The present

double-wide home, numbered 150 Beacon Street, was built in 1904. It was later home of Alvan T. Fuller, a governor of Massachusetts and a well-known car dealer.

16 Victorian architecture wasn't appreciated in 1965, when the apartment tower at 180 Beacon Street was erected. Not long afterwards, the residential section of the Back Bay was declared a historic district, precluding future high-rises.

17 Make a left on Clarendon Street and continue past Commonwealth Avenue. The "church of the holy bean blowers" (dedicated in 1873) got its nickname from the carved angels on its tower, whose trumpets resemble peashooters aimed down at passersby. The angels and the friezes between them portraying the sacraments were sculpted by French artist Frédéric Bartholdi a few years before he created the Statue of Liberty. Originally built for a Unitarian parish, the church was one of architect H. H. Richardson's earliest designs. But the costs of the new building proved too great for the struggling congregation, which went bankrupt and "became extinct" just three years later. The edifice was then bought by the First Baptist Church.

Trinity Church, 1920

18 At the corner of Clarendon and Newbury streets is the rectory for Trinity Church, also designed by Richardson. From its doorstep you can also see Trinity Church itself—the only place in the world where you can see three of Richardson's buildings from the same spot.

19 Initially a residential thoroughfare, Newbury Street has evolved into Boston's leading shopping stroll. Enjoy the avenue for a block before turning right on Dartmouth.

20 "One of the most palatial and most elaborately furnished hotels in the world," the Hotel Vendome hosted Mark Twain, P. T. Barnum, Oscar Wilde and Sarah Bernhardt over the years. Erected in two stages in 1871 and 1881, it was in the latest French style and bore the name of the elegant Parisian square. It was also Boston's first public building with electric lights. With its hotel days over, a condominium conversion was underway when a disastrous fire broke out on June 17, 1972. Nine firefighters died when part of the building collapsed on a ladder truck.

Hotel Vendome

21 In the Commonwealth Avenue Mall (to your right off of Dartmouth Street) is a moving memorial to the men who were killed in the Hotel Vendome fire, created by sculptor Ted Clausen in 1997.

22 Turn left up the mall, and look to your right to see the Back Bay's grandest single-family house— that of Frederick L. Ames, an 1882 enlargement of an 1872 residence. To make a proper entrance, arriving guests would alight from their carriages under the porte-cochère, take the elevator up to the second floor, then descend the oak-paneled staircase into the mural-lined great ballroom, 36 feet long by 18 feet wide by 18 feet high. Ames was a scion of the family that owned the Ames Shovel Works in Easton, Mass., which at one time made 60 percent of the world's shovels.

23 Because the Back Bay was filled in from east to west, it's a chronological history of Victorian architectural tastes. Each block represents approximately five years. In the Dartmouth–Exeter block, for example, are mostly houses erected between 1878 and 1883, with a few later apartment buildings. This block of the Mall is

24

25

26

27

Old South Meeting House, 1874

also adorned by an 1885 statue of William Lloyd Garrison, abolitionist publisher of the newspaper *The Liberator*.

24 At Exeter Street turn left. The First Spiritualist Temple (1885) was an independent Christian Spiritualist Church for those who believed in communications with the dead. In 1914 its interior was modified so that it could double as a movie theater: films were shown six days a week, but the sanctuary was reserved for church services on Sundays. The Spiritualists moved to Brookline in 1975, although the movies remained for some years after that.

25 Boylston Street is the main commercial street of the Back Bay. Directly in front of you is the new wing of the Boston Public Library, designed in 1971 by Philip Johnson. Turn left onto Boylston Street.

26 Boylston Street also represents the last 3½ blocks of the Boston Marathon, run every year on Patriots Day (now the third Monday in April). The finish line is in front of a dental clinic at 665 Boylston St.; the starting line is in Hopkinton, 26 miles and 385 yards west. In 2011 Geoffrey Mutai of Kenya won the men's Boston Marathon with a time of 2:03:02, the fastest marathon ever run. But Mutai's time isn't considered a world record, since the course doesn't meet technical requirements of international athletic federations.

27 Old South Church (1875), also called "New Old South," was built for the congregation that moved here from the Old South Meeting House on Washington Street. Its high Victorian design is modeled on north Italian Gothic, with walls of Roxbury puddingstone, quarried from a site near

today's Brigham Circle. The sanctuary, with its polychromed walls, is open most days for visitation and prayer.

28

28 Turn right on Darthmouth Street. Boston Public Library is America's second-largest municipal library, and the world's first public library to allow patrons to borrow books without paying a fee (1854). Their present building (1898) was the work of architects McKim, Mead & White; both Charles Follen McKim and Stanford White had been protégés of H. H. Richardson, working as draftsmen on the plans for Trinity Church. The library's interior is noted for its murals and sculpture.

29

29 Enter the library. In the courtyard is a casting of Frederick MacMonnies' bronze *Bacchante*. The original sculpture, an 1896 gift from architect McKim, was rejected by the library trustees—banned in Boston because the dancing mother, naked and holding a bunch of grapes, was seen as a corrupting influence on her child. A duplicate was finally installed here a century later.

30

30 Across from the library, Copley Square is named for John Singleton Copley, whose 2002 statue faces Boylston Street. In deference to the adjacent Museum of Fine Arts, the square was initially known simply as "Art Square" or "Museum Square." In 1883 it was officially named after the Colonial era portrait painter.

31

31 The first public building erected in the square was the Museum of Fine Arts, which opened in 1869. When a 10-story apartment building was erected across the street (on the site of today's Hancock Tower) in 1898, the museum's trustees worried about the dangers of fire and decided to move their

Museum of Fine Arts, 1875

Copley Square, 1941

treasures to Huntington Avenue in 1909. The old museum was then demolished to make way for the Copley Plaza Hotel (1912), erected by the investors responsible for the Plaza Hotel in New York City.

32 The congregation of Trinity Church had already purchased land here for their new building when their building on Summer Street was consumed by the Great Boston Fire of 1872. Dedicated in 1877, the church is open daily for tours.

33 When the 60-story John Hancock Tower was under construction in 1973, some 3,000 of its windowpanes cracked, broke or fell to the ground; for a year, one side of the tower was mostly covered with plywood. Eventually all 10,344 of the skyscraper's "lites" had to be replaced due to the defective design of their metal frames. Designed by architect I. M. Pei, who studied at M.I.T., it's the tallest building in New England. The older John Hancock Building, at the southeast corner of St. James Avenue and Clarendon Street, was the site of the Coliseum for the first Peace Jubilee in 1869.

Exterior view of coliseum for the Grand National Peace Jubilee, 1869

34 We began this walk with a beloved sculpture by Nancy Schön, and we shall end with one. Next to the fountain in Copley Square are a bronze tortoise and hare (1996), a double allusion to Æsop's fable and to the annual running of the Boston Marathon.

Then & Now

Boston Public Library, 1923

Library Courtyard, 1923

FENWAY

1 Mass. Ave. and Columbus Ave.
2 Wally's Café
3 Western Lunch Box
4 Savoy Cafe
5 King Apartment
6 New Haven Railroad Tracks
7 View Towards Downtown
8 First King Apartment
9 Boston Arena
10 Cotting School
11 New England Conservatory of Music
12 NEC Huntington Avenue Steps
13 Mass. Ave. Underpass
14 Symphony Hall
15 Horticultural Hall
16 Christian Science Center
17 Mother Church
18 Sunday School Building
19 Administration Building
20 Prudential Center
21 Christian Science Monitor and Mapparium
22 Sharaf's Cafeteria
23 Berklee College of Music

Above: View of the city along the railroad tracks, from present-day Mass. Ave., 1848

 ■ Exisiting Building or Reconstruction ■ Building No Longer Exists

Newbury St
90
90
Massachusetts Turnpike
Hynes Convention Center
Boylston St
Berklee College of Music
Scotia St
23
Hemenway St
Edgerly Road Playground
Belvidere St
Dalton St
St Germain St
Edgerly Rd
22
Norway St
Clearway St
21
Symphony Community Park
Massachusetts Ave
Burbank St
Christian Science Center
17
16
20
Prudential
19
W Newton St
Durham St
Cumberland St
18
Westland Ave
Huntington Ave
15
St Botolph St
14
Symphony
Symphony Rd
8
Albemarle St
SW Corridor Path
13
St Stephen St
10
St Botolph St
7
Wellington St
Massachusetts Avenue
6
5
4
9
Massachusetts Ave
3
Huntington Ave
12
11
Gainsborough St
2
1
Columbus Ave
Northeastern
Saranac/New Castle Garden
28
Northampton St
Northeastern University
Carter Playground
Camden St
250 ft
100 m

START:
Corner of Massachusetts and Columbus Avenues

METRO:
Orange Line to Massachusetts Avenue

END:
Corner of Massachusetts Avenue and Boylston Street

METRO:
Green Line at Hynes

Columbus Ave. Anniversary of Battle of Bunker Hill, 1875

The last part of central Boston to be developed, Huntington Avenue became home to large-scale educational and cultural institutions, giving it a far different feeling from the rest of the city. Across the railroad tracks, the junction of Mass. and Columbus Avenues was for many years the symbolic heart of Boston's African-American community. Combine the two, and you have a unique section of the city that few people ever examine in detail.

1 "You could stand at Mass. Ave. and Columbus in those days and see five clubs in either direction," reminisced Charles Walker, a tenor sax player who performed at many of them. When jazz became popular in the 1930s and '40s, this corner of the South End became Boston's hip place to be, a place where blacks and whites enjoyed the new style of music. Clubs came in all varieties—large, small; dance clubs and music clubs; illegal after-hours places down back alleys that didn't close 'til sunrise. Among the fanciest was the Hi-Hat—officially the "Hi-Hat Barbecue of Boston"—which presented black musicians to wealthier, mostly white audiences. Opened shortly after World War II, it was claimed by fire in 1959. A mural on a first floor wall now honors its memory.

2 The lone survivor of the South End jazz clubs is Wally's Café, established in 1947 by Joseph L. "Wally" Walcott, a Barbadian immigrant who was the first African-American to own a nightclub in New England. It's always featured a combination of student musicians from nearby colleges and seasoned professionals. Originally across the street, Wally's Paradise was forced to relocate here in 1979. Since Wally's death at age 101 in 1998, the club has been run by his daughter and grandchildren.

3 In her 1969 autobiography, Coretta Scott King remembered the Western Lunch Box as a restaurant "where black students attending the various institutions of learning often gathered. It specialized in Southern cooking—we would call it soul food now." Operated by Mrs. Mary C. Jackson, it was on the ground floor of 415–417 Mass. Ave.

4 Another legendary jazz club was the Savoy Cafe, "Boston's Original Home of Jazz," whose building now houses a barber shop at 410 Massachusetts Ave.

5 In January 1952, Martin Luther King, Jr., rented an apartment at 397 Massachusetts Ave. with a friend. He lived here in Apartment 6 for a year and a half, during the time when he met and courted Coretta Scott. (After their marriage the couple moved into a now-demolished apartment building at 396 Northampton Street, just behind this building.)

The Boston Arena, 1920 - 1929 (approximate)

6 For the first two-thirds of the 20th century, the New Haven Railroad's tracks were the unofficial boundary between white Boston (in the Back Bay and Fenway) and black Boston (in the South End and Lower Roxbury). African-Americans first settled along Columbus Avenue in the 1890s, drawn there by the railroad yards—now the site of the Prudential Center—where many black men found employment as Pullman porters. Churches, restaurants, music clubs, and beauty parlors made the neighborhood the center of Boston's black community.

7 The Boston & Providence Rail Road opened in 1835, built on a trestle across the Back Bay. By the turn of the century, the Back Bay had been filled, and the line had become the main rail route between Boston and New York City. When the MBTA's Orange Line was rerouted to share this alignment in 1987, the tracks were put in a tunnel with a park above it. Look east for a fine view of the city skyline.

8 Make a right onto Saint Botolph Street, named after the patron saint of Boston, England, which in turn lent its name to Massachusetts's capital city. Martin Luther King's first residence in Boston, in fall of 1951, was a rooming house at 170 St. Botolph St.

9 Walk the opposite direction on Saint Botolph Street, past Mass. Ave. Erected in 1910, the Boston Arena was the first home of both the Boston Bruins (1924) and the Boston Celtics (1946). Since 1979 it's been owned by Northeastern University, which has renamed it the Matthews Arena.

10 Across the street, The Industrial School for Crippled and Deformed Children—the nation's first private day school for children with physical disabilities—moved to this imposing structure in 1904, and built an addition in 1923. Renamed the Cotting School, it moved to Lexington in 1988. The building is now occupied by the New England Conservatory.

10

11 Continue on Saint Botolph Street and make a right onto Gainsborough Street. Founded in 1867, New England Conservatory of Music was one of the nation's first colleges of music, modeled after Mendelssohn's Conservatorium in Leipzig. Eben Tourjée, the school's founder, was a close friend of Eben Jordan, owner of the Jordan Marsh department store, and Jordan became one of the school's early financial backers. When the Conservatory needed to expand three decades later, Jordan's son, Eben Jordan, Jr.—who was also a music lover—purchased land here on Huntington Avenue for its new campus, which was dedicated in 1903. In gratitude, the school's main concert hall is named Jordan Hall. Like Horticultural Hall, it was designed by Wheelwright and Haven.

11

12 Turn left on Huntington Avenue. Following some matchmaking by a mutual acquaintance, and after a lengthy phone conversation in which they explored their shared interests, Coretta Scott agreed to meet Martin Luther King for a lunch date on a February day in 1952. Since she was a voice student at the New England Conservatory, Coretta said that she'd wait for Martin on the Conservatory's Huntington Avenue steps; he told her to watch for his green Chevrolet, which he drove here from his classes at Boston University.

12

Symphony Hall, 1916

Mother Church, 1906

13 Turn around and walk east on Huntington. Laid out when the Back Bay was being filled, the avenue was named for Ralph Huntington, a large stockholder in the Boston Water Power Company, and an early benefactor of M.I.T. The underpass under Massachusetts Avenue was a 1940 WPA project, which included an extension of the Green Line subway.

14 Turn left on Mass. Avenue. Symphony Hall (1900) is home to the Boston Symphony Orchestra and the Boston Pops, who are essentially the same musicians but playing different kinds of music at different times of the year. One of the world's premier concert venues for classical music, it's known for its perfect acoustics. The architects were McKim, Mead and White, who also designed the Boston Public Library in Copley Square; Harvard physicist Wallace Sabine consulted on the acoustics.

15 In size, materials and its neoclassic design, Horticultural Hall (1901) is a near twin to Symphony Hall across the street. That's not surprising because its architect, Edward M. Wheelwright, had previously worked for the McKim firm. Originally home to the Massachusetts Horticultural Society, the building's interior features a large, unadorned hall once used for the Society's annual flower show.

16 Surrounding Horticultural Hall is a large, open complex of buildings erected for the Church of Christ, Scientist. Founded by Mary Baker Eddy in 1879, the church is based on the healing powers of Christ, or, as Mrs. Eddy put it, a desire to "reinstate primitive Christianity and its lost element of healing." World headquarters of the religion are here at the Mother Church, which has two

connected buildings. In front of you is the domed Extension of 1906; behind that is the Original Edifice, a Romanesque structure of gray New Hampshire granite, erected in 1894.

17 Prior to 1974, the Mother Church building wasn't visible from Massachusetts Avenue. A row of apartment buildings and a city street were removed to create the landscaped plaza that you see today, and the modern portico with colossal Corinthian columns was added to the church's Extension, as part of architect I. M. Pei's master plan for the Christian Science Center.

Mary Baker Eddy

Sunday School Building, 1975

18 Walk behind Horticultural Hall to get a full view of the Christian Science Center, Boston's only successful example of modern urban planning on a monumental scale. To your right is the quarter-round Sunday School Building. Architect Pei chose white concrete for the Center's new buildings, to match the limestone of the Mother Church.

19 Ahead, the 1½-acre reflecting pool forms a frontispiece for two other buildings of the Christian Science Center—the long, low Colonnade Building at left, and the tall Administration Building at the far right corner. (As this book was going to press, church officials were planning to alter the reflecting pool, a proposal that's aroused much opposition from city residents.)

20 In the background are the high-rise buildings of the Prudential Center, begun in the early 1960s and still expanding nearly 50 years later.

21 After being a target of attacks from Joseph Pulitzer's *New York World*, Mary Baker Eddy started the *Christian Science Monitor* newspaper in 1908, its stated goal "to injure no man, but to bless all mankind." The Publishing House building was erected in 1934 as the *Monitor*'s office; inside it is the Mapparium, a stained glass globe of the earth, 30 feet in diameter, that one can walk through. (Enter through the garden, facing Massachusetts Avenue.)

Christian Science Center, 1975

22 Across the street, the green-awninged "Carillon" apartment building marks the site once occupied by a branch of Sharaf's, a local cafeteria chain at the middle of the 20th century. Their store at 187 Massachusetts Ave. was where Martin Luther King and Coretta Scott went on their first date, discussing politics over lunch.

23 Of Greater Boston's more than 35 colleges and universities, Berklee College stands alone as the world's only higher learning institution devoted entirely to popular music. Founded in 1945 as Schillinger House, it was later renamed for the school's founder, Lawrence Berk, and his son Lee. Originally focusing on jazz, the school now teaches all forms of contemporary popular music, emphasizing not only the music itself but also the skills needed to develop a musical career. Continuing a decades-long tradition, many Berklee students still sit in on the nightly sessions at Wally's Café just down the street.

THE CHARLES RIVER ESPLANADE

1. Massachusetts Avenue
2. Fenway Park
3. Ames House
4. Hotel Marlborough
5. Church Court
6. Back Street
7. Storrow Memorial Drive
8. Harvard Bridge
9. Smoots
10. Citgo Sign
11. Boston University
12. M.I.T.
13. Boston Skyline
14. Esplanade
15. Embankment
16. Great Dome
17. Storrow Memorial
18. Green Building
19. Embankment Island
20. Riverbank
21. Lagoon
22. Stone Home
23. Longfellow Bridge
24. Fiedler Sculpture
25. Ducklings Islands
26. Hatch Memorial Shell
27. Cannon
28. Commissioners Landing
29. Community Boating
30. Embankment Road
31. West Hill Place
32. Fields Garden
33. View of Back Bay Skyline

 ■ Exisiting Building or Reconstruction ■ Building No Longer Exists

Museum of Science
Bent St
Charles St
Rogers St
Bent St
Binney St
Hampshire St
Binney St
Broadway
3rd St
2nd St
1st St
Munroe St
5th St
Linskey St
Edwin H Land Blvd
Cambridge Parkway
Galileo Galilei Way
Kendall St
Broad Canal St
Kendall/MIT
Charlesbank Playground
Main St
Vassar St
Hayward St
Wadsworth St
Carleton St
Ames St
Longfellow Bridge
Massachusetts Institute of Technology
Amherst St
Memorial Dr
McDermott Court
Memorial Dr
Killian Court
Charles/MGH
David G Mugar Way
Lime St
River St
Charles St
Chestnut St
Beaver Pl
Charles River Basin
Gibson House Museum
Back St
Clarendon St
Arlington St
Storrow Dr
Exeter St
Marlborough St
First Church in Boston
Fairfield St
Gloucester St
Arlington Street Church
Beacon St
Commonwealth Ave
Arlington
Dartmouth St
Charlesgate W
Charlesgate E
Massachusetts Ave
Hereford St
Commonwealth Ave
Old South Church
St James Ave
Boylston St
Copley
Newbury St
Stuart St
Hynes Convention Center
Massachusetts Turnpike
Boston Back Bay Station
Berklee College of Music
Dalton St
Prudential Center
Back Bay
Belvidere St
Chandler St
Back Bay Fens
Prudential
Appleton St
Clearway St
SW Corridor Path
Hemenway St
Edgerly Rd
Norway St
Columbus Ave
Fenway
Burbank St
Christian Science Center
Huntington Ave
W Newton St
Hayes Park
Westland Ave
Titus Sparrow Park
Tremont St
Agassiz Rd
Symphony Rd
Symphony
500 ft
200 m

START:
Entrance to Hynes subway station, Massachusetts Avenue near Newbury Street

METRO:
Green Line to Hynes

END:
Charles Circle

METRO:
Red Line at Charles/MGH

1

2

Think of the Esplanade as Boston's family room—beloved by locals, yet undiscovered by visitors unless they're here for the big party on the Fourth of July. Come on a sunny summer weekend and the place will be mobbed with sunbathers, skaters, joggers and bikers, but at other times it may be almost deserted. Stroll along the river and discover Boston's sapphire jewel.

1 Massachusetts Avenue in the Back Bay was originally called West Chester Park, an extension of a street in the South End. In 1894, after the Harvard Bridge was opened, some 15 miles of streets in four municipalities were renamed, creating a continuous thoroughfare from Dorchester to Lexington.

2 At the corner of Newbury Street, look left (west) to see the light towers and scoreboard of Fenway Park.

3 The house at the northeast corner of Commonwealth Avenue was built in 1882 for Oliver

Ames, later to be the Governor of Massachusetts (1887–1890). His cousin, Frederick Ames, lived in an equally opulent mansion just five blocks away at the corner of Comm. Ave. and Dartmouth Street (see the Back Bay tour).

4 At the end of the 1890s, demand for luxury apartment buildings in the Back Bay was outpacing the desire to build single-family townhouses. Real estate investor Washington B. Thomas and architect Willard T. Sears joined to erect the eight-story Hotel Marlborough at the corner of Mass. Ave. and Marlborough Street in 1895, then followed with the 10-story Hotel Cambridge at the corner of Mass. and Beacon three years later.

5 After a 1978 fire destroyed the Mount Vernon Congregational Church (1891), architect Graham Gund salvaged two walls and grafted the new Church Court condo complex onto them. The old bell tower is now one residence, seven rooms on seven floors. There's no elevator, but a pulley and basket system is used to haul up packages.

6 The alley behind the Beacon Street houses is called, appropriately, Back Street. Just beyond it, look down to your right to see a glimpse of the granite retaining wall erected when the Back Bay was first being filled, in the 1860s. Since the Charles River was tidal, the wall had to be high; later landfill projects, for the park and the highway, are at a lower grade.

7 Next to that retaining wall is James J. Storrow Memorial Drive, the highway that Helen Storrow never wanted when she donated money to build a park in honor of her late husband. The road opened in 1951 and was widened in 1955.

8 The bridge crossing the river next to the M.I.T. campus is called the Harvard Bridge; engineering students at the Institute sometimes joke that the span was named after their rival school because it was so poorly designed. In fact, it was built almost two decades before M.I.T. even thought of locating near it. Opened in 1891, it's been completely rebuilt several times, while keeping its original appearance.

9 Painted numbers on the bridge sidewalk mark the distances in *smoots*, a unit unique to this location. One night in October 1958, the pledge class at M.I.T.'s Lambda Chi Alpha fraternity was ordered, as part of their pledge rituals, to measure the bridge in terms of their shortest classmate—one Oliver R. Smoot, Jr., all of 5′ 7″ high. At first, Smoot lay down, got up, and lay down again, while his fellow freshmen chalked off the measurements. But an upperclass student, supervising the job, told the pledges to carry Smoot from one marking to the next. The prank has since been enshrined as a legend, and each new class of LCA pledges must repaint the markings twice a year. The bridge is 364.4 smoots long, ± 1 ear.

10 Walk out to about the 50-smoot mark and look upstream (left, or west) for a view of Boston's famed Citgo sign. As late as the 1970s, the river waters shimmered every evening with reflections of a dozen neon signs advertising oil companies, food, appliances and more. Now only the Citgo billboard survives alongside the main river basin. It was erected atop a Kenmore Square building in 1965, replacing a sign promoting Cities Service, the petroleum company's earlier name.

11 Also to your left, on the Boston side, twin pointed towers mark the campus of Boston University;

the tower to your right is the School of Theology where Martin Luther King studied for his Doctor of Divinity degree. The many tall buildings next to these spires are also part of the B.U. campus.

12 At the far end of the bridge is the Massachusetts Institute of Technology. Tech's original Cambridge campus was east of Massachusetts Avenue; the land west of the avenue was purchased later and is used mostly for student dormitories and athletic facilities.

13 To the east is the Boston skyline. Atop Beacon Hill, the golden dome of the State House glistens, with downtown skyscrapers as a backdrop; to the far right, towers of the Back Bay punctuate the horizon. On a nice day, a bevy of sailboats will usually be navigating the river basin.

Proposed Park, 1875

14 Return to the Boston shore and take the pedestrian ramp next to Storrow Drive, leading down to the park below; then turn east (toward Boston) along the Esplanade.

15 Before the river was dammed, its tidal variations—about 10 feet up and down, twice each day—made landscaping at the water's edge impractical. The first attempt at a riverbank park was the Embankment, just a hundred feet wide, parallel to Back Street. It was completed in 1910 as part of the dam project. Visionary and chief advocate for the dam, and for the park, had been James Jackson Storrow, a prominent banker and philanthropist.

16 As you walk, look across the river to see the original buildings of M.I.T.'s Cambridge campus (1916), including the Great Dome.

17 In 1929, Helen Osborne Storrow donated a million dollars to widen the Embankment, in tribute to her late husband, James. At Gloucester Street a stone overlook and boat landing were erected; a large bronze medallion, set in the ground, honors the Storrows.

18 Directly opposite the Storrow memorial is the tallest building at M.I.T.: the Green Building, or Earth Sciences Building, with weather radar domes at its top. It was designed by I. M. Pei in 1966.

19 Cross the footbridge onto the island. The 1929 plan for the Storrow Memorial Embankment included one small island, surrounding an oval lagoon, centered on the block between Exeter and Fairfield Streets.

20 The 1910 Embankment had a granite seawall that reflected waves, making the water surface choppy for boaters. The expanded Storrow Embankment has a sloping gravel riverbank that absorbs the waves instead of bouncing them back. With the dam, the river level rarely varies more than a foot, allowing landscaping to extend to the water's edge.

21 To make up for parkland destroyed when Storrow Drive was built in the 1950s, state planners extended the island 2,000 feet to the east, from Exeter Street to the Hatch Shell. A network of small lagoons sets the islands apart from highway traffic; the lagoons are a popular place for the launching of radio-controlled model boats.

22 Look to your right, toward the Back Bay neighborhood. In February 1909, Charles A. Stone, an M.I.T. alumnus and cofounder of the Stone & Webster engineering firm, invited incoming M.I.T. president Richard Cockburn Maclaurin to dinner at his Beacon Street home. Looking across the river, Maclaurin spied a vast area of recently filled, but still vacant land on the Cambridge shore, and realized that it would be the perfect location for the institute's new campus. Within two years the school had purchased 50 acres on the Cambridge side of the river.

23 Upstream you can see the arched Longfellow Bridge (1907), with Red Line trains rumbling over it. The first fixed span erected across the Charles—without a draw to allow passage for ships—this bridge required special permission from the U. S. Army, which had a large arsenal in Watertown. Twenty years after its opening, it was renamed after the poet, in honor of his poem "The Bridge." When Longfellow was courting his fiancée, Fanny

Longfellow Bridge, 1931 (approximate)

The Shell, 1940

Appleton, he made many late-night crossings of the older bridge on this site, walking home to Cambridge after visiting his future bride's house on Beacon Hill.

24 Arthur Fiedler, the beloved conductor of the Boston Pops, and initiator of the Esplanade Concerts, is memorialized in Ralph Helmick's 1984 sculpture. As sculpted here, Fiedler's giant disembodied head adds emphasis to his already prominent brow, receding hairline and enormous moustache.

25 Two small, crescent-shaped islands, with no pedestrian access, are nicknamed the "Ducklings Islands" because they are where Mrs. Mallard hatched her brood in Robert McCloskey's story *Make Way for Ducklings*. The islands provide shelter for nearby boat docks.

26 The Hatch Memorial Shell was donated by Maria Hatch in 1940, in honor of her brother Edward, replacing a temporary bandstand that had been on this site. Ever since, it's been the home of Boston Pops summer concerts. Designed by Richard Shaw, it's one of Boston's few Art Deco structures.

27 An Army cannon stands beside the Hatch Shell, ready to provide percussion for Tchaikovsky's *1812 Overture* in the Pops' annual Fourth of July extravaganza. Church bells ring from the nearby Church of the Advent, on Brimmer Street.

28 Commissioners Landing offers a formal connection between the river and the shore, and a dock for private boats.

29 The first public community sailing program in America began here in 1937, with seven boats. Today Community Boating still offers inexpensive sailing for all, serving over 6,000 people a year with a fleet of 120 sailboats.

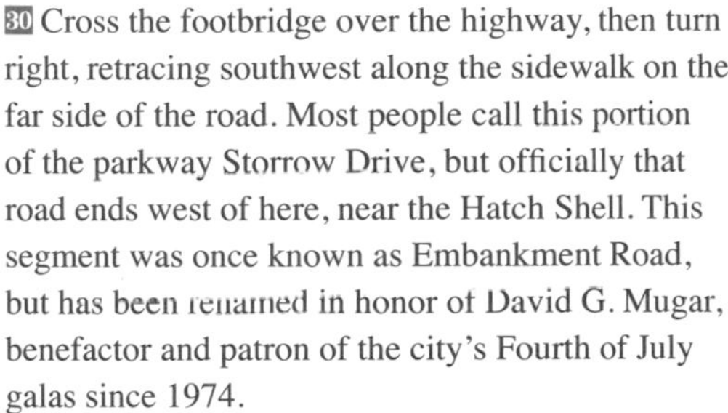

30 Cross the footbridge over the highway, then turn right, retracing southwest along the sidewalk on the far side of the road. Most people call this portion of the parkway Storrow Drive, but officially that road ends west of here, near the Hatch Shell. This segment was once known as Embankment Road, but has been renamed in honor of David G. Mugar, benefactor and patron of the city's Fourth of July galas since 1974.

31 Turn left on West Hill Place, laid out in 1916 on land formerly occupied by a giant gas tank accessed by docks from the river. The grouping of rowhouses is reminiscent of London, and of Boston's early garden squares. Walk into the cul-de-sac, then through the archway at its end, and out to Charles Street.

32 As you pass through the archway, look to your right for a glimpse of Boston's literary history. Hidden here is the garden of Annie Adams Fields, wife of publisher James T. Fields and a writer in her own right, known for the intellectual salons that she hosted in their Charles Street home. Following Annie's passing, the house was demolished; miraculously, her garden endures.

33 For an even more spectacular view of the river and the Back Bay skyline, take a walk across the Longfellow Bridge, or hop aboard a Red Line train and take a ride to Cambridge.

HARVARD SQUARE AND ENVIRONS

1 Newsstand
2 Click and Clack Office
3 Wadsworth House
4 Eaton House
5 Porcellian Club
6 Harvard Yard Fence
7 Harvard Yard
8 Harvard Statue
9 Massachusetts Hall
10 Harvard Hall
11 Hollis Hall
12 Widener Library
13 Sever Hall
14 Tercentenary Theatre
15 Memorial Church
16 Memorial Hall
17 Tanner Fountain
18 Science Center
19 Pooh's House
20 Austin Hall
21 Cambridge Common
22 First Church, Congregational
23 Washington Elm
24 Radcliffe College
25 Christ Church
26 Old Burying Ground
27 First Parish, Unitarian
28 Harvard Square Theatre
29 Club Passim
30 Brattle House
31 Brattle Hall

Conant Hall
Harvard Museum of Natural History
Semitic Museum
Longy School of Music
Follen St
Massachusetts Ave
Concord Ave
Waterhouse St
2A
Harvard Law School
Harvard University
Oxford St
Cambridge Common
20
21
22
23
Mason St
Harvard University Science Center
19
18
17
Sanders Theatre
16
24
Radcliffe Yard
Garden St
Appian Way
Cambridge St
Broadway
25
26
11
American Repertory Theater
Farwell Pl
Old Burying Ground
10
Harvard Yard
15
27
Brattle St
Church St
9
8
14
13
Sever Quadrangle
28
29
Palmer St
7
Story St
Harvard Coop
12
Pusey Library
Quincy St
30
Mifflin Pl
1
Widener Library
31
Harvard
3
Brattle St
2
6
4
Mt Auburn St
Massachusetts Ave
5
University Rd
Harvard Book Store
Harvard St
Dunster St
Winthrop St
Linden St
Holyoke St
Bow St
2A
Eliot St
Mount Auburn St
South St
JFK St
Quincy House
John F Kennedy Park
Mill St
N
Memorial Dr
Charles River
250 ft
100 m

START:
Harvard Square

METRO:
Red Line to Harvard

END:
Harvard Square

METRO:
Red Line

Whether you call it the Left Bank of the Charles or the University City, Cambridge has always been the counterpoint to Boston's point. Named after the English college town (where many Puritans attended Cambridge University), it's been an intellectual and cultural center for 375 years. And it was military headquarters for the Continental Army for the first eleven months of the American Revolution.

1 When the subway from Boston opened in 1912, the first station entrance was an oval structure made of stone, in the center of the intersection. After many accidents and near-misses, it was replaced in 1928 by a brick and glass kiosk, whose large windows allowed exiting subway riders to see the approaching autos. With the Red Line extension to Alewife in the 1980s, the old brick kiosk became a newsstand.

2 Look to the left to the corner of Brattle and J. F. Kennedy Streets and the brick office building at the point of the intersection. On a third-floor window are gilt letters, like those on a law office, proclaiming "DEWEY, CHEETHAM & HOWE." It's the office of Click and Clack, the Tappet Brothers (Tom and Ray Magliozzi), hosts of the popular public radio show *Car Talk*.

3

3 Cross behind the newsstand and follow the curving street to the right. The yellow wooden Wadsworth House was built in 1726 as the college president's home. Arriving in Cambridge on July 2, 1775, to assume command of the American Army, George Washington was informed that this house would be his headquarters. Realizing that it would be inadequate for his needs, Washington moved two weeks later to the grander Vassall house on Brattle Street.

4

4 In the street pavement in front of Wadsworth House, look for some L-shaped brass plates in the middle of the traffic lanes. One, labeled EATON, indicates the site of the rented house where Nathaniel Eaton taught (and abused) Harvard's first nine students, until he was fired in 1639. (A second EATON marker is missing.) Two markers labeled GOFFE show the corners of a 1651 dormitory.

5

5 Instead of fraternities, Harvard has secretive "final clubs," where students of the social elite can eat, drink and party—and make connections they will use after graduation. At pledge time, one negative vote is sufficient to blackball a prospective member or "embryo." Highest-ranking on Harvard's social ladder is the Porcellian Club, nicknamed "the Pork" or "the Pig Club." Located anonymously above J. August's Harvard Shirt Shop, the club's name comes from a roast pig (*porcellus* in Latin) served at a memorable dinner in 1794.

Johnston Gate, 1899

John Harvard Statue

McKean Gate

6 The ornamental fence around Harvard Yard was erected beginning in 1890. Opposite the Porcellian Club is the McKean Gate, funded by the club's alumni, and named for the club's founder, Joseph McKean. Atop its arch is a carved boar's head.

7 In the 1630s a row of houses faced the street (now Massachusetts Ave.), with long, skinny cowyards behind them. The yard purchased by the college naturally became known as "Harvard's Yard." The lawn on your left, in front of Grays Hall, was the site of the first building erected by the college, known as the Old College or Harvard Hall. It stood here from 1642 to 1679.

8 Seated in front of University Hall, a bronze "John Harvard" surveys the students who pass by en route to classes and the tourists who gather to gawk at him. Since no one knows what John Harvard really looked like, the artwork is a speculative image, crafted by sculptor Daniel Chester French in 1884.

9 Massachusetts Hall (1720) is the oldest building now standing on the campus. Today it's the office of the University President.

10 Harvard Hall (1766), with its cupola, is the third building of that name. The second Harvard Hall, also on this site, burned on the night of January 24, 1764, destroying the college library, including all but one of the books bequeathed by John Harvard in 1638.

11 Like many of the redbrick buildings in Harvard Yard, Hollis Hall (1764) is now a freshman dormitory. All first-year undergraduates live in the Yard; upperclassmen reside in "houses" (as Harvard's main dormitories are called), a few blocks away.

12 With 16 million volumes, Harvard has the largest university library in the world. About a fifth of its collections are in the Widener Library building (1914), which dominates the New Yard. Harry Elkins Widener, Harvard class of 1907 and the only child of a wealthy Philadelphia family, was an avid book collector. After he died aboard the *Titanic*, his mother donated this new library to his *alma mater*. At its center is a memorial room dedicated to Harry, containing his personal library of 3,300 rare and beautiful books (including a Gutenberg Bible), a portrait of Harry, and a vase of fresh flowers at all times.

13 Sever Hall (1880), with its distinctive arched entrance, is one of two Harvard buildings by the noted architect H. H. Richardson.

HARVARD COOPERATIVE SOCIETY
THE COOP
HARVARD
Coop Café

14 The quadrangle here, known as Tercentenary Theatre, is the site of Harvard's annual graduation ceremonies.

15 Memorial Church (1932) was erected in honor of Harvard students and alumni who died in the first World War. Plaques honoring those who died in later conflicts have since been added. The steps beside the church, facing Widener Library, serve double duty as the speakers' platform for Harvard graduations.

16 Perhaps the finest example of Ruskinian Gothic architecture in America, Memorial Hall (1876) is Harvard's tribute to its Civil War dead. But only the 136 students and alumni who fought and died on the Union side are honored here; efforts to provide a memorial to the Harvard men who died for the Confederate cause have been repeatedly rebuffed. The slate-roofed tower is a modern creation. A half-century ago, Victorian architecture was widely disliked; when a fire destroyed the top of the original tower in 1956, some university officials called for removal of the remainder of Mem Hall. The tower was finally restored 43 years after it had burned.

Then & Now

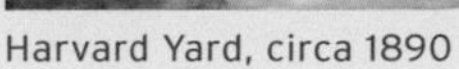

Harvard Yard, circa 1890

17 Obert C. Tanner was a businessman, a university professor and a philanthropist in his home state of Utah. He gave dozens of fountains to schools and communities around the nation, including this one (1984) in front of the Science Center. A basin-less rock fountain, it sprays a cooling mist of water in summer, and low-pressure steam in winter.

18 Harvard's Science Center (1972) was funded in part by Edwin Land, inventor of the Polaroid camera, who attended but never graduated from Harvard. Observers often joke that the Science Center's design, with its stepped terraces, resembles one of Land's old-style cameras with bellows. The building was designed by Josep Lluís Sert, a Spanish émigré who was Dean of Harvard's architecture school, known as the Graduate School of Design.

19 How the Bear of Very Little Brain came to reside at Harvard is unknown, but he's had a house here for decades. Outside the Science Center, look at the base of a nearby tree to see Pooh's House with its tiny door.

20 Austin Hall (1881) is the main building of Harvard Law School, where Barack Obama studied from 1988 to 1991. The edifice is another creation of architect H. H. Richardson. Most of the law school's buildings are behind it.

21 Like Boston Common, Cambridge Common was set aside as a common cow pasture in the 1630s. During the Revolution, it was camp for thousands of Continental Army soldiers. At its center is the city's Civil War Memorial, featuring a statue of Abraham Lincoln and one of an anonymous Union soldier.

22 On the far side of the Common is the "big brown church with the rooster on top," officially the First Church, Congregational (1870). Its golden weathervane (1721) is one of the oldest still in use in New England; it was originally atop the Cockerel Church in Boston's North End, where Paul Revere once worshipped.

23 In the middle of the intersection of Garden and Mason Streets, what appears to be a manhole cover is actually a historical marker, denoting the site of the Washington Elm. A legend once developed that General Washington stood under this tree on July 3, 1775, to review his troops, after assuming command of the army earlier that day. Modern historians have debunked the legend, but elements of it persist. The elm fell over in 1923 as workers were trying to remove yet another dead branch. A cutting, or scion, of the tree now stands nearby in the Common.

24 So that female students could obtain a Harvard education, the Society for the Collegiate Instruction of Women—known informally as Harvard Annex—was founded in 1879. In 1894 the school was named Radcliffe College in honor of Lady Ann Radcliffe, an Englishwoman who'd donated Harvard's first scholarship fund (for men) in 1643. For 60 years, Harvard professors taught separate classes for women here at Radcliffe Yard; then walked back to Harvard to teach the men. During World War II a shortage of male students led to the introduction of coed classes. As of 2011, Harvard counts slightly more women than men among its undergraduate student body.

25 Christ Church (1761) is the oldest church building in Cambridge, designed by Newport (R.I.) architect Peter Harrison. Financed by a London

25

26

27

28

missionary group, it provided a place of worship for Anglican students at Harvard, and for a small group of Anglican families in the town. Virtually all of the congregation members were loyalists who fled Massachusetts during the Revolution. George and Martha Washington worshipped here on December 31, 1775; Theodore Roosevelt, a Harvard student, taught Sunday School here in the late 1870s.

26 The Old Burying Ground (1636) was the only graveyard in Cambridge until 1811. It contains the remains of virtually everyone who died in the town in that era, including seven of the first eight Harvard College presidents, and at least 19 Cambridge residents who fought in the Revolution, including two slaves. Near the corner of Garden Street and Massachusetts Avenue is the old milestone, proclaiming on one side eight miles to Boston (through Allston, Brookline, and Roxbury) in 1734, and on the other side 2 ¼ miles to the "new bridge" (on the present site of the Longfellow Bridge) in 1794.

27 Cambridge has a First Parish, a First Church and an oldest church building; Zero Church Street is the official address of the First Parish (Unitarian). Both the First Parish and the First Church trace their roots to the same congregation, which was organized in 1633. Following a theological split in 1829, the Unitarians erected this new place of worship in 1833.

28 On May 9, 1974, Bruce Springsteen played the Harvard Square Theatre as opening act for Bonnie Raitt; reviewer Jon Landau wrote in Cambridge's *Real Paper* that "I have seen rock 'n' roll's future and its name is Bruce Springsteen." Landau subsequently quit journalism and became

Springsteen's manager, giving a jump-start to Springsteen's career. For most of its history, entrance to the theatre was through a storefront at 1436 Massachusetts Ave.; the mural on the present Church St. façade is by Joshua Winer.

29 Club Passim at 47 Palmer St. is the current incarnation of the legendary Club 47 folk music club, which opened in 1958 at 47 Mount Auburn St. on the other side of the square. At first Club 47 was a jazz coffeehouse, but one night it took a gamble on a 17-year-old folksinger, a college freshman from suburban Belmont named Joan Baez. In 1963 Club 47 moved here to Palmer Street, taking its street number with it. From 1968 to 1995 it was called Passim; the current name is an amalgam of the two earlier appellations.

30 William Brattle built his house in 1727. A loyalist, Brattle fled to Boston, then to Halifax during the Revolution. Like other loyalists' houses in Cambridge, his house served as officers' quarters for the Continental Army. In the early 1830s, it was briefly the home of a young Margaret Fuller, later to be a well-known writer, philosopher and early feminist. Today it's home to the Cambridge Center for Adult Education.

31 Brattle Hall (1889) was built as a theater for live drama, where T. S. Eliot performed in 1912–13 and Paul Robeson played Othello in 1942. In 1953 it was converted to a movie theater with an emphasis on foreign films and art movies. The Brattle Theatre played a major role in the emergence of the Humphrey Bogart-starring *Casablanca* as a cult film.

INDEX

PHOTO CREDITS

4-5 Popular Graphic Arts, Prints & Photographs Division, Library of Congress, LC-DIG-pga-03789

14 Detroit Publishing Company, Prints & Photographs Division, Library of Congress, LC-D4-17103

12 Miscellaneous Items in High Demand, Prints & Photographs Division, Library of Congress LC-USZ62-53343

16 Miscellaneous Items in High Demand, Prints & Photographs Division, Library of Congress LC-USZ62-86631

20 Photograph by Leon Abdalian. Courtesy of Boston Public Library, Print Department, Leon Abdalian Photographs

28 Miscellaneous Items in High Demand, Prints & Photographs Division, Library of Congress LC-USZ62-96218

32 Cartoon Prints, American, Prints & Photographs Division, Library of Congress, LC-USZC4-4600

40 Butterworth, Hezekia, ed. Young Folks History of America. Boston: Estes and Lauriate, 1881

64 Lithograph by J.H. Bufford & Co. Courtesy of Boston Public Library, Print Department, Old Boston Photograph Collection

67 Photo from Keystone View Co., Inc. of N.Y. Courtesy of Boston Public Library, Print Department, Parades, Tercentenary & Misc. Celebrations

79 Print by William Comely Sharp. Courtesy of Boston Public Library, Print Department, Colleges & Universities

88 Courtesy of Boston Public Library, Print Department, North End

90 Courtesy of Boston Public Library, Print Department, Neighborhoods Misc.

92 Photograph by Thomas E. Marr. Courtesy of Boston Public Library, Print Department, North End

93 Courtesy of Boston Public Library, Print Department, North End

94 Detroit Publishing Company, Prints & Photographs Division, Library of Congress, LC-D4-11969

98 Courtesy of Boston Public Library, Print Department, Old Corner Bookstore

100 Courtesy of Boston Public Library, Print Department, Old South Church & Meeting House

102 Lithograph published by Haskell & Allen. Courtesy of Boston Public Library, Print Department, Great Fire of 1872

104 Photograph by D. W. Butterfield. Courtesy of Boston Public Library, Print Department, Great Fire of 1872

106 Etching by W. Harry Smith. Courtesy of Boston Public Library, Print Department, Trinity Church

109 Courtesy of Boston Public Library, Print Department, Great Fire of 1872

110 Courtesy of Boston Public Library, Print Department, Great Fire of 1872

111 Portrait of H. H. Richardson by Sir Hubert von Herkomer (1886). National Portrait Gallery, Smithsonian Institution

114 Miscellaneous Items in High Demand, Prints & Photographs Division, Library of Congress, LC-G9-Z4-116,794-T

116 Courtesy of Boston Public Library, Print Department, Commercial Buildings Misc.

118 Posters: Performing Arts Posters, Prints & Photographs Division, Library of Congress, LC-USZC4-4959

121 Theatrical Poster Collection, Prints & Photographs Division, Library of Congress, LC-USZC4-12307

122 Historic American Buildings Survey/ Historic American Engineering Record/ Historic American Landscapes Survey, Prints & Photographs Divisions, Library of Congress, HABS MASS,13-BOST,69-

123 Courtesy of Boston Public Library, Print Department, Music Halls & Theatres

126 Courtesy of Boston Public Library, Print Department, Railroads & Subways Misc.

128 Wood Engraving by John Andrew. Courtesy of Boston Public Library, Prints Department, Railroads & Subways Misc.

129 Courtesy of Boston Public Library, Print Department, Street Views: Boylston Street

130 Courtesy of Boston Public Library, Print Department, Railroads & Subways Misc.

132 Courtesy of Boston Public Library, Print Department, Parades, Tercentenary & Misc. Celebrations

135 Photograph by Andrew Zalewski. Courtesy of Boston Public Library, Print Department, Commercial Buildings Misc.

142 Photograph by Thomas Lingner, Courtesy of the Isabella Stewart Gardner Museum

144 National Photo Company Collection, Prints & Photographs Division, Library of Congress, LC-DIG-npcc-00317

147 Photograph by Leslie Jones. Courtesy of Boston Public Library, Print Department, Leslie Jones Collection

149 Bain Collection, Prints & Photographs Division, Library of Congress, LC-DIG-ppmsca-18459

152 Photography by Fairchild Aerial Surveys, inc. Courtesy of Boston Public Library, Prints Department, Aerial Photographs

153 Photograph by Luther H. Shattuck. Courtesy of Boston Public Library, Prints Department, Bridges & Tunnels

154 Courtesy of Boston Public Library, Print Department, Statues, Plaques & Monuments

155 Courtesy of Boston Public Library, Print Department, Parks Misc

156 Photograph by Leslie Jones. Courtesy of Boston Public Library, Print Department, Leslie Jones Collection

158 William Barton Rogers Courtesy of MIT Museum

159 Courtesy of Boston Public Library, Print Department, Colleges & Universities

160 Photograph by Michael Bauer

162 Courtesy of Boston Public Library 02337 Huge molasses tank explodes in North End; 11 dead, 50 hurt [Boston Post, January 16, 1919]

164 Photograph by Globe Newspaper Co. Courtesy of Boston Public Library, Print Department, Molasses Disaster, Boston, Mass., 1919

168 Photo by Yoichi R. Okamoto, White House Press Office

170 World Telegram & Sun photo by Herman Hiller. Miscellaneous Items in High Demand, Prints & Photographs Division, Library of Congress, LC-USZ62-116775

172 Highsmith (Carol M.) Archive, Prints & Photographs Division, Library of Congress, LC-DIG-highsm-05751

176 Courtesy of Boston Public Library, Print Department, City Hall

180 Photograph by Robert Knudsen, White House, in the John F. Kennedy Presidential Library and Museum, Boston.

182 Photograph by Richard Sears in the John F. Kennedy Presidential Library and Museum, Boston.

183 Highsmith (Carol M.) Archive, Prints & Photographs Division, Library of Congress, LC-DIG-highsm-11956

184 Miscellaneous Items in High Demand, Prints & Photographs Division, Library of Congress, LC-USZC4-4892

185 Photograph in the John F. Kennedy Presidential Library and Museum, Boston.

186 Photograph in the John F. Kennedy Presidential Library and Museum, Boston.

190 Long Wharf LOC

193 Park Street Church 1904 LOC 4a11380u

195 Courtesy of Boston Public Library, Print Department, Public Buildings Misc.

196 Engraving by Abel Brown. Courtesy of Boston Public Library, Print Department, Commercial Buildings Misc.

197 Photograph by Leon H. Abdalian. Courtesy of Boston Public Library, Print Department, Leon Abdalian Photographs Courtesy of Boston Public Library, Print Department, Churches Misc. Detroit Publishing Company, Prints & Photographs Division, Library of Congress, LC-D4-71592

200 Lithograph by Francis E. Getty; Forbes Lithograph Manufacturing Company. Courtesy of Boston Public Library, Print Department, Neighborhoods Misc.

203 Courtesy of Boston Public Library, Print Department, Faneuil Hall & Quincy Marketplace

205 United States National Archive

206 Courtesy of Boston Public Library, Print Department, North End

209 Courtesy of Boston Public Library, Print Department, North End

210 Courtesy of Boston Public Library, Print Department, Old North Church

211 Courtesy of Boston Public Library, Print Department, North End

212 Courtesy of Boston Public Library, Print Department, Street Views

215 Courtesy of Historic New England

216 Detroit Publishing Company Photograph Collection, Prints & Photographs Division, Library of Congress, LC-D4-19609

219 Courtesy of Historic New England

219 Courtesy of Historic New England

227 Courtesy of Boston Public Library, Print Department, Boston Common & Public Garden

228 Courtesy of Boston Public Library, Print Department, Hancock House

230 Popular Graphic Arts, Prints & Photographs Division, Library of Congress, LC-DIG-pga-03621

239 Courtesy of Historic New England

241 Photograph by Leon H. Abdalian. Courtesy of Boston Public Library, Print Department, Leon Abdalian Photographs.

242 Photograph by Leon H. Abdalian. Courtesy of Boston Public Library, Print Department, Leon Abdalian Photographs.

243 Courtesy of Boston Public Library, Print Department, Hotels.

244 Photograph by James Wallace Black. Courtesy of Boston Public Library, Print Department, James Wallace Black Photographs.

245 Courtesy of Boston Public Library, Print Department, Museum of Fine Arts

246 Photograph by James Walker Kenny. Courtesy of Boston Public Library, Print Department, Boylston Street & Copley Square

246 Lithograph by New England Lith. Co. Courtesy of Boston Public Library, Print Department

247 Courtesy of Boston Public Library, Print Department, Exterior & Courtyard

247 Courtesy of Boston Public Library, Print Department, Interiors

248 Courtesy of the Author

250 Photograph by James Wallance Black. Courtesy of Boston Public Library, J.W. Black Photographs: Boston

252 Courtesy of the Boston Public Library, Print Department. Public Buildings.

254 Courtesy of Boston Public Library, Churches Misc.

254 Photograph by Thomas E. Marr & Son. Courtesy of Boston Public Library, Print Department, Street Views, Misc.

255 Miscellaneous Items in High Demand, Prints & Photographs Division, Library of Congress, LC-USZ61-215

256 Courtesy of Boston Public Library, Churches Misc.

257 Courtesy of Boston Public Library, Churches Misc.

264 Courtesy of Boston Public Library, Parks Misc.

265 Painting by Francis E. Getty. Courtesy of the Boston Public Library, Print Department. Bridge & Tunnels

266 Drawing by George F. Bosworth. Courtesy of Boston Public Library, Parks Misc.

275 Courtesy of Harvard University.

275 Detroit Publishing Company, Prints & Photographs Division, Library of Congress, LC-D4-10086 L

288 Photo by Glenna Lang

Unless listed, all tour photos by Misaki Matsui and Heather Corcoran

ACKNOWLEDGMENTS

The author would like to thank J. L. Bell for making this book possible; Heather for her persistence and encouragement; and Ginny for her patience.

In addition, Museyon Guides would like to thank the following the following organizations for their guidance and assistance in creating *Chronicles of Old Boston*.

Boston Public Library
Harvard University
Historic New England
John F. Kennedy Presidential Library and Museum
Library of Congress, Prints & Photographs Division
MIT Museum
Museum of African American History

SUGGESTED READING

Allison, Robert J. ***A Short History of Boston.*** Commonwealth Editions, Beverly, Mass., 2004.

Archer, Richard. *As if an Enemy's Country: The British Occupation of Boston and the Origins of Revolution.* Oxford University Press, New York, 2010.

Bailyn, Bernard. *The Ordeal of Thomas Hutchinson.* Harvard University Press, Cambridge, 1974.
Beatty, Jack. *The Rascal King: The Life and Times of James Michael Curley, 1874-1958.* Addison-Wesley, Reading, Mass., 1992.

Beauchamp, Cari. *Joseph P. Kennedy Presents: His Hollywood Years.* Alfred A. Knopf, New York, 2009.

Bremer, Francis J. *The Puritan Experiment: New England Society from Bradford to Edwards,* revised ed. University Press of New England, Hanover, N.H., 1995.

Bruce, Robert V. *Bell: Alexander Graham Bell and the Conquest of Solitude.* Cornell University Press, Ithaca, N.Y., 1973.
Carp, Benjamin L. *Defiance of the Patriots: The Boston Tea Party & the Making of America.* Yale University Press, New Haven, Conn., 2010.

Clarke, Bradley H., and O. R. Cummings. *Tremont Street Subway: A Century of Public Service.* Boston Street Railway Association, Boston, 1997.

Cudahy, Brian J. *Change at Park Street Under: The Story of Boston's Subways.* Stephen Greene Press, Brattleboro, Vt., 1972.

Daniels, John. *In Freedom's Birthplace.* Arno Press, New York, 1969.

Fisher, Sean M., and Carolyn Hughes, eds. *The Last Tenement: Confronting Community and Urban Renewal in Boston's West End.* The Bostonian Society, Boston, 1992.

Forbes, Esther. *Paul Revere & the World He Lived In.* Houghton Mifflin, Boston, 1942.

Fischer, David Hackett. *Paul Revere's Ride.* Oxford University Press, New York, 1994.

French, Allen. *General Gage's Informers: New Material Upon Lexington & Concord, Benjamin Thompson as Loyalist & the Treachery of Benjamin Church, Jr.* University of Michigan Press, Ann Arbor, 1932.

Goodwin, Doris Kearns. *The Fitzgeralds and the Kennedys.* Simon and Schuster, New York, 1987.

Haglund, Karl. *Inventing the Charles River.* The MIT Press, Cambridge, 2003.
Harris, John. *America Rebels.* Globe Newspaper Co., Boston, 1976.

Johnson, Richard A., and Glenn Stout. *Red Sox Century: The Definitive History of Baseball's Most Storied Franchise,* revised and expanded ed. Houghton Mifflin, Boston, 2005.

Kamensky, Jane. *The Exchange Artist: A Tale of High-Flying Speculation and America's First Banking Collapse.* Viking, New York, 2008.

Kirker, Harold and James. *Bulfinch's Boston, 1787-1817.* Oxford University Press, New York, 1964.

Kruh, David. *Always Something Doing: A History of Boston's Infamous Scollay Square.* Faber and Faber, Boston, 1990.

LaPlante, Eve. *American Jezebel: The Uncommon Life of Anne Hutchinson, the Woman Who Defied the Puritans.* HarperSanFrancisco, New York, 2004.

Morison, Samuel Eliot. *The Founding of Harvard College.* Harvard University Press, Cambridge, 1935.

Norton, Elliot. *Broadway Down East: An Informal Account of the Plays, Players and Playhouses of Boston from Puritan Times to the Present.* Trustees of the Public Library of the City of Boston, 1978.

O'Connor, Thomas H. *Boston A to Z.* Harvard University Press, Cambridge, 2000.

O'Connor, Thomas H. *Building a New Boston: Politics and Urban Renewal, 1950-1970.* Northeastern University Press, Boston, 1993.

O'Donnell, David G. *The Old Corner Bookstore.* Pocket Metro, Cambridge, 2010.

O'Gorman, James F. *Living Architecture: A Biography of H. H. Richardson.* Simon & Schuster, New York, 1997.

O'Gorman, James F., ed. *The Makers of Trinity Church in the City of Boston.* University of Massachusetts Press, Amherst, 2004.

Petronella, Mary Melvin, ed. *Victorian Boston Today: Twelve Walking Tours.* Northeastern University Press, Boston, 2004.

Prescott, Samuel C. *When M.I.T. was "Boston Tech," 1861-1916.* The Technology Press, Cambridge, 1954.

Puleo, Stephen. *A City So Grand: The Rise of an American Metropolis, 1850-1900.* Beacon Press, Boston, 2010.

Puleo, Stephen. *Dark Tide: The Great Boston Molasses Flood of 1919.* Beacon Press, Boston, 2003.

Quincy, John, Jr. *Quincy's Market: A Boston Landmark.* Northeastern University Press, Boston, 2003.
Rutman, Darrett B. *Winthrop's Boston: Portrait of a Puritan Town, 1630-1649.* W. W. Norton, New York, 1975.

Sammarco, Anthony Mitchell. *The Great Boston Fire of 1872.* Arcadia, Dover, N.H., 1997.

Schorow, Stephanie. *Boston on Fire: A History of Fires and Firefighting in Boston.* Commonwealth Editions, Beverly, Mass., 2003.

Seasholes, Nancy S. *Gaining Ground: A History of Landmaking in Boston.* The MIT Press, Cambridge, 2003.

Shand-Tucci, Douglass. *The Art of Scandal: The Life and Times of Isabella Stewart Gardner.* HarperCollins, New York, 1997.

Shand-Tucci, Douglass. *Built in Boston: City and Suburb, 1800-2000,* revised ed. University of Massachusetts Press, Amherst, 1999.

Shaughnessy, Dan. *The Curse of the Bambino,* enlarged ed. Penguin Books, New York, 2004.

Shulman, Seth. *The Telephone Gambit: Chasing Alexander Graham Bell's Secret.* W. W. Norton, New York, 2008.

Southworth, Susan and Michael. *AIA Guide to Boston,* 3rd ed. Globe Pequot Press, Guilford, Conn., 2008.

Strangis, Joel. *Lewis Hayden and the War Against Slavery.* Linnet Books, North Haven, Conn., 1999.

Sullivan, Robert. *The Disappearance of Dr. Parkman.* Little, Brown & Co., Boston, 1971.

Tryon, Warren S. *Parnassus Corner: A Life of James T. Fields, Publisher to the Victorians.* Houghton Mifflin, Boston, 1963.

Unger, Harlow Giles. *John Hancock: Merchant King and American Patriot.* John Wiley & Sons, Hoboken, N.J., 2000.

Whitehill, Walter Muir, and Lawrence W. Kennedy. *Boston: A Topographical History,* 3rd ed. Harvard University Press, Cambridge, 2000.

ABOUT MUSEYON

Named after the Museion, the ancient Egyptian institute dedicated to the muses, Museyon Guides is an independent publisher that explores the world through the lens of cultural obsessions. Intended for frequent fliers and armchair travelers alike, our books are expert-curated and carefully researched, offering rich visuals, practical tips and quality information.

MUSEYON'S OTHER TITLES

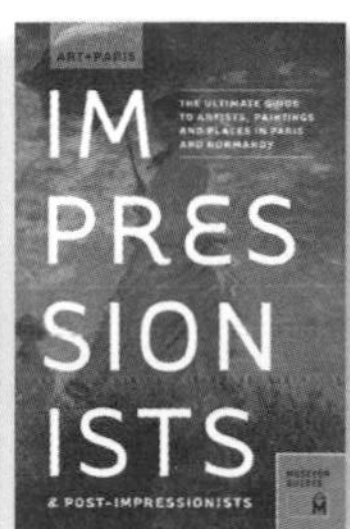

Film + Travel Europe 9780982232002
Film + Travel Asia, Oceania, Africa 9780982232019
Film + Travel North America, South America 9780982232026
Music + Travel Worldwide 9780982232033
Art + Travel Europe 9780982232057
Chronicles of Old New York 9780982232064
City Style 9780982232071
Art + NYC 9780982232088
Art + Paris: Impressionists and Post Impressionists 9780982232095
Chronicles of Old Las Vegas 9780984633418
Chronicles of Old Paris 9780984633425

Pick one up and follow your interests...wherever they might go.
For more information vist www.museyon.com

Publisher: Akira Chiba
Editor-in-Chief: Heather Corcoran
Art Director: Ray Yuen
Cover Design: José Antonio Contreras
Photographer: Misaki Matsui
Maps & Illustration Design: EPI Design Network, Inc.
Copy Editor: Carrie Funk

ABOUT THE AUTHOR

As a college student, Charles Bahne was captivated by Boston and its history. For three decades since then, he's shared his enthusiasm about the city he loves, working as a tour guide, lecturer, and even a park ranger. A graduate of MIT's Urban Studies program, Charlie is also the author of The Complete Guide to Boston's Freedom Trail. Charlie lives in Cambridge with his wife Ginny and their beloved cat Angie.